MW01708677

It Certainly Was God's Grace and Mercy

NOW A STREET FIGHTER FOR THE LORD

MINISTER CAROLIN JONET MORGAN

***Personal names have been omitted from this book to protect the guilty and the innocent.**

RBT Press
www.rbtpress.com

ISBN: 978-0-9776345-2-1

Preface

I was beaten and raped, and they tried to put me on the block for prostitution, but even in my mess! God had His hands on me. I should have been dead or in prison for life.

My existence was like a roller coaster that never stopped. I was up and down, from serving God, to living in sin.

I was living [the] fast life, I thought I was unstoppable, I knew how to evade the law. I had the glamor, the jewels, the money and the kudos (the fine cars, whatever I wanted, I got); greed had set in. The more money I made, the more MM (my man) and I wanted.

Self-indulgence was destroying my life and those around me. The guilt began to eat me alive, and I became weary of destroying lives. Addictions were all around me. Friends and family were suffering; many were strung out on drugs.

Getting busted was the best thing that could have happen to me. Prison saved my life. To this day I am forever thankful that God's grace and His mercy covered me.

God's word reveals His nature, His work, and His plan for our lives. The ones who are willing to submit to [HIS WILL] come under HIS care, the LORD God promised that He would lead us, strengthen us, and bless all who answers to His call of obedience.

When we trust God completely we: relinquish all of our rights, and we allow Him to direct the course of each part of our lives.

The mountains are a special place I love to go to commune with the our heavenly FATHER. There's something extraordinary about **Lookout Mountain** in Colorado. I would go to a rock that looked out over Colorado and I would pray. It's beautiful to see God's magnificent work. The splendor of it all is Amazing!

The passion that God has given me [for Him], is revealed in my [new life]. I had been a hardened criminal; I really truly thought that I was unstoppable! But God's plans for my life changed me; thank God I am not that same person.

God said in 1 Corinthians 5: 17, "that I am a new creation and the old things have passed away, and behold all things become new."

Our lives are a walking testimony for the world to see! GOD's "Grace" and "Mercy," it truly covered, and is still covering my life today.

Here's my life's testimony, how about yours! Are you willing to share your life to save someone else's?

It was God's grace and mercy

God really loves and cares for us all. That is why He died for you and for me. He gave us a way to live our lives stress free. All we have to do is trust and believe, and live out the word that He has given us to live by. "Obedience" is the key.

We are all one of God's children! Always remember, we all are special! God put us on this earth to do His will.
The Harvest is plentiful but the laborers are few. We have to work while it is day.
If you are not saved read, ***Romans 10:9-13***

Minister Carolin J Morgan

Contents

Special Thanks & Dedication..vi
Mothers that impacted my life ix
Women Mentors & Parayer Partners/Friendship...x
Spiritual Leaders
Introduction xv
Perseverance with Patience in the mist of
Persecuted...xx
Chapter 1. My Childhood Growing up...1
Grateful with a Thankful Heart
Chapter 2. My Teenage year 13
Praises
Chapter 3. The Crimes began 24
God's Grace and Mercy
Chapter 4. Life as a Drug dealer 43
Greed
Chapter 5. Busted! To Parallax 53
Addiction/Co-Dependency
Chapter 6. Jail to Prison..76
Reaching Beyond the Bars
Chapter 7. Freedom..103
Change& Transiting back into Life after Prison
Testing of your Faith
Making right Decision
Chapter 8. Having a Personal Relationship with Christ...........................132
Our Identity & Blessing God's Gift
Chapter 9. The Call on my Life..147
Knowing God's Will
Obedience
Be a Positive Thinker
Chapter 10. The Lost of my Father and Mother..174
Grief
Chapter 11. Prayer..198
Our Words are our Battle Ground
Love with a Pure Heart
The Lord's Prayer for His Disciples
Chapter 12. From Prison to Purpose...206
Following Jesus
Surrendering to God in Love
Be Prepared to Serve
Using God's Gift of Time Stepping out on Faith

Special Thanks and Dedication

My Friend

I want to dedicate this book to a friend of mine, who was my inspiration to write this book. Bro. Oscar Jones II. He is truly an awesome man of God! He has been a blessing in my life since the day I met him. He has been there as a friend, a spiritual advisor, and somewhat a mentor. He has always encouraged me in everything that I put forth in my life to do.

He also challenges me to look at the things that have come into my path, and to see them from God's point of view, not my own. He tells me what I need to hear, not what I want to hear; he is a man of integrity. He walks in the fruit of the spirit and he gives me the answers I need, through the word of God. He is not a person that voices his own opinions; he comes directly from God's Word. If he hadn't stayed on me, I would not have written this book. He is a very strong and loving man of God. So I just want to thank him from the bottom of my heart. I will always be grateful to him and his friendship, and for the part that he has played in my life.
He continues to pray for me and encourage me.

Much love and respect goes to this Holy man of God, a man God allowed to come into my life at the right time. He is a teacher and a doer of the word. He has a love for God that is rare in this world today among Christians, especially men. He is very respectful towards people, and is always reaching out to help and pray for others; he is a true servant of the Lord. I have so much respect for Bro Jones.

Thank you Oscar for coming into my life and being my friend, I will always have love and respect for you. Thank you. May God continue to bless you and your family.

My parents

To my mother and father whose prayers kept us covered and safe in the arms of God. My father was my spiritual advisor, a strong man, a solid father figure.

Even though we had problems when we were growing up, he

never failed to tell us what God said through His word. He was a man of great faith until the day he died.

It is a blessing to have your father in your life, because, fathers are absent from many homes today. I'm thankful for the time that God had our father in our lives to teach and to raise us to always believe and trust in HIM.

My mother was always there for her children. She would fuss curses, or whatever she thought she had to do, but I know she loved us, and she loved the LORD. She always made sure that we were clean and fed, and she provided a good safe and clean environment, regardless of our situation. She taught us how to clean, cook and be good responsible home makers.

Living in the country, we raised a lot of our food from a garden. I miss both of my parents a lot. My mother has also gone home to be with the Lord. I thank God for the time that He allowed us to have our parents here with us. No one should ever take their parents for granted. God tells us to honor our father and our mother that our days will be long; Exodus 20:12.

If your parents are still alive, tell them often, how much you love them. Always find ways to show them you love them. You never really know what you have until they are gone.

Give them their flowers while they are alive; I can never say this enough. Never, ever see them as just being your parents. They are special people that God allows us to enjoy on this earth!

I miss my parents so much, it still feels like they are supposed to be here! But I know that they are resting in the LORD. You never stop missing your loved ones, but it does get easier.

My oldest sister

My oldest sister has also passed on; this is for her also. She went through a lot (with me), when I was dealing drugs. I'll always remember her as the wonderful sister she was. She was a caring and loving sister, and a friend to me. She was kind to everyone she met. Sometimes I wonder what it would be like if she was still alive. She died at the age of 38, quite young, huh! But God knows best for us.

My daughter and grand daughter

To my daughter Terri, who has been a rock in my life, since the day of her birth. I was blessed the day she was born, and I thank God for her. She was my birthday present. I went in the hospital on my birthday, and gave birth to her, two days later.

She and my granddaughter Tradeja, both are the joy of my life! Thank you baby girl for being the young lady you are. I love the woman that God is molding her to be.

Terri has never been a problem child, like what I took my parents through. She was God's gift to me, even though I had her out of wedlock; we all should know that our children are truly a very special gift.

Tradeja/Deja, is an awesome granddaughter; as a baby, Tradeja was always around me. She loved having praise and worship with me. We would walk all over the house having a good time in the Lord! She would go on prayer missions with me; and as a baby she would [lay on hands] and pray for people!

God tells us to train a child in the way they should go, and when they are old they will not depart from it; *Proverbs 22:6.* They may stray for a while, but they'll always come back; I did.

Hard as I was in the streets, that's the way I am for the Lord, now. "To God be the glory."

Father, I thank you for the person who's reading this book. I pray that they see You through it all (and not myself).

I pray and I thank You for deliverance for them and their families in every area of their lives. God You made us all in Your own image. Your word says that You have given us the same power and authority that You gave Your Son (in HIS Name). Father I thank You that Your plan for our lives are revealed to us all; and thank You for helping us to realize that You bring freedom to our lives when we obey Your word. Trusting and Understanding that You are God and You really don't need our help (being GOD); just our obedience, our praise and worship. Help us to remember to give You thanks for all You have done and are still doing for us. We continue to be grateful. In Jesus Name, AMEN!

Mother's that impacted my life

Lennie Jean Nelson: Was a beautiful woman who would always discipline me (and the others) about the things we were doing. She had her own unique way, but I know it was all out of love. I will always remember her.

Louise Wilson: Was a special woman in my life. She also stayed on all of us to do the right things in life. Much love goes to her.

Mamie Johnson: This woman always had a special love for me from the day that I met her; I love her too. She and big mama will forever be in my heart.

Lula Calhoun: Wonderful woman and mentor. She would always encourage me to do better. Helping and shaping us to be beautiful women of God. Through her Alteration Shop she helped us to become beautiful models, through all that she did.

Jo-Mae Mullins: She was special in my life. She always knew what we were doing; she accepted us for who we were and she loved us anyway. I worked with her for a while and I really got to know her in a very special way. I will always remember her.

Sal Finley: She was a loving mother and grandmother; she loved everybody; I admired her for how she took care of her family. She died saving her grand kids. I'll forever remember her for the hero she was.

Ms. Faye Oliver: She was a quiet and laid back woman (to me). But when she spoke she would say something that really encouraged you. She has always cared about everyone she met (that was around all of her children).

Mother Brown: Very inspirational woman of God. She came into my life later, but she loved and had a great respect for me as a person, and she accepted me into her family as one of her own.

Mrs. Irene Bailey: I became one of her children. I enjoy talking and having fellowship with her. The family gatherings at her home are awesome. I blend in very well! I love her very much. She'll call me sometimes and tell me that she thought about me "so I called you" she'd say. That is a blessing to me.

All of the mothers were women I knew who cared about what the young people were doing. They all (in a very special way) played a unique part in my life to make me the woman I am today; for that, I thank them. I thank God that I met all of their children, because if I had never met them I would not have met these wonderful women that God placed in my life to encourage me. I love them all very much.

Women Mentors

Prophetess Edwina Jones: She always prays with me and for me. She has not only been a spiritual blessing; she is like a second mother to me. She has been in my life and my family's life for many, many years. I have much love and respect for her. I will always hold her close to my heart. When I was released from prison, she encouraged me to believe in myself, and she believed in me and told me that I could make it. She saw the woman that God wanted me to be. She has a love for God that is so real that you can't help but be blessed in her presence! Prayer-My God! This one is a prayer warrior! Her voice is like an angel from heaven; when she sings, deliverance takes place! I love her with all my heart. "Mama Pumpkin."

Minister Lola Simons: She would pray with me, fast with me, and just encourage me. She has been a great inspiration in my life.

I thank her from the bottom of my heart. She would always invite me to her prayer groups. When I got out of prison, she was always there to give the truth of what God said in His word; she helped me to not dwell on where I had been. My love and thanks to you.

Rev Billy Mosley: She is a praying woman of God. She is very encouraging and she ministers to me a lot through her singing.

I just love her! She has always been there for my family; she was a very close friend to my mother. When my mother took ill, she really stepped in and supported me with whatever I needed, in order to help take care for her. I will never forget her loving and giving spirit. Much love to you.

Pastor Grace Miles: when I went to Restoration Ministries Church, she [just] took me under her wings. I'll be forever grateful for her friendship and her love for me, both as a woman of God and as a friend. She prayed with me and for me through a lot of the trials and tests that came into my life. She has helped me to see things through God's eyes instead of my own. We did a lot of things together. I really love, respect and enjoy this woman of God. I will always remember her for the way she encourages me to fight [in] the Spirit.

Apostle Ruth White: She is a mighty woman of God. Her teaching was awesome! The anointing she carries is so great! Everything changes when she walks into the room! WOW!!!! A power house! I love her teachings! They are life changing (if you embrace them). She was raw, but real. A woman who doesn't mind getting you [in order], because she sets order wherever she goes.

Elder Susan Hurst: Is a true woman of God. She reminds me (a lot) of her mother. A powerful woman of God. Now Susan carries her anointing. I'm blessed whenever I am in her presence.

Pastor Sherian Cook: When I met her, I knew she was a true woman of God. She was there as a spiritual advisor. She always gave me sound advice from the word of God. She is a prayer warrior. I have a lot of love and respect for this woman of God.

Prayer Partners/Friendships

Terry Hutton: She has faith, to [no] fault. She is a woman who walks in integrity. She loves and is very devoted to whatever she does. She is a woman of great faith in God. She has always been a true friend. I mean a friend to no end. She and her family have played a big part in my life. She is a powerful woman of God. I love her

Jan Chandler: She is a great warrior. She takes on things like a pit bull...in the spirit! And she doesn't let it go until she has prayed you through. She is true to the call that God chose for her life. Her life is a walking testimony. Jan and her family are special to me.

Apostle Rita Montgomery: We met for a short season; she made a great impact in my life. She is true to her calling.

Sharene Thompson: It was amazing the way that we met. Our friendship was a setup, "A setup by God." She has always been there for me, ever since the day we met. She is one of a kind.

Much love to her and her husband and sons. They are very special
Phyllis Murphy; She is a mighty woman of God who never fails to pray. She is always encouraging you and has a great love for God.
Minnie Chambers: Love you much. She always gives me sound advice from the word.
Phyllis Burley: She is my favorite sister-in-law. She holds a very special place in my heart and in my family. Love her much.
Bernia Williams Kelly: This is a woman that when God changed her, He really brought out the fullness of Him in her life! From the streets, to walking into her destiny, she embraced Him.
Sheila Walker, Cherri, Nenya and mother Brown: They were my extended family. When I met them, I just fell in love with the whole family, they-love-God! They were a family that prayed together. Mother Brown was so special to me. She and Nenya are gone home to be with the Lord. I will always remember them.
Bernastine Williams: She is meek, and she has a spirit of humility like no other, and she is very loving. She is a person you can count on always and she never has anything bad to say about anyone. She loves God. She has endured a lot. Always wanting to help someone and getting what was needed to help her family.
Denell Corner: She is my friend who will just cut to the chase. If she is for you, she's for you. She loves God and she lives for God. You always know that she is praying for you.
She and her husband have been a true blessing to me. I love them as my own family. They are the same two people that I met many years ago. These are the kinds of friendships we need to always cherish.
Jonell Ross: Since the first time I met her, she has never changed. She became my friend in spite of how we met; I love her. She's passed on also, and I truly miss her.
Janet Betts: I admire her for being consistent (with me) no matter when or where we meet. I have always been in contact with her from the streets until now. She has always been the same person in my life. No matter how many years we don't see each other, when we do, it is like we never left.

Spiritual Leaders

Pastor A.G Jones: Macedonia Missionary Baptist Church. This was where I was raised. I was under his teaching for 20 years. He always prayed for me, and was a blessing to my whole family. I grew up in this church from 8 years old (until I went to prison). I understood that God loved me at an early age. Pastor Jones baptized me; I understood why I got baptized (in water). This is where I first spoke of my life [living as a drug dealer].

Prophet Ron Miles: Restoration Ministries. A man that through the anointing changed my life. This is where I first knew what it was to go out under the power of God. I learned a lot from Prophet Miles a man of God. All the things that I am walking in now, he is one of the ones that God used to help me grow in Him. He has always been right there in my life. He walked in a boldness that was passed down in my life. He & his wife will always hold a very special part in my heart.

Apostle Cornelius Sanders: Revelation Ministry. This is a holy man of God. He has an apostolic anointing on his life. I learned through his teaching a "A Newness" of the word of God. The last year before I left Wichita, God directed me to his ministry to embrace his teaching. It prepared me to venture out. I'm thankful for Apostle Sanders (a true man of God). His ministry has been a blessing for many people, and it still is.

Bishop Kevin Foreman: Harvest Christian Center. Bishop Foreman is: A Holy Man of God, he has been a blessing to me. God is changing this generation through him and his ministry. God connected me to Bishop Foreman (a man of God) when I moved to Colorado. Bishop Foreman taught me Bible truths while attending Harvest Christian Center Bible College. I will always be grateful to him for how he loves and cares for God's people; He is a life changer. He is very gifted in all areas in his life. He teaches you how to walk in excellence because he is a man of excellence and he sets order wherever he goes. He flows in the 5 fold ministry

gifts, and he walks in all of them with the spirit of excellence. You can learn a lot under the covering of this Holy Man of God.

[Each Man of God] that God purposed me to sit under has helped me to become the person I am today. I thank God that they have all been a part of my life. It really matters who you bond with, because every man or woman of God are not meant to cross our path.

* Allow God to send people your way who will make a positive impact in your life; be prepared to embrace them. Allow them to give you good advice and always be open to positive criticism. God knows what is best for us even when we don't understand His ways.

* Be teachable, you never know what you might learn. Listen to where the Lord is sending you, and make sure you get under the right man of God so you care truly walk in your purpose.

1 Thessalonians 5:12-13, say's: "And we beseech you, brethren, to know them which labor among you, and are over you in the Lord, and admonish you; V13. And to esteem them very highly in love for their work's sake. And be at peace among yourselves."

We should appreciate our leaders and let them know how they have helped us. Give them the respect and the honor due them.

God wants us to pray and always encourage them. Hold them up at all times in prayer. They are a blessing from God.

Introduction

I wrote this book with the hope, that my [past struggles] will save others from the hell of the streets, and all of its crimes. Satan's purpose is to: steal, kill and destroy.

Looking back and seeing the things that I went through, [most of it could have been avoided if, I had listened] to the men and women God put in my path. It would have saved me from the pain and suffering that I endured, and caused to others due to my drug dealing (and occasionally trying to use), but I could never get the full hang of drugs, and I thank God I didn't!

If only I had heeded the voice of God; if only I had been obedient; if only I had, the courage to sanctify self! And later: If only I had published my journal after God [first] told me to write this book.

I was like Jonah when God told him what to do, instead he decided to flee. God wanted him to go and call the people to repentance, but he ran in the opposite direction. I, also moved in the reverse direction, all the while knowing that God had called me. I really did not want people to know, all that I had done; especially those in the church that had watched me grow up from a child! I hid behind pretense. In my youth I was known as the "goodie two shoes" girl. I was in rebellion but God was constructing a beneficial testimony through me.

My abase is someone else's gain, and I have done both in my life (abased and abounded). Knowing what I know now, I wouldn't change my experiences for anything; without the [trials and the tests], I would not be where I am today. My life in prison was a blessing in disguise (at the time). Prison saved my life! I could have been dead or locked up for life if it had not been for: "God's Grace and Mercy."

So this is a book of hope, to let you know that if God did it for me! He'll certainly do it for you! I want you to know that prayer does change things. I don't know about you, but I cannot live without God (I am totally dependent on Him)! Prison is really where I truly met Him. I received the Baptism of the Holy Ghost in the El-Dorado County Jail!

As you read this story of my life, you will see how I made it through the hard times growing up, and how God covered me and my family, back then. I believe that as you read this book with an open heart, you will see how God can calm the storms and change the circumstances.

God gave me Jeremiah 1:5-10 in the El Dorado County Jail in 1981. As you read you'll see how God has changed my life (from lost to found)! Sometimes we don't understand why things happen. If we look [to] God in every situation that we find ourselves facing, He will bring us through.

If you truly love God, then Romans 8:28 will bless you. It says: "And we know that all things work together for good to them that love God, to them who are called according to his purpose." The key is: we have to love Him, and be obedient to what His word says. Our lives are special and precious in God's eyes. I am certain that your life will change for the better when you totally depend on Him. Remember, we all have gifts and talents that God has given us to use, so let's not waste time saying: I should of, would of, and could of.

I pray that God will truly bless you as you read this book. This book will show you how the power of prayer has worked for me; I have since learned a lot from the people around me, but most of all, I have learned through God's Word.

Praying people introduced me to prayer, God saved me because praying people never stopped praying for me! We have to understand the power that God has given us!

The Father gave the Apostles the same power and authority that HE gave His Son; we also have that same power (in JESUS NAME). JESUS is our Mediator to the FATHER (through prayer, according to His Word, there's power in His spoken Word).

Follow these steps and you'll know how to get your prayers answered. *We have to first acknowledge our sins; Romans 3:10.*

Then we have to realize that our sins deserve eternal punishment: Romans 6:23a. We must believe that Christ died on the Cross for our sin 1 Corinthians 15:3, 4. We must believe that through Christ we shall have eternal life; Romans 6:23b. We must repent; confessing our sins to the Lord; 1 John 1:9. We must realize that our salvation is based on faith in JESUS, not our feelings. Also, realize that we cannot earn nor do we deserve to be saved; Eph. 2:8, 9.

Everyone has sinned both past and present (all of us have sinned). No one born of a man is perfect (in this life) the only sinless man was Jesus Christ, we all have fallen short. God loves us all, any way we come to Him; no matter what we have done, or where we have been. Whosoever will, can be saved; God will change our hearts and turn us around (HE changed me). I thank God for the things He allowed me to go through because it made me the woman I am today.

Our life is not our own, we were bought with a price. God sacrificed His Son's (physical, incarnate) life on the cross for me and you; John 3:16. Sometimes we suffer persecution; people will gossip about you, they will lie about you, stab you in the back, they will even try to make others think that you are a bad person.

There were lots of 'so called friends' in my life who did bad things against me; but through it all, God has kept me sane (in my right mind), and in perfect peace! (Thank You Lord)! I still love them even though they speak all manner of evil towards me. God tells us we must pray for those who despitefully use us and say all kinds of bad things against us. I thank God that He delivered me from (those kinds of people). Praise God! God's word taught me "How to endure Persecution."

Your experience might be different, but what I'm saying is that, I had to learn to read and study God's Word, and be obedient to what it says; God's word works! We have to trust and understand that God knows what trials and tests we need to endure in order to get us where we should to be. Don't allow yourself to get caught up in the things of this world!

John 10:10 says "The enemy only comes but to kill steal, and destroy, but I have come that you may have life and have it abundantly."

We have to know who we are in Christ; we are all special people who were put on this earth for a special purpose; no one can give your testimony, but you! We must not allow ourselves to be quiet in this day and time! People need what we have (what we have learned the hard way)! There are people who are waiting for you to minister to them. Sometimes our lives are the only bible that people will read! God says in ***Matthew 9: 37-38, "That the harvest is plentiful, but the laborers are few, therefore send out laborers into his harvest. [That's you and me.]***

When we become a child of God, we not only inherit God's blessings, but, HIS enemies as well. As a child of God, He gives us His Armor to wear daily. The LORD's foremost enemy is Satan, and he's our worst enemy also. He tries to destroy God's people and their good works, but Jesus came in order to "destroy the works of the devil;" Satan is in no way equal to the LORD God our Creator. Satan is inferior to God in every way. We have the power of the resurrected Christ and His protection over us. ***1 John 4:4 tells us: That greater is He (God) who is in us than he (the devil) who is in the world. Eph. 6:11-17 teaches us how to put on the [whole] Armor.*** Each piece has its own meaning that will help each part of our mind, body, and our spirit.

1. ***'Gird your loins with Truth.'*** The lions are the seat of our emotions. To gird this area with truth is to commit our emotions to believing the truth of God's Word,

2. ***Put on the Breastplate of Righteousness***. John 8:32 says, "And you shall know the truth, and the truth shall make you free." Breast: is thought of as the place of our soul. The heart must be kept pure and righteous because sin gives hold to the enemy. We must confess our sins, and forgive on the basis of the blood of Christ. It cleanses our heart. 1John 1:9 says that "If we confess our sins, He is faithful and just to forgive us our sins and cleanse us from all unrighteousness."

3. ***Your Feet shod with the Gospel of Peace***. The proper shoes (on our feet) will allow us to move around in order to spread the gospel of peace and reconciliation to the entire world.
Matt. 28:19 says: "Go therefore and make disciples of all nations, baptizing them in the name of the Father, Son, and the Holy Spirit."
4. ***The Shield of Faith.*** Faith is like an invisible shield that deflects untrue accusations. Heb. 11:6 says "Without faith it is impossible to please Him, for he who comes to God must believe, that He is and that He is a rewarder of those who diligently seek Him."
5. ***The Helmet of Salvation***. The helmet protects our minds...that is: our spiritual brain and thoughts. Satan wants us to doubt God (our Salvation through Christ Jesus). 1 John 5:11-13. Says: "And this is a testimony: that God has given us eternal life, and this life is in His Son." Verse 12: "He who has the Son has life; he who does not have the Son of God does not have life." Verse 13: "These things I have written to you who believe in the name of the Son of God that you may know that you have eternal life and that you may continue to believe in the name of the Son of God."
6. ***The Sword of the Spirit.*** It was the only weapon of the armor, (which was the word) that was used by Jesus against Satan. It is the weapon of defense. Read. Luke 4:1-13. Jesus was tempted by Satan. That chapter will show you how the word cancels every trick the enemy tries to use. God's word is powerful, it's effective, and gives us instructions. Heb. 4:12 says: "For the word of God is living and it's powerful, and sharper than any two edge sword piercing even to the division of soul and spirit, and joints and marrow, and is a discerner of thoughts and intents of the heart."
7. ***Praying Always with all prayer and supplications in the Spirit***. Prayer is our only open communication with God. In all our battles we have to always keep in constant communication with Him to allow Him to give us directions and encouragement to help us along the way. We must pray for one another. James 5:16 says: "Confess your trespasses to one another, and pray for another, that you may be healed. The effective, fervent prayer of a righteous man avails much."

It is important for us to allow God to change our lives; He changed my life. It was His word that helped change me to who I am today.

I have met a lot of people in my life; some were good and some were bad. But we all have something we can give back to someone in this life. God has blessed me in [such] a way, that all I want, is to see everyone come to know Christ.

The next 2 pages teaches us about Persecution. We have to go beyond ourselves. We have to allow God to mold us to be who He wants us to become. Life can be a struggle, but with God, we can make it through. We may suffer hardships sometimes, but our God is an awesome God, who will see us through everything we face, if we would only allow Him to be LORD of our lives.

Some people will try to discourage you, and make you feel you can't make it. All you have to do is look to the hills from which comes our help, because our help comes from the Lord. God loves us [Trust] HIM and you will never go wrong.

Proverbs 3: 5, 6 says, "Trust in the Lord with all your heart, and lean not to your own understanding". Verse 6: "In all thy ways acknowledge Him and he shall direct thy path."

*Reading this book: along the way you may encounter a mistake or two, you might even see a few errors but I hope you receive the message from it all. This is my first book and I thank God for giving me the courage to write it to help someone else. God bless.

Perseverance with Patience in the mists of Persecuted

Perseverance: Is to endure and stay steadfast in anything that comes your way. We have all kinds of opposition coming at us. Sometimes we face discouragement, or all kinds of attacks. We have to endure as the Christians/People we are. Stay steadfast and focus on Jesus. Staying focused on the things of God can help us to endure any and everything. ***To persevere we have to have patience to continue, without complaining***. *James 1:2-4 says: "My brethren, count it all joy when you fall into various trials."*

V3. "Knowing that the testing of your faith produces patience." V4, "But let patience have its perfect work, that you may be perfect (meaning: mature), and complete, lacking nothing." Having a daily commitment will lead us to be disciplined.

As a believer we have to be wise in knowing the real and true source of being persecuted and the motives that cause it. This is asking: what did we do to bring this upon ourselves?

Here are some scriptures to help in persecution:

1. 2 Peter 1:5-7: "But also for this very reason giving all diligence, add to your faith virtue, and to virtue knowledge, and to knowledge self-control, to self-control perseverance godliness."
2. Romans 8:35-37: "Who can separate us from the love of God? Shall tribulation, or distress, or persecution, or famine, or nakedness, or peril, or sword? As it is written For Your sake we are killed all day long; we are accounted as sheep for the slaughter. Yet in all these things we are more than conquerors through Him who loved us."
3. John 5:16: "For this reason the Jews persecuted Jesus, and sought to kill Him, because He had done these things on the Sabbath." So this is telling us that we are going to be persecuted, also. Sometimes people don't even know why they are coming at you. But Jesus knew and He always spoke the Word to disqualify everything evil. We can know this, "that the sinful world hated God*."* of the Spirit."
4. Galatians 4:29: "In the mist of living righteous, tribulation will come."
5. Matthew 5:10: "We have to persevere in our prayer life."
6. Ephesians 6:18: "in faith"
7. Hebrew 12:1, 2: "in our obedience to God, and in serving."
8. John 15:18: Also, "the things of the flesh always try to battle the things of the spirit.

CHAPTER 1

My Child Hood Growing Up

I can remember way back in the 1950's when I was just a little girl we lived in a small town called Bodcaw, Arkansas; it is about 15 miles outside of Hope Arkansas.

My father and mother had five girls and one boy. We lived in a house that, at the time looked very big! **It wasn't big at all**! My grandma, uncle, his daughter, and her son also lived there.

I can remember those big beds, they were piled high with the large quilts that grandma used to make. We had what was called an out-house; that's where we would go to use the toilet; and we would have to bathe on the back porch in huge wash tubs.

My mother and grandma would wash our clothes in the creek, scrubbing them by using a wash board and then they would beat them with rocks. We had a potbellied stove that burned wood to cook our food and boil our water, and we had a wooden fire place that kept us warm.

As I look back on those early days, it was God's grace that got us through it all. Back then it was only me, my sister under me (who was born in 1954), my brother (born in 1951) and my oldest sister (born in 1950).

I remember all the good home cooked meals (that we had). We raised our own chickens. My father, and uncle would hunt and catch different kinds of animals. (the kinds you could clean and eat).

We didn't have a whole lot, but I remember my people, making do with what we had; they were certainly prayer warriors! They would pray about everything without hesitating.

Whenever a storm came through, we would always have to be still. They had a saying back then that: "God was doing His work." They would blow out the lanterns and sit quietly in the dark.

One time a tornado blew off half our house. (I think) my father and some other men rebuilt the part that we lost; it was just a shack (as I now see it), but it was home!

God has kept me and my family through some very difficult and trying times. My mother (and grandma) hired themselves out [to iron clothes] for wealthy families to make money. Back in the day; Blacks weren't allowed to enter certain parts of Arkansas.

I can remember when there would be white paint on the trees, and wherever we saw the white on the trees, we knew that we couldn't go past that point unless we were with a white person.

We used to play in the woods all the time; I was born in those [woods]. My mother was out there one day (according to what I was told) and a raccoon scared her into labor!

I really loved the country life. The LORD was prominent in our family (having a praying grandma was a blessing)! God's anointing was always in our home; my family knew how to call on God! Our home was peaceful and filled with love. We used to call our grandma, [grandma Dug-ga]. It was lots of fun living in that house, and we had many happy days in that little house.

We had a deep water-well in our backyard. We always had enough to eat; talking about some good eating...when they would wring off, one of the chickens necks, that chicken would run all over the yard until it died! I knew [then] that we were going to have some good O'll fried chicken for breakfast or dinner! Those homemade biscuits along with apple, peach, or pear preserves, awe, man; that was so good!!!!

Life didn't seem hard at all, although I would sometimes over hear my parents say that things were rough (but they did not let it show). God always kept us with plenty of the things we needed! (People totally trusted in the Lord back then).

I remember going to this church in Arkansas; they really knew how to Praise and Worship the LORD! It was awesome!! Those people would grab hold to the anointing and the power of the LORD would move throughout the building. Christians back then really appreciated [the power that God moved in]. I remember hearing them pray all night long (sometimes). Life seemed very good to me back then!

I remember when my sister and I would sit on the side of the road and eat clay dirt; that dirt was so good! There were trees that had black berries on them and we would eat the berries until our faces were purple from the juice! (LoL!) Everything was [like] fresh! We used to have that [cured out ham] hanging on the back porch; they'd make homemade butter and ice cream (everything was made from scratch).

As I look back I see that we were very rich! Sometimes I miss those days because there was a lot of love in that small country house. My aunts and uncles lived in the area; my favorite aunt lived in Texarkana, Arkansas. I used to love going to her house; she was a true woman of God! I loved hearing her talk about the Lord; she always tried to encourage us to know and trust in HIM; she was a very wise woman. Going to aunt Rubies house, was the [big thing] in my life!

Church was awesome! Looking back to see how people loved and served God: It's a whole lot different in this day and time. People really worshiped and praised God back then! Aunt Ruby was the mother of 11 children, and we all played together and loved each other. My aunt Augusta and her kids were around also, she had much older kids than we were; she was also a wise woman of God. I loved all of my aunts and uncles, and their families.

All of a sudden my father packed us up and we left Arkansas; well, it was all of a sudden to me I'm sure that it had been planned. We had a 1949 black Chevy; my father loaded us up and we moved to Los Angles California. We went from the country, straight to the city! You talk about a change; WOW, that was a change! California was gigantic (in my eyes).

When we were riding into LA, I remember being very excited to see all of the lights! It made Arkansas look like a tiny town.

I was scared and excited at the same time! My parents had already made arrangement for our living quarters (I suspect) because we moved right into a place).

I remember riding with my father one day and I saw the Three Stooges they were filming on a corner street. That was amazing to me! Lots of things happened out there!

I remember we were playing in daddy's car and mama told us to [get out of the car] and come in the house. Well we jumped out and I can't remember if it was me or my brother, but one of us slammed the door and my sister's finger got caught in it; it cut the tip of her finger off! We were so scared! They had to take her to the hospital; we got in BIG trouble! My mother was pregnant at the time, with her fifth child. My father was gone [like] always.

I did not know why he was away so much. It's funny now, because I found out after he passed away that he had been a truck driver during that time (I thought he was just gone all the time); I guess when you're a kid the reason doesn't really matter.

My oldest sister would help my mother around the house; one day she was trying to wash some clothes in one of those Wringer Washing machines; she was trying to put some pieces of clothing between the rollers and her arm got caught; (that was a very sad day). Back then you had to call the telephone operator to get help.

They had to break the machine loose to free her arm! It was smashed real bad, you could see her bones, so they rushed her to the hospital; she had to have a lot of surgeries. They had to take skin from both of her sides, and both of her legs, and they grafted it to her arm; it was really bad and we were sad. I did not like California very much I wanted to go back to Arkansas.

In 1957 my mother went to General Hospital; she gave birth to another baby girl. Not long after that, I remember mama packing us up and we got on a Greyhound Bus and we finally went back to Arkansas, (the bus had an upper and lower deck); we went to the top of the bus (the upper deck). We stayed in Arkansas for a while I don't remember what was going on with my father, but I was real glad to be back in Arkansas.

One day we were playing in the house on a cold day and somehow, my sister (the one that got part of one of her fingers cut off) slipped and fell into the fire place, it burned the side of her leg! She used to catch hell back then (no pun intended)! We also have two older brothers (my father's sons) and my father also had a daughter that was older than my mother! (They are my father's children from his first marriage); but never the less, they are still my brothers, and my sister. They didn't live with us, but we all loved each other. My father was 18 years older than my mother.

Our family ended up moving to Wichita, Kansas in 1959 and that's where we settled. In 1960, I got another sister. We stayed in a two bedroom house on 12th and Ash. I can remember that dirt road on the side of our house; even with all the dust and dirt, my mother still kept the house spotless clean; she was one of the cleanest people I've ever known and she loved cooking! I used to be in the kitchen with her a lot (just watching her).

We attended Ingalls Elementary school on 10th and Grove, we walked to school.

(Time passed.) We moved again, so I had to get used to another school. I was in the fourth grade and attending Isley Elementary School when President Kennedy was killed; and somewhere during that tlme Martln Luther King got killed also; we had moved to 16th and Poplar Street and that's when my mother and father started to fight a lot.

One evening we went to pick my mother up from work (at the Shimmley Inn Hotel, she was a cook there); my father had been drinking, and when my mother walked out the door, she was laughing and talking with a male coworker; my father got mad and when she got to the car he started asking her who the man was: she replied that he was just a friend she worked with. My dad said that she was too friendly with him; he was steaming! They started talking real bad to each other, so my mother refused to get into the car. My sister and I were lying down in the back seat (I was crying). My mother walked all the way home from Kellogg, to where we lived on 16th and Poplar, which was around 8 to 10 miles.

We drove beside her in the car and they argued all the way to the house. Once we got home a big fight broke out; I jumped on my father's back to keep him from hitting mama and I got thrown into the bath tub. My mother took a milk jug and hit him so hard he was knocked into a daze! The police came and stopped the fight; they told my mother that another half an inch would have killed him. (Those were unhappy days) my father's drinking is what caused his peculiar behavior.

Things were bad between them, but we still went to church (with my dad). Church was always a big part of our lives I don't know what happened!

All of us kids used to play church, my brother would play the preacher, and we would pretend to be the women shouting. We were well taken care of. My mother made sure that we learned how to help keep the house clean (we all had chores).

My father would get on us, if we brought home bad report cards. Back in elementary school I was considered a nerd; I would spend recess alone because I didn't have anything in common with the other girls, plus I didn't like doing the things they thought was fun (and I was chubby too)! They would always make fun of me and pick fights with me, for no reason.

I can remember not getting any valentine cards from the kids in my class [to put in my big heart that hung on the classroom wall]. I would give [everyone] in my class, a card; I used to cry a lot; I felt so isolated, and my feelings were easily hurt. I truly loved people but they didn't seem to like me.

I didn't like [that] school; some of the kids were bullies, I thought to myself: "how can people be so cruel!" I was glad when we moved; this time we moved to 20th and Piatt Street. The remainder of my elementary school years, wasn't quite as bad; I was talked about, but I only had to fight a few times (with kids who thought they were all of that).

I tried to stay focused (and keep my grades up), so that I wouldn't be worrying about: [what people thought of me]. My father was a stickler when it came to bad grades (as I indicated before). A bad report card was not an option; we knew that our dad would give us a whipping and we'd have to stay in the house if we brought home a bad grade. We used to try and change our grades but, we always got caught.

Unlike my siblings I didn't get a lot of whippings from my dad because he thought that I could do no wrong. I was always getting away with things that my sisters and brother couldn't. Anytime they tried to tell daddy that I did something wrong, he didn't believe them (although they were telling the truth); I got away with a lot of things.

Back then, school was where children could feel safe; you didn't have to worry about guns and gangs; the most people would do was fight and run home; people just didn't go around shooting and killing one another. We didn't have school buses; we used to walk to school, but we never had to worry about gun fire. This was a time when we could play outdoors and have fun without any worries. I liked all of my teachers they were very concerned about the students and they made sure you learned your lessons I don't think it was just a job (to them). I'm thankful to God that I grew up in that era. Now-a-days, some schools are like war zones with teachers fearing for their lives; all kinds of bad things are happening. Life is hard for our young people today. As I look back on my own childhood I can say with all sincerity that I was truly blessed; things were rarely as bad as they appeared to be at the time. God always protected us from dangers, seen and unseen. Halleluiah!!!!

Even though my parents would fight (sometimes) they loved us enough to not let what affected them, distress us. I always saw (or heard) them praying. The drinking (with my father as I stated before) is what caused a lot of things that went wrong, but I truly knew he loved us. The enemy has always tried to interfere with and destroy families.

We had very good Christmases when both our parents were living in our home together. I loved the Nativity programs at church and I loved Easter (as it was called back then) I always had a speech to recite; and I always sang in the choir. Our family attended Macedonia Missionary Baptist Church on the corner of 21st and Grove; that church was a blessing to my family when we were younger.

Just about the time I'd get used to living in a community; we'd move (this time it was to a beautiful neighborhood, so it didn't bother me). My parents and one other family moved cross 21st street; we moved to 22nd street. (Blacks weren't allowed [cross] 21st, we weren't allowed to live pass 20th street for a long time). I had always thought that the homes across 21st were nice (I was very happy when we moved into one). I had thought that after we left the south, we were through with all of that racial stuff but *Jim Crow* was still alive and well. I had attended Isley Elementary School, but after we moved, I transferred to Mueller Elementary.

Our [past] lives had been centered on God, we were happy for a moment, until one day everything turned counter clockwise (and then some). My parents were not getting along (again); they finally separated and he moved out of the house. My mother started going out clubbing with the woman next door (and some other [new] acquaintances). When they would go to the clubs my oldest sister would take care of us. My mother completely stopped going to church, and it seemed to me that our lives were altered even more. My mother met this guy who would come over all the time (he did hair). Some black men [back in the day] would wear hairdos called [processes]; most of the time their hair looked better than the women's! My mother's boyfriend began to do hair out of our garage, and they went partying a lot.

My father met a lady at church, and they started dating; she was very nice, so we would continue to go to church with him (I attended church as much as possible). I really loved being in the house of the Lord. My oldest sister (and her friends), would have parties at the house when mama was away. I am not real clear why things got so bad but, we had to apply for welfare. I can remember getting (all that) government cheese and spam meat, and all the other stuff that came with it; things were complicated. I remember hating to leave Mueller Elementary School (we planted a tree there, when I was in the 6th grade) I always tell people when we pass by: "I helped plant That Tree!"

Truly God's grace got us through those trying times. We had lived at that house for a long time (lots of secret partying and drinking went on there).

The summer of 1964 was different I was glad to be going to the 7th grade in the fall. We had lots of friends in the neighborhood we would go to each other's houses and play for hours. I had some cousins who lived on Minnesota Street; I loved going to their house, and I loved the sleepovers; it seemed as though it was more fun over there than being at home. The community was changing. I don't know why we as black people can't keep things looking the way they were [before] we were stewards over them.

(Time passed).

It was January sixteenth nineteen sixty-six; we awoke around eight o'clock; at approximately 8:30 AM we heard a loud noise, it sounded (and felt), as though a giant plane was landing in our front yard; it was such a force that things were falling out of the cabinets, and the pressure knocked my mother to the floor. We ran outside and saw an amazing sight! A plane was flying low over our house and one of its doors appeared to be open. We were so scared!!! We watched it fly over 21slStreet; a few seconds later it crashed and exploded!

We thought it had hit our father's house so we all began to run in that direction. When we got there, we saw that it had not hit our father's house, but! I shall never ever forget that deadly day. People were running, screaming, and crying; bodies were burning and there were pieces of fingers, arms and things were floating in fuel (that came from the plane)! I saw them bring a woman out of the area with a baby in her lap (they both were on fire)! I am thankful to God that we weren't [physical victims] of the disaster. I hate, that it crashed on the street where we used to live (first house on the corner). That was one of the saddest things I've ever had to witness.

We later learned: the plane was loaded with jet fuel (engine failure caused the crash).

Life is precious and children should not have to witness such devastation. The pilot had a chance to bail out, but, he wouldn't. He tried to land the plane in the field behind a store called: Razooks on 21st and Piatt. I heard that the control tower was trying to get the pilot to abort the plane, but he wouldn't, he said that he was going to try and land the plane. So in fact he saved many lives that day including (possibly) ours it was a heart breaking event for the whole city. God spared us that day and we are grateful!!! A Memorial Park was later erected at the site; it is called: "Piatt Plane Crash Memorial."

Sometimes we don't realize how blessed we are, until we look around and see what other people have had to endure. I think about that pilot's family and how they had to carry on without him; in my opinion he was a hero. It was in the pilots heart to save as many people as he could; some were lost, but many were saved. The victims of that plane crash didn't have an option to choose life or death, but! Jesus gave us a choice when He gave His life for us on the cross (who-so-ever-will let him come). When adversity comes we do not understand the reasons and so we ask: Why? All we know is that God "sees and cares."

Thank you Father for all you have done.

You are our Alpha and Omega; The Beginning and the End of all things; Rev 21:6

You are our Chief Cornerstone: A sure foundation of life; Ephesians 2:20

You are our Shepherd: One who gives guidance and protection John 10:11, 1 Peter 5:4

You are our Savior: One who delivers from sin and death John 4:42.

You are Immanuel; "God with us;" The One who always stands with us Matthew 1:23.

The separation of my parents caused us kids to struggle both emotionally and financially. Before we moved across 21st street I used to love going to the candy store; they seemed to be everywhere in our neighborhoods. Some people would sell candy out of their homes. Candy was very cheap, back then. You could get 3 pieces of candy for a penny and candy bars were 5 cents (big candy bars). I can remember gas being 19 cent a gallon! I look back and praise God for those days.

Family was important back then even though I felt like we were going through hell at the time I know with all my heart my parents loved us kids.

I can remember this one chapter in the bible when growing up; Psalm 100 [a Psalm of Thanksgiving], it said: "Make a joyful noise unto the LORD. Serve the LORD with Gladness. Come before His presence with singing, Know that the LORD He is God. It is He who has made us, and not we ourselves. We are His people and the sheep of His pasture. Enter into His gates with thanksgiving, and His courts with praise. Be thankful to Him, and bless His name. For the LORD is good. His mercy is everlasting, And His truth endure to all generations." That lets me know we should always be thankful.

1. ***Remember that a grateful person is a humble person and focused on God.***
2. ***Also remember that we are to thank God even in the mist of adversity and trials.***
3. ***God's word wlll always stand no matter what we're going through.***
4. ***We have to thank God in the good times, and also in the bad times. His word will never fail.***
5. ***We must always remember to be grateful for whatever circumstances we find ourselves in.***

Our family was blessed through all we had to go through. I'm truly grateful to my parents for how they loved and kept us covered in spite of all odds. I'm truly grateful.

Here is something God taught me about having an attitude of gratitude, having a thankful spirit.

Grateful with a Thankful Heart

Being grateful is an acknowledgement of who God truly is (and of all the things that He has done for us). Life is a gift from God and there is no gratitude except that which is built on a solid foundation. We must embrace gratitude and learn to pass it on to our brothers and sisters. That's what God wants us to do.

Things to remember

1. ***We must always thank God in the midst of everything; every trial, every test that we go through.*** 1 Corinthians 10:31 says: "Therefore, whether you eat or drink, or whatever you do, do all to the glory of God."
2. ***Write down the blessings that God has given you***.
3. ***Remember all of his faithfulness.*** Hebrews 10:23 says: "Let's hold fast the confession of our hope without wavering, for He who promised is faithful."
4. ***We should express gratitude to God and others***. Never take anyone for granted. Openly do it. Psalms 35:18 says: "I will give You thanks in the great assembly; I will praise You among many people."

God has plans for our lives. We will have interruptions; but we should not allow disruptions or distractions make us lose sight of where God is leading us. A grateful person is humble and [focused] on God, and not his or herself. When we are truly thankful we have a heart full of praise and gratitude.

[An] attitude of gratefulness brings blessings to us and to everyone around us.

Always remember, to be grateful for what God does (in your life).

We should always keep an attitude of gratitude at ***all times; be thankful for what God has done for you.***

1 Thessalonians 5:18 says: "In everything give thanks: for this is the will of God in Christ Jesus concerning you."
Believe me! God truly cares about every situation we find ourselves in.

CHAPTER 2

My Teenage Year

What a wonderful time in my life! Junior High School!!

I attended Brooks Junior High School; it was mostly whites. My brother (who was a year and a half older than me) also went there.

I was glad to be in the 8th grade. Classes got a little harder, but that was OK with me. I was becoming a young lady and I was heavily into sports: running track, jumping hurdles, shock pit and basketball. I won a ribbon in track, I was one of the schools fastest runners.

I was finally old enough to go to the "Tarp" (it was a place where young people (age 12 to 17) would go on Friday nights: from 7 to 9 PM, to dance and have big fun!!!

I met some girls and we began to hang out, they attended Mathewson Junior High. It was the, so called: "HIP" school. Anyone who didn't go there, wanted to! I really didn't know it at the time, but this is where my troubles would begin.

As I can remember, Mathewson was an all-Black School, so that's where I wanted to go, but we were not in that district. I'd hang out with the people from Mathewson, and go to the Tarp on Friday night (with my big sister). Very often we went without parental consent because my mother wasn't at home and my oldest sister was watching us (we had to go where she took us). One time we got caught! I saw my father come in there because my mother had called him and told him what we had done. I ran to the side of the walls, so he couldn't see me, but he caught my oldest sister. It was kind of funny to me; she was so embarrassed! She got in a lot of trouble that night.

My brother used to hang out with some teenage boys that he

had met over by our house; some of them lived on Minnesota Street; it seemed like the happening street.

One weekend my mother went out of town, and my oldest sister and a friend of hers decided to have a party! All of their friends came over (our garage and backyard was full of teenagers); they were having a good time and I was too.

About 11:00 o'clock mama came home unexpectedly (we had thought that she'd be gone overnight). My mother and some of her friends came in there and began telling people to leave. She was waiving around the stool plunger and telling the kids to get out of her yard, and out of her garage. My sister was humiliated, and mad at the same time! I felt bad for her that night, she did not want to go to school on Monday; all of the boys teased her about the mother with the stool plunger!

My sister met a young man. I don't know how long they dated, but they were married in our living room. She and her girlfriend friend (next door neighbor) married two brothers. She could not wait to leave home; her husband and his two brothers had moved to Wichita from Memphis Tennessee.

I remember having a school girl crush on my brother-in-laws friend. He was the finest person I had ever seen! It was funny; I used to go over to their house just to see if he was there.

Throughout the summer, I continued to hang out with all of the Mathewson Junior High School girls; I would go to the Tarp, with them (instead of my big sister).

I met a guy that I liked, he was my girlfriend's brother's friend; I looked forward to going to the Tarp on Friday nights (so that I could see him); he really knew how to dance, and I loved dancing! All of his homeboys were awesome dancing machines! That was a fun summer!

School started again; I was a 9th grader; and I still wanted to go to Mathewson Junior High; the guy I liked went there, and I wanted to be near him (stupid huh?).

We ended up moving to the corner of 14th and Hillside; I don't know why we moved during the school year, but I was GLAD because, I was finally going to attend Mathewson; we were just 7 blocks from the school, so I started the end of 9th grade, at Mathewson, YEA!!!

There was a lot of fighting and other bad things going on at that school I tried to stay out of trouble, but it just did not happen. The girls that I would run around with were always into something, and I would be right there with them, because I did not want to feel the way I felt in grade school, (I really wanted to fit in and not look like a nerd), so whatever they did, I did.

I used to wear the same skirt every day; I had four different blouses to rotate. I would feel ashamed because my friends wore pretty clothes that matched, and I had to wear the same thing all the time. So one day, one of the girls asked me if I wanted to go downtown with them to get some new clothes, I said yes!

One Saturday we caught the bus and went down town, and when I saw what they were doing, I got scared. One of the girls grabbed my bag and helped me put some items in it, I was scared we'd get caught, but we got on the bus. I looked out the back window of that bus until we got out of sight (fearing someone saw us and that they would catch us).

As time passed I got used to shoplifting, we began to catch the bus downtown, and stealing became a habit. We would go into stores with shopping bags and fill them with clothes, earrings, perfume and everything we wanted to wear; we were stealing big time! When we went to the Tarp we would all be dressed to the max. I would hide the stuff from my mother. I'd wear what I had at home and then when I got to school or wherever I was going I would change clothes.

I liked (the dancing guy), but one Friday night he didn't show up at the Tarp, and I met another guy, (he didn't do much dancing, so we sat down and talked). His friend wanted to be introduced to one of the girls I was with; we all walked home together that night (there were a lot of us and we had fun).

I had to be home by 10:00, or I would get in trouble, but I didn't want my friends to know that. Even though my parents were divorced, my mother would still call our father to tell on us. I tried to keep in good and close contact with my father, as I mentioned before, he always thought that I was [the good one].

I never wanted to disrespect my parents; I didn't want them to know some of the things I was doing; so I would always hide everything from them.

There was a downtown store called Woolworths, it had clothes and personal stuff, and it had a food counter where you could sit on a stool and order food, and eat. We would go in there and get a big shopping bag, and buy one thing each, and put it in our bag, and then we would go to all the stores downtown (we became regular thieves). Looking back at how much loot we took, it was shameful! We never got caught, during that time.

There was always something bad (like fights), going on at Mathewson; we had our own little click, and if one of us got into a fight; it became our fight. Mathewson is where I began to have to get whippings (if I got caught).

I remember one Friday night, I wanted to go to the Tarp, but we couldn't leave the house. My mother went to bed early that night, I can't remember why, but anyway, around 7pm, my sister and I (the one that was up under me), went upstairs to our bedroom; we climbed out the window by grabbing hold to the tree outside our bedroom. (We would climb out, and back up again, unnoticed).

My mother got up just as I was climbing back in the window (that night); I was able to get into bed before she saw me. My sister was coming through the window just as mama was looking in our bedroom; (she was BUSTED)! She...got...into...BIG TROUBLE!!! She tried to tell mama that I had gone out with her (I had already jumped in the bed). My mother called my father and told him what my sister had done, they didn't believe that I had left the house also; they thought she was lying. In between the time she went to call my father I jumped out of the bed and took my clothes off so they did not know that I had been out with my sister. My sister got a whipping that I'll never forget!!! She ran out of the house, and my father ran after her, and caught her. After the WHIPPING, my father cut off that tree limb (that we had been using to pull over to our window); my sister was on punishment for a long time. Those days were very exciting and fun!

The school started giving dances; we'd try to go to everything that was happening. I was talking to two guys during that time. There were two groups of boys, and I and all my friends had a boyfriend in each group (that was a hot mess)! We didn't think anything of it at the time; nothing serious, just kids having fun and hanging out.

Suddenly before I knew it, it was the summer of 1969 and we were all going to the 10th grade in the fall.

It was time to [move again] this time we moved to 10th and Volusia, we all enrolled at East High (everybody wanted to go there, and as it happened, I lived in that district). We didn't stay on Hillside very long I don't know why, but we did our thing during that summer, and we were ready for High School. I had the clothes and the look (at least I thought I did).

School was about to start and my mother took us shopping and bought us some new clothes; I felt so bad because I had all those stolen clothes hidden in my room. I couldn't tell her, that I didn't need any new clothes, I did not want them to know how bad I had been, and that I had taken their trust for granted (because that's what it really boiled down to). I was lying to them, myself, and to God (and I would still go to church). For some reason I just had to be at church; I really liked being there.

I was still singing in the choir, and I was in all the programs (all of us were). It was funny how all the ladies would shout in church as I stated before. I used to love to see my aunt (my father's sister) shout; she would jump up and shout, and turn around screaming all down the row that she was sitting in, and then she would go back and sit down. She was a graceful woman to me; they say: I look a lot like her, and that I act and dress the way she did (my aunt Cleo).

I continued to do bad things and I always felt guilty when I did something wrong, but I did it anyway. As I got older, I would hang out with my friends more and more and we'd walk home from school together. I was 15 years old and that was pretty awesome to me! I was dating and having fun!

One day I was walking home after a school party with a friend. The party had been at a place called: "the Met-Sect center;" It was on Wichita State University (WSU) Campus. My girlfriend and I were walking down 17th street and all of a sudden: I got pulled into a car; the guys were men that we knew; they put one of those old potato sacks over my head; I was kicking and screaming and they just told me to: "shut up!" some of the thugs were boys who used to get mad at me because I would not [just give up my body to them]. They took me out to this place called the "Mills" that's where they used to take girls to rape!!! I was screaming and fighting them, and one of them said: "this is a cock strong "B>>>>." They had a really hard time raping me.

In the middle of my disarray God was [still] watching over me.] All of a sudden, I heard my mother coming, she was hollering: "you better let her out or I'll shoot all of you." She shot the gun once and they pushed me out of car, and they took off! My friend had run all the way over to my house to tell my mother and she told my mother where those boys would take girls to rape. My mother didn't have a car at the time so she hitchhiked a ride (a nice white man picked her up and he drove her to the spot). I was crying and my mother was too; she and the man picked me up off the ground; my clothes were all torn and hanging off me. The man gave me his shirt to put on to cover my body. We went to the hospital and the police came and took my statement (one of the males had done five years for rape before) he was already known for raping women and girls.

After that incident, I did not like boys for a long time after that. One of my attackers was the brother of one of the girls I hung out with; I guess boys will be boys but it's sad that they feel they have to rape someone. As time went on I healed; but it was hard to forget.

It Was God's grace and mercy

The second group of guys was bad too they would steal; not only did they shoplift, but they were also, car thieves. One night they picked us up in some [stolen cars] we didn't know at the time that they were stolen. Three of us got in one of the cars (me, my sister and a girlfriend of ours); we were riding down Cleveland street, laughing and having a good time. Next thing I knew, one of the guys said: "when I say jump out; jump and run." I saw him looking through his rear view mirror as the police passed by us, all of a sudden they made a U-turn right in the middle of the street, and they jumped out of the car; we got stuck in the back seat (we were supposed to lift up to make the seat go up) I panicked; it was a two door GTO; the three of us girls were caught in the car.

The police took us downtown to Juvenile Detention. They called our parents but couldn't reach them so they took us to a place called: Friendly Gables a girl's detention home).

The police were mad because we would not tell them who the boys were. We were laughing and saying we hope they didn't catch them; that was a very stupid statement we made. My sister was crying saying she was going to tell my mother on me if I didn't tell the truth. The police knew who the boys were (they just couldn't catch them).

The next morning my mother came to pick us up; she was so mad at us! (My friend's mother brought her suitcase and told them to keep her)! It was funny to me at the time (they couldn't keep her) so her mother had to take her home, we used to hang out over at her house a lot. I think her mother was sick of us.

[**Time passed**]

We used to go out dancing (a lot) at different places; one time I won a dance contest I was very excited! The guys we hung out with (the first group, as I said before) could dance! All of them; I mean could really dance! Anyway, my partner and I was given the opportunity to be on Hi-Fi Hop (a local TV teenage dance program). I thought I was something! They put us up on this platform in the spot light; boy I had it going on! We used to love to dance the two step. Those were some good times and some bad times.

When I went to the eleventh grade I started skipping school; It got so bad that they charged me with truancy; I had to go to court and I was sent to Friendly Gables (I was 15 years old, and I was hurt to say the least). My mother got so mad that she chased the Judge off the bench! They arrested her for trying to attack him (that was a sad day). Some of her friends got her out of jail (I was very glad that mama was released in a hurry). I spent 4 months in Friendly Gables.

One of my friends ended up in there for stealing (so I had someone to hang with). I went back to court and I was released [to] my father. The stipulation (of my release) was that I had to stay in school, or go back (I was on probation). I ended up being transferred to West High School.

I started having parties at my father's house; he was never there because he spent most of his time at his girlfriend's house although he always came home late at night; he would never stay at her house overnight (he was really into the church, and he didn't believe in shacking up). I did not like the lady he was dating at all! She was much younger than my father, I felt she was only with him for what she could get.

My father was a very nice looking man (all the men in my family were). At the time I wished that he had stayed with the nice woman he met at church (I don't know what happened there). This woman and her sisters would come over and think that they had control over my dad's house.

One time I was not at home and she and her sister (from Oklahoma) came to visit my dad; her sister had the nerve to steal some of my clothes and she took them back to Oklahoma with her! I told my dad and he went over there and told them that they had better get my clothes back where they belong! His girlfriend told him that they were all gone (he went off on her). I heard my daddy say to her: "this is my child and you don't mess with my kids!" My mother was going to get her, because the woman thought that she could run over me; they backed up off of me. After that, I knew then that my father didn't need me trying to defend him (he was not to be used), not one bit! My father let me know (by his actions), I got this! One thing I can say is that my father loved his children.

When I turned sixteen, I dropped out of school I was in the 11th grade. After you turn 16 you didn't have to go to school.

During this time I met this guy, and one of my friends liked his friend (they played basketball). He (BP basketball player) was so fine to me!!

One weekend I thought my father was out of town (for the weekend), so I decided to throw a CO-ED all night party. They used to call my father's house, 809 goodtime! He came back home that night and boy! Did I get it! Everybody started running including me; the boys jumped in their cars and drove off; I was really embarrassed I got grounded for a long time.

Well, my father ended up marrying the woman he was dating (she became my step mother). As the years went by I grew to love her. I saw that she really loved my dad and that's what was important to me. She already had 3 children when she met my father, and after they got married, they had three babies together.

We all went to church as a family. There were still times when I would go out with my friends; we had many fun clubs, back then, you could have good clean fun; even the back yard parties were good.

[Time passed]

I got older and went on to older things. My friends and I had begun to make money from selling things we would steal, such as: cartons of cigarettes to sell to different "fences" (men who would buy them in large quantities). We would make something like 100 to 300 dollars a day. This one Italian man who worked at a club would buy everything we would bring to him.

I bought my first car at 17; it was a pretty white 1959 Buick. I thought I was something back then (we would all get in it and ride around doing things that we had no business doing; we were chases out of stores a lot).

My father didn't have a clue as to what I was doing; he would have put a hurting on me; he was a good man who tried to teach me about the things of the world, and how to respect myself. After he stopped drinking, you couldn't ask for a better father. God was first in his life, and as I look back over the years I can see how and why he wanted us to live for God. When you're young you want to experience things for yourself (I would go out a lot).

The basketball player was a big part of my life; I was also (kind of) still seeing the guy in the second group (that was a mess). The things that I did in my life, when I look back; all **I can say is: My God!!! Father, I thank and I praise You for keeping me safe, even in the midst of my foolishness. I thank and I praise You that You kept me here, to be a blessing to other people coming up around me; help me to teach them through my trials and tests to do what is right and to trust in You, in Jesus Name, Amen**.

Praise is what I do. When we praise God with our whole heart, we can see a break through like no other. Even with all the bad things we have done. I always sing praises to God. That has always been in my spirit. The section called Praise will bless you.

Praises

Praise sometimes stands in the way our human nature (our flesh). Interference sometimes occurs. ***Praising does not always come naturally.**

Praising God must be genuine. It must come from our hearts; even when we are going through tough times (trials and tests). **Praise** is a weapon we can use (to release us from bondage). **Praise** brings victory.

Acts 16:22-25 teaches us how Paul and Silas were beaten (striped), and thrown into the dungeon (prison); through it all they praised God! The other prisoners heard them as they were singing and praising God.

(You never know what your praise might do for yourself or someone else.)

Music played an important part in the battle between Jehoshaphat and Judah's enemies. *2 Chronicles 20:20-22, says: "And they rose early in the morning, and went forth into the wilderness of Tekoa: and as they went forth, Jehoshaphat stood and said, Hear me, O Judah, and ye inhabitants of Jerusalem; Believe in the LORD your God, so shall ye be established; believe in his prophets, so ye shall prosper." Verse 21 "And when he had consulted with the people, he appointed singers unto the LORD, and that should praise the beauty of holiness, as they went out before the army, and to say, Praise the LORD; for his mercy endures forever." Verse 22 "And when they began to sing and to praise, the LORD set ambushments against the children of Ammon, Moab, and mount Seir, which were come against Judah; and they were smitten."* ***The music strengthened the Hebrew soldiers. It signified the defeat of Gods enemies.***

Music gives me courage to defeat (in JESUS NAME) [any evil] that comes my way. I sing and I praise God, a lot. I love singing; praise gives me the breakthrough that I need (for me and those around me). It gives me a melody in my heart. *Ephesians 5:13 says: "But all things that are reproved are made manifest by the light: for whatsoever doth make manifest is light."* ***Praise exposes evil; it brings it to the light (surface). Praise is our weapon against Satan. Praise is power against all principalities on earth.*** God is worthy to be praised at all times; regardless of our circumstances. He is worthy, worthy, to be praised (in good times and in bad).

Here are some scriptures you can read,

Psalm 145:4, 5	1 Chr. 15:16-25	Psalm 33:1-3	1 Peter 2:12
Luke 11:1-4	Psalm 42:5	Psalm 96:3	Isaiah 55:12
Hebrew 13:15-16	Psalm 148:5	Psalm 61:8	Rev 5:12
Ezra 3:10-11 (2)	Psalm 103:1		

Embrace the word of God. Let it become real in your spirit.

IT WAS GOD'S GRACE AND MERCY

Chapter 3

The Crimes began

Finally! I was turning eighteen! I went and got my very first apartment; it was located on seventeenth and Lorraine. All of my cohorts [friends] had their own apartments (also).

My boyfriend (in the second group) moved in with me; he started getting high. His uncle was off into the "big times" (crime), and we got in the middle of it. UG (uncle gangster) was the one who first introduced me to heroin; I began to sell it; he was dealing with some big time people (gangsters). (If I'm remembering correctly) during that time UG was going with a lady that was with a Well-known poplar band group. (in some capacity); he also knew Sly and the Family Stones. I liked being around him.

My boyfriend became an extensive dope user; he got on it real bad and we started fighting a lot. I came home one day and he had sold everything in the house. I had rented that furniture from a place called: Home Furniture, and I still had to continue to pay for it. My life was going from bad to worst.

One day he came in the kitchen while I was washing dishes and I told him that I didn't want him anymore; he spit...up the side of my face! I was so humiliated; all I could do was cry. I moved out of that apartment and moved on. I got another apartment, this time by myself.

[Time passed]

I messed up my car and had to buy another one, so I bought a 1967 navy blue Chevy. My two friends and I started stealing cartons of cigarettes again. One day we had 298 cartons in the car and we needed 2 more to make it 300 (to divide equally); so, we went into a store; my friend was spotted stealing something. We ran out the door and jumped into the car (my girlfriend was d people from getting the tag number. The police ended up seeing us driving); we drove that car in reverse for 3 blocks to keep the store anyway, so we jumped out the car and ran. The police confiscated the car and all of the cigarettes.

I called and reported my car stolen as soon as I got to a phone; I told them that I went in this place and came out and my car was gone. The police came to my house and asked me so many questions (I really didn't know how to answer), but we escaped jail that time; oh, I was glad, because that would have been a felony!

We may have gotten away that time, **but God still sees everything**. The Bible tells us that we reap what we sow. Eventually you will end up paying for everything you've ever done wrong, and I mean everything. ***God's love is unconditional.***

By that time in my life, I had really gotten off into selling drugs; it started with just weed, and later hash, pills, acid, and eventually dealing heroin (big time). We were smoking weed (taking it with some pills and other kinds of drugs; we tried everything).

[I didn't like the way any of it made me feel] I took drugs to fit in with the crowd. I remember one night we all took a tab of acid, called: window pane; we were on a street called Hillside; we're laughing and playing in the street. We took our shoes off, and started throwing them into the middle of the street; the cars were running over them; it was funny (to us) because we were under the influence. Everyone threw their shoes, except for one of my friends; she loved her footwear; she had very small feet, and her shoes were very important to her. We had just stolen the shoes from a store called: Models (down town); the store had just got them in. I'll never forget those shoes; they were a pretty beige color with wooden cork heals, we all had a pair. (We dressed alike a lot back then.)

After our expedition in the street we went to my friend's house on Spruce Street (we hung out in the yard a lot in those days) we did many immature things back then (we were out of control). I was heavily into dealing drugs and still doing a [little stealing] on the side. Sometimes I would buy stolen goods from other people, or I'd barter drugs for clothing, and household goods (whatever I wanted).

I was moving a lot because I was getting into the dope life, really, really heavy now! There was a doctor who would write a prescription for whatever kind of pills you wanted; anything from: speed, sleeping pills, valium, red devil (reds), Quaaludes and the list goes on and on; we would sell them one pill or by the bottle.

We liked to hang out at Skate-land north (back then) we were good skaters. I was dating BP during that time (and so were a lot of other girls) he thought he was all of that (and he was); he and one of his friends hung out at the skating ring, looking good, showing out and dancing on their skates: I would just melt when he was around!

We had lots of fights at Skate-land and the guy who stood at the door hated to see us coming; he thought we were the worst bunch he'd ever come across. (It was us against the other group of girls that our 'boyfriends' messed around with; we would fight all the time.) We'd put our claim on someone or something, and we thought they or it belonged to us. We didn't take a lot of stuff off anyone. We started going to jail, for a lot of petty things (breaking the law became a habit and an occupation to us).

As years passed we all used to go to Kansas City on weekends to party, and just hangout (we'd stay with my friend's sister) we had some good times in Kansas City.

A few more years went by and one of my friends moved there and got with a guy who was into drugs; I went there with some other friends and stayed for a while; I was introduced to an older hustler: KCG (Kansas City Guy); he was a friend of a friend of mine; I ended up dating him. KCG was at least 20 years older than me (I think he was 42 and I was 22); a big age difference huh! After a few months of being in Kansas City he talked me into moving in with him; Guess what! He was a dope dealer too! It seemed like everyone I met were into drugs.

I was introduced to his friends and began to live a life of [more] drugs. I took to stealing again (like I'd done before). I had thought that I graduated from larceny, but it was not a reality; this time I was shoplifting with KCG's friends-girlfriends (most of them got high).

Two of my friends came to Kansas City from Wichita, and I would take KCG's dope and give it to them (to get high on, and then I would give them drugs to take back home).

KCG used to take me to concerts; I saw many of the hit musical artists of the day. Life seems (on the surface) to be: all that.

I met up with some other ladies from Wichita who had moved to Kansas City; one of them introduced me to a younger guy (YG) who was about my age, I liked him. I had a ten speed bike that I'd ride a lot for exercise. YG would come over on his bike and we would go riding together. It was fun to be with him, just doing normal things.

One day the KCG got home early and caught me with YG (we were not in a sexual relationship he was just someone I had fun being around). KCG thought I was sleeping around on him;
(I wasn't, but I could not make him believe that), so he locked me in the basement. One of his friends came over and convinced him that-that was not cool, so he let me out.

We went to a concert that night; I did not enjoy it at all. After that he began to 'look' at other women. He was smoking almost an ounce of weed a day; he didn't do the hard stuff, he just sold it.

One night he brought another woman home and told me to go to the other room. I left the house and called my mother and told her that I wanted to come home and to please come and get me.
I stayed at a store on Prospect Street, until my mother and my brother-in-law arrived to take me back to Wichita. I left everything that I had; I did not care I was just ready to get away from that life.

I was back in Wichita only a few weeks before I went right back into that same old life style. I don't remember the details, but I came in contact with some fellows I had known before (they used to live in Wichita and they were back in town for a visit). These guys were dealing dope out of California; I think this was in 1975 I was with my sister (under me), along with one of my friends when we met up with them. We [like fools] ended up going to California with them.

They lived in Kensington Hills in a big beautiful home. We had lots of fun in that house (until we got busted). My sister had a habit of going to the bottom of the hill to steal a Chinese ladies wigs.

It was the day after Thanksgiving; If the police had come to the house on Thanksgiving Day, a [lot] of people would have gone to jail because there was so much dope in that house it was unbelievable!

It was early in the day when all of a sudden all the windows and doors came falling in; it seemed like all of the police and narcotic agents in California were out there. My sister, my friend and I were the only women in the house and they made us take off our clothes in front of all those cops! We had to stand before them buck naked! Guess what was on the search warrant? Thirteen Wigs! My sister was stealing that ladies wigs! Those wigs got us busted! The cops said they'd been trying to find justification to come in there, and those wigs were their excuse; we were really upset with my sister.

They searched the house (they went through everything), they did not find the drugs they were looking for. I had hid some dope [up under a piece of wood] that I had taken out of the floor, and I put the carpet back over it. We had a lot of money in that house; the police said we made a big donation to the Nixon campaign that year.

They took us to the Martinis California, county jail. While we were locked up my sister had all kinds of people wanting to fight us (she was a feisty one); she and a cell mate got thrown in the hole.

My sister and my friend ended up getting out, but I was sent to San Aretha; they claimed that I had sold drugs to an agent; they were mistaken, it was not me. It was another female drug dealer who had sold dope to an undercover agent, but they could not do anything with the case because the agent was [also a junky], who shot-up all of the dope that he was supposed be to taking to give to his brother (the narcotics agent).

These guys had been under investigation for 3 years so, we

were caught in a trap. San-Aretha was a jail that was in the desert I was there for several hours: It was scary. There was a big woman there that loved women and she said that I was going to be her girlfriend; I started crying. About five hours later they called my name and I was released I was happy as a lark. After that, we all ended up back in Wichita, Kansas we all just left, and went back to where we belonged: "AT HOME."

[Time Passed]

I had moved back home with my mother. She left for work about 7:00 AM that morning; a little later two men knocked on our door I opened the door; the two men had a picture of me, they said that I had jumped bail in California. Yes! I had jumped bail because I felt that it was not my case; so why would I have to deal with it! They said they could take me back willingly, or they could just drag me back. I told them that I would go to jail here, and let Wichita send me back to California. They told me: "No! Get dressed we're taking you back to California." I told them I had to call my mother because my younger sisters were there and I could not leave them alone. One of the men walked with me to the back and I got my clothes and went into the bathroom; I told him he was not coming in with me to change my clothes.

I took the phone in there with me and I called my mother I told her what was going on I told her they were bounty hunters and she asked me if I could get out of the house and I told her that I was going to jump out the window and run. She said that she was going to call my aunt and then she'd call the police. The men were trying to tell me to hurry up...and...come on; I told them to wait a minute.

I had locked the bathroom door I raised the window up real slow I looked out and saw one standing at the end of the house. I knew I only had one chance to escape, so I kicked the screen off and jumped out, then I took off running, and they could not catch me; remember, in my junior high days I ran track! I ran down the back alley and on to the dirt road; as I turned the corner, the police drove up; they got the men and took them to jail I never saw or heard from them again.

Hustlers were always trying to date me because I knew how to make money dealing drugs.

I started going down on 21st (I used to love going down there): BJ's Steak house, the Inn-Crowd, a club call The Apollo, and a restaurant called Chat & Chew where my mother was the cook; all those clubs were on twenty first street. Everybody loved my mother's cooking! When the clubs let out, Chat & Chew would really be jumping; it was a popular hangout.

I was in my middle 20's, hanging out, and making money was my thing. I did not like being around a lot of fighting anymore, so I became a loner.

My sister got with a guy that I couldn't stand. He was very crazy (to me); he and I didn't get along; I did not like what my sister was doing for him. (There were a lot of pimps in Wichita.) He used to tell me: "you think you're too good the sell your body!"
I told him: "I damn show is!" He had a friend that was a big time drug dealer that they wanted me to [play on]. My sister said: "you don't want to sell your body; just look pretty for this Fat Man (FM) and he'll give you anything you like:" I was very petite at the time so I decided to meet FM when he came into town. He liked me right off, and I ended up flying to California with my sister and that crazy man (that's what I called him) they put us in a nice hotel.

I began transporting drugs for FM, and my sister would do her thing; I was very scared for her. One time she got wrapped in barbed wire she still did not let that stop her. I was waiting for her to come out of a room one time (it was during the time when the Zodiac Killer was loose in California); I waited and waited. The man she went in there with had tied her up and taken her money; at the same time I was walking down the street; and a man was getting ready the slit my throat. My sister's man drove up and stopped him (I guess he thought that I was a prostitute.) He told me I needed to get the F>>> off the streets before I got my dumb a>> killed.

Anyway, the four of us would get [dressed up] and go to the Speakeasies along the strip (they were after hour clubs). Anybody who was anybody, hung out "on the strip." One night we were hanging out and I went to the restroom (people know when you're new). While I was in there, some women came in and corned me They were going to jump me and take my money; my sister walked in and said: "I knew your a>> was in trouble." She told them B>>>> to back off! They knew her! As I mention before my sister was fearless; we got out of there.

It was time to go home; we walked outside, all of a sudden some shooting started [FM had a wife] I said: "what the hell is going on?" My sister's man said: "ya'll had better run cause that B>>>> is crazy." The man was too fat to run; he was backing up, telling her to wait a minute, let me explain! We got in the car and left him there. He called me and said: "you just going to run off and leave me huh!" I told him: "hell yea! I was not getting ready to get shot." I asked him: "why didn't you tell me you were married?"

The next day he came to the hotel, I was getting ready to take some drugs back to Kansas; he came in and gave me the [stuff] and some money, and put me in a cab; I left.

Well!!! Dumb as it sounds, I had the cab driver take me to the wrong airport. I was supposed to leave out of San Francisco, but I went to East Oakland. The cab driver knew that I was not from there, so he told me that he had to charge me 30 percent extra for going out of the way (how can you go out of the way when you're paying a cab)? I was dumb enough to fall for it. He turned the cab around and took me to San Francisco; when I got there, my plane had left.

I called FM and a woman answered the phone; said she was his sister, I told her what happen and she said to catch a cab back to the hotel. Oh my God!!! When I got there she was waiting for me...it was his wife! She was a big woman, very tall over me. She and one of her friends got out of the car and walked me to the room. She told me to open the door and she pushed me in; I was so scared! She had a gun and she said she had two bullets in it, one for me, and one for him. She said she was so tired of these young B<<<< talking all of her money. I tried to tell her I didn't know he had a wife. She asks me, if I was planning on coming back? I told her I was supposed to; she said: "the hell you are!"

She said: "get everything you have in this room and pack it, when you get on that plane you better not come back; I'm going to take you back to the airport and wait for you to get on the plane."

So I did as she said I had to drag all that stuff down the stairs, she said she'd pay for whatever else it would take, so I checked out of the hotel and got in her car and left.

It was misty outside, and they had their windows down. I asked them if they would roll up the windows, and her friend replied: "Do you hear anybody talking in here?" She said: "no!" (Answering her own question) I felt so humiliated. We got to the airport, finally. I didn't care about what they were doing or saying, I just wanted to get away from that woman.

I had about an hour before my plane left, so we went in the restaurant and sat down; she ordered me a glass of milk!

When they called my flight, I was so glad! They walked me to the terminal (where you go through the door to the plane). I got to where I knew they could not come without a ticket, and I turned around and said to the woman: "You Big Old B, I'll be back" she tried to get on that plane, but she couldn't. Talking about dangerous! I was playing with fire. When I told my sister what had happened she laughed her head off. I called him and told him about her (I think he was scared of her).

Well like a fool I ended up going back out there again; my sister and I were staying at a hotel in East Oakland and one day I was driving FM's car on the freeway we pulled up to a light while getting off on an exit; Guess who we ran into? That woman! After I had talked crazy to her, I knew she was ready to kill me!! My sister said: "you better hit it," really laughing her head off. I took off in that Cadillac; we were going in and out of traffic like a high speed chase; my sister thought it was funny. I managed to get away from her and I said: "I'm through with this; I cannot live like this!" We started going places, just hanging out, but I was always watching my back.

One night I met a guy who had played a pimp in a Blaxploitation movie: Guess what! He really was a pimp in real life!

He had about 14 women working for him! I thought I was something special because he was wining and dining me. My sister said: "he's baiting you in" I said: "no he's not; he really likes me!" She said" "OK! You know, they whip their women with clothes hangers, out here!" I did not pay her any attention. So this went on for about 3 months.

One day he came to pick me up and told me he wanted me to meet the family I said: "OK!" I was happy, because I really thought that I was going to meet his family (his immediate family). We got to this big beautiful home and walked in; there were all these women in evening wear and looking glamorous! They were all his women; my mouth dropped! He took me around the entire room and introduced me, and then he told me who I would be going to work with. He had spent a lot of money on me; I guess he figured it was coming back, I said: "oh God, what have I done!!! I can't sell my body!" I said: "God you've got to get me out of this!" When the pimp took me back to the hotel, he told me to be ready: "they will pick you up tonight."

I was scared; I moved from that room and disappeared. My sister said: "he will find you, and he is going to get back all that money he spent on you." You know pimps don't ask for sex from you, when they are trying to catch you, they treat you like a perfect lady, strange huh?

[Time Passed]

A few months went by, and I was hanging out with some friends who lived up in the mountains, the [road winded] up to their house. My girlfriend was driving us up there one day, she used drugs a lot, she was so high I was scared that she was going to drive us off the cliff (I still prayed a lot in my past and God's mercy covered us even though I did not deserve it).

One night they had a big party up there and I went to help host it, and help with the food (I always loved to cook). It was a formal event so I got dressed at their house. I was greeting everybody at the entrance door while she and her husband entertained. They had someone at the bottom of the stairs to open the door, and I stood at the top. The way their house was built you had to come up the stairs to their living room (it was beautiful).

Well about 8:00 PM the doorbell rang, guess who was at the door? It was the [movie pimp] and all of his women he had one on each arm, and the rest were walking behind them. I froze like no body's business!!! He walked up those stairs looking directly at me, we had eye contact until he got to the top. He told the ladies to go on in. I held my head down, and he took his hand and lifted my head back up (so he could look me in the eye), he told me he was not going to bother me because he knew I didn't know any better he said: "you are just a pretty little country girl that was out here in the fast life, getting ready to get lost if you did not go home." He said: "this life is not for you" and then he kisses me on the forehead and said: "YOU GO HOME!" He walked away I was so relieved, but I still did not hang out at that party (I stayed in the back).

Eventually, I went back to Wichita (but not right away). Once I got back to Kansas I started hanging out again. I would have money and I'd always try to turn it to make a profit.

One night I went down to BJ's Steak House, I walked in and I saw this guy! Oh man! He was sitting at the bar; I thought: that's the finest man I've ever seen! The basketball player was nothing compared to him (as far as looks were concerned). Oh boy! I played it cool; every woman in the place looked at him when he walked by; I stayed cool although I was dying to say something to him I just sat at the end of the bar (he was about 5 seats over from me); I was looking good: I thought. I was wearing a black and peach (two piece) outfit with a big black flop hat, I looked like a model I had a shape that was out of this world, back then (smile) all of a sudden, he spoke to me. Gosh! I could have melted! But was cool; I was so glad I did not act like a nut, wanting to talk to him; carrying yourself like a lady pays off.

We talked and danced the whole night. He had beautiful hair that went down to the middle of his back, that man was sexy, and fine! I really thought I was something back then when I was with him. We'd go out on the town and, we'd spend time at one another's house.

When he realized that I was the woman people were talking about who could really make money selling drugs; he would give me money and I would buy heroin for us to resell. I could really sell drugs (because I was not a "user").

I began to like the money we were making. We became a big time couple I would dress us alike (meaning the same colors) and we would go out to have a good time, we were inseparable.

I've always loved to dress, and I would pick out clothes for him also. I had good taste in choosing men's clothes (as well as my own). I knew what would look right, just by looking at you. A lot of woman wanted him I found out after a year, that he was married (his wife lived in California) he told me that they were "separated." I loved that man a lot.

Seems like I was always drawing married men and drugs. He began getting other people (mostly women) to sell drugs for us; they would get strung out and would make money so they could get high. He lived with me and he never stayed away from home, except when he was out [gambling all night].

He started going back and forth to California a lot. He had a brother who would always look after me whenever he was away. His brother was like my protector (from other men, who would try to "catch me"). I was well known in the fast life because of what I did, and how I did it.

One day I was on 21st Street, and there was [this] guy who had been trying for a long time to "catch me" he pulled up in his car, and said: "come here for a minute with you fine a>>." I walked over there and he tried to pull me in his car and take off with me, and some people stopped him! He was very crazy.

When my man (MM), was out of town every man who was [off into that life] tried to "catch me." One even went crazy, because I stayed over at his girlfriend's house. He told people that I was there because I was: "his woman." I was in the Apollo one night and he came in talking wild; he had a gun in his hand, and he was drinking. [His woman] and I were sitting at the bar; he walked over and said: if I didn't choose him, he would blow my head off! She and I both were scared; she had always been afraid of him.

All of a sudden, MM's brother walked in (the one I referred to as my protector) and ran up on the guy; oh boy! He put a gun in the back of his head and told him to back off! "That's my brother's woman you can't F...with her! Leave her alone or I'll blow your head off!" Everybody in the club started running for the door. The [crazy] guy's father (the owner of the place) came in and things calmed down a bit; he never bothered me again.

MM came back to town; I was so glad to see him, he didn't go out of town again for a while after that.

[Timed Passed]

The next time MM left town, he was gone much too long. I went down on 21st met a guy who was well known; he'd pop in and out of town all the time he drove a beautiful Rolls-Royce. I started talking to him, because MM was gone too long (he had told me that he and his wife weren't together but I didn't believe him anymore and I wanted to make him jealous).

I started going out of town getting drugs for this [new guy (NG). By me doing this, I got an even bigger connection. NG would give me money to buy cocaine and heroin. One time (I can't remember if I lost his dope, or if it got stolen) he came to my house around 7:30 in the morning with a male friend (of one of the girls that I ran around with); he said: "come take a ride with me." I said: "ok" I got in the car and when he turned the corner from my house, he hit me in the mouth and broke my front tooth (on the right side); that's why I have a gold crown. He got mad because I made him look like a fool. He knew that I was still with MM. When you play around with fire, you get burned yourself. He thought he messed me up, but, the gold tooth made me more appealing (he's dead now). I was told that some dope dealers killed him in Kansas City.

I was angry with MM for going back to California, and when I tried to make him jealous, it backfired on me.

I met two ladies and we became good friends; we started working at: McConnell Air force Base (in the NCO Club) together. I worked in the dining room (it was fun out there). I was still with MM, but I got tired with him dealing with other women, he told me it was only "about the money," so I just started seeing other people for fun.

I met this sergeant at the NCO club; he was a very nice person I saw him for a while, but it did not get serious because I was so in love with MM that I really could not fall for anyone else.

His wife came to Wichita because she wanted to know who I was. I noticed a car following me one day as I was driving to my cousin's house (on Kellogg & Elpyco); the car pulled up behind me. This woman jumped out of that car and came up to me and tried take my keys out of my hand; she told me to: give her that car. I looked at her and said are you crazy! I sold most of the dope that bought [this] car. She started crying about her husband and I told her that MM said that the two of them were through and are getting a divorced. Someone pulled her back (away from me) I got in the car, and drove off. I went to find MM; when I found him, I told him what had taken place (I don't know what happened when he saw her).

Things were getting a little ugly in our 'relationship' with her in Wichita (and some other unpleasant things were going on as well). He was the love of my life (back then). After I found out he was married I should have [bailed out] right then and there, but I didn't. I was mad a lot; because women were constantly in the background because of the drugs we were dealing. And, I was frequently approached by men who knew that I dealt drugs.

All the hustlers wanted me to be their woman; there was one in particular who would come to my house, he was MM's best friends brother. He was always saying that I was going to be his woman. He was a Pimp! I didn't like him; I wasn't going to sell my body for anyone (that was one thing I really despised). I always knew in my heart (even back then) that "women," should not allow [men] to rent (out) "their" bodies in order to put money in [their] pockets.

I'd go out to clubs by myself if I wasn't with MM. I was addicted to making money by selling drugs (that was my thing). I met a lot of folks in that profession, both dealers and addicts; many people were strung out on drugs and they would do anything to get [a high]. A lot of bad things were happening. My life was taking a turn for the worst and I was always looking over my shoulder.

One day MM and I (and someone whose name I don't remember) drove to California in an old Chrysler. Anyway, our air conditioner broke down in the desert; that was one of the most horrible experiences I had ever had. It was so hot! It was like: HELL!!! We stopped to get a hotel until night fall and all their air conditioning was out of order, also. We checked into the hotel anyway because we figured it would still be better than riding in that heat. After we checked in, we decided to go swimming, and guess what! The water was so hot you could have boiled something in it.

We left, when the sun went down and drove all night; we finally made it to California. We arrived in CA and did what we went there to do. MM ended up selling the car and we had to fly back to Wichita. He left me alone again; he was constantly in and out of town during that time, and I was busy selling drugs.

In order to fool people into thinking that I worked for a living, I started waitressing at a club on 9th street called: 904. During that time I was running around with a girl that I met at the club (we'd do things together).

One night a guy from Junction City came to the 904, he had a lot of people at his table with him; he was spending lots of money and he tipped me very well (I was his waitress for the 3 nights he came to the club that weekend). The last night he was there he gave me his phone number on a ten dollar bill and told me to call him. MM was out of town so I decided to call JC (Junction City Guy); he asks me to come to Junction City. I talked my friend into going with me.

We didn't have a way up there so we hitchhiked. MM had taken the car and drove it out of town (he had sold the one we drove to California). Hitchhiking was a very stupid thing to do but we made it to Junction City. He was off into big time drug dealing; I didn't know whether to be fascinated or scared! So, I high tailed it back to Wichita he had someone drive us back home; I was glad. More than likely he had heard that I was a 'good drug dealer' (as I said before, I really could make the money because I was not a user).

I tried again to get high; I thank God I never liked the way it made me feel. That heroin was one of the worst highs that anyone could have, all it did was make a person nod and get sick.; I always got sick I really didn't see what people saw in that stuff but you could buy anything you desired if you had some dope to sell. I became [big, big, time pusher] and then I started getting robbed (a lot). People would break into my house; it got so common that I would just walk in, look around to see what they took or were taking, and just leave, and move someplace else; and buy more stuff. One time when I returned from out of town, someone had piled my clothes on the middle of my bed and set them on fire [I knew who had done it]. I had let [this girl] move in with me, she was a dancer who worked at the strip clubs and her boyfriend was a dope dealer.

One day some men came out of Kansas City looking for him. He was not there the night they robbed us, but he was [the target]. The stripper girl, tried to hold on to his stuff, but I told her to give them anything they wanted because I was not going to die for anybody. She was really trying to save his belongings! I thought to myself: 'this girl has got to be out of her mind!' No man is worth dying for because you are trying to hold on to his [stuff] especially, if he's not your husband and doesn't have any intention of looking at you, that way! She (and a lot of other women), was crazy over that guy. He was very young, but he rolled with the big boys! They both were mad at me: like I cared!

A short time later it became pretty obvious that they were the ones who set the fire in the middle of my bed, because nothing in her room was touched! I was really upset about the whole thing. She moved out shortly after that. I took whatever furniture wasn't burned or scorched and moved to another apartment. Things were simple back then (you could move anywhere, as long as you had the money to pay the rent) your credit history wasn't important. I moved to a community called: Shadow Lakes, it was a beautiful location; JC moved me there and paid my rent (for a year in advance); he even bought me a car and put it in my name.

I was still emotionally attached with MM; but he was in California again, and he [would] be gone for months on end. JC was [big stuff] in the drug world and I thought that I was living it up, like: Ms. Queen Bee. Everyone knew to come to me if they wanted dope (because I had the Right Connections).

I was transporting drugs in, and out of Wichita, and other places, not comprehending that my freedom could be taken away from me at any given moment. (I didn't realize how important liberty really was until I [later] lost mind.) I used to be the drop-off person for most of the people that were dealing for JC.

Most of my friends began to get high [off the hard stuff]. I am very sad for people who were, and are still on dope. Back then (as I said before) people would do anything to get drugs. I learned all about cocaine and heroin; I knew how to cut it to make more money, I would make as much money for myself, as I made for the person I was selling it for; it became a regular business for me.

I would still go to church, ha! Isn't that something? God was still (partly) in my life. I think that's why I felt so bad about what I was doing. I felt sorry for the people who were hooked on illegal drugs; if they didn't have money I would just give the dope, or I'd tell them that they could pay me later.

This was funny at the time: one night I hid all the dope that I had in a pond behind the apartment complex; there were big rocks around it (that you could pull out); I guess I didn't properly put the rocks back in place and the ducks in the pond pecked and busted all of the bags (dope was floating in the water). Thank God none of the ducks died!

I started exchanging lots of money (out of town; in my father's name). I figured that since he was a business man no one would be the wiser. I got to where I felt unstoppable and I began to want to make (more) money for myself; so, I taught to myself how...I felt: 'why do all of this (buying and selling dope) for someone else!' It wasn't my body I was selling, but it was still a form of prostitution. (I was giving money to a darn man); so, I couldn't look down on anyone who was selling their body to support a man, because if you look at it clearly; I was selling my SOUL.

I truly thank God for covering me even in the midst of my foolhardiness. My life was out of control. I can say assuredly that it was **God's Grace and Mercy** that kept me. As I think back to some of the things I did! I am still alive to tell it, all I can say is: "MY GOD!!!" **It was truly God's Grace and Mercy!**

Mercy does not give us what we do deserve. **Grace** gives us what we do not deserve.

Let's look at **"Grace:"** it denotes goodwill, kindness, and benefits. It gives us favor that we don't deserve (undeserved favor from God). The LORD God accepts us with unconditional love. Who else can do that but God? *John 1:14-17 says; "And the word became flesh and dwelt among us, and we beheld His glory, the glory as for the only begotten of the Father, full of grace and truth." V15 "John bore witness of Him and cried out, saying, This was He of whom I said. He who comes after me is preferred before me, for He was before me." V16. "And of His fullness we have all received, and grace for grace." V17 "For the law was given through Moses, but grace and truth came through Jesus Christ."*

"Mercy:" *Psalm 5:7-12 says: "But for me, I will come into your house in the multitude of Your mercy. In fear of You I will worship toward Your Holy temple." V8 "Lead me, O LORD, in Your righteousness because of my enemies. Make Your way straight before my face." V9. "For there is no faithfulness in their mouth; their inward part is destruction; their throat is an open tomb; they flatter with their tongue;" V10 "Pronounce them guilty, O God! Let* *them fall by their own counsels; Cast them out in the multitude of their transgressions, for they have rebelled against You." V11 "But let those rejoice who put their trust in You. Let them ever shout for joy, because You defend them; Let those also who love Your name be joyful in You." V12 "For You, O LORD, will bless the righteous with favor You will, surround him as with a shield."* David was in trouble because his enemies were lying about him. He prayed, with confidence; he knew God's love would not only console him, but defend and shield him. God will judge evildoers!

GOD'S LOVE IS STRONGER THAN ANY EVIL WE WILL FACE. REMEMBER THAT.

Grace includes:

Salvation; Ephesians: 2:8
Adoption; Ephesians: 1:5
Inheritance; Ephesians 1:11
Holiness; Ephesians 1:4
Heavenly Citizenship; Phil 3:20

Grace is one of God's great pleasures.

The sin we commit is not a match for God's grace. That's why His mercy is new every morning. God loves us so much! I thank God for all I have been through to get me to this point. I express that a lot in this book. We all have done things we're ashamed of (if we are honest with ourselves). We know that if it wasn't for God's grace and mercy we probably would not have made it through some of the situations that we have found ourselves in.

I thank the LORD everyday (all day). I know He loves me in spite of the things I have done.

THANK YOU JESUS!!!

Chapter 4

Life as a Dope dealer

I was rolling big time. I got so good at what I was doing; people called me the, "Lady with the Bag!" [High rollers] thought the world of me, they liked the way I carried myself. I was always a lady thanks to my father who taught me to respect myself; and yet, in spite of his teaching my life became: "all about the money."

I met two white girls who were the women of two "brothers." I can't remember the exact time they came into my life, but those women were two of the best friends you could ask for (considering our lifestyles). The guys were in the adult entertainment business (strip clubs, adult video stores, and massage parlors). They started buying drugs from me; they would purchase quite a bit of it, to get high on (themselves).

The women's boyfriends, and the guy I was with, didn't like one another (very much); as a matter of fact, they did not like each other at all. The "brothers" thought that we were getting too much of their money.

One day one of the women came to my house and said that her man was going to [drop a dime on us]. Both women showed up at my door on the day that their men were going to send the police to arrest us (they told their men that if we were busted (because of them), that they were going to leave them). They were some money making girls, for real!

I was coming and going. I was dealing with all the major players in the dope game, and I became an "Addicted drug dealer" (myself). I was well into my twenties by that time I thought of myself as a seasoned pro. I was looked up to by those in the "under" world. I was still with the man (MM) that I had fallen in love with, plus I was still playing JC. I was wheeling and dealing [BIG TIME].

I was going out of town a lot, bringing drugs back for diverse buyers and sellers; dropping them off to dealers along the way.

At some point I started to be stressed out all the time. I was always having to watch my back. People loved to rob you, back then (if you blinked). I had lots of protectors while MM was in California; his friends and his brother watched out for me, and I stayed busy making money. I had tons of associates during that time; [Maybe] just maybe, it was only because I always had an abundant supply of drugs.

One time I returned home and someone had kicked my apartment door off its hinges! I couldn't understand how none of the neighbors heard a thing! If they saw what happened, they were too terrified to speak up; whoever broke into my apartment took a lot of my jewelry. I had diamonds: for days! So...they took those things! I think they thought that I had drugs in the house.

A few months went by and one of my close friends (the one that I talked about earlier who went with me to Junction City), started getting high real bad (her and another friend); I was really hurt by that, I hated seeing them strung out. I always felt bad for people who were hooked on that stuff, even when I was the one selling it. (Drug money is extremely addictive.) The guilt was breaking my heart. People were being destroyed. Buying and/or selling dope is wrong; I was hurting people!

One day a guy took his mother's gold teeth to trade for some dope; I was out done with that one! It was hard seeing a lot of stuff that was happening because of the love of dope and money. I had furnished my entire house because people brought me things they had stolen in order to barter (televisions, furniture, whatever you needed, they would get it to trade for a fix).

One day a junkie showed us some very nice coats and MM bought them all (he had come back into town). That weekend I went to the Inn Crowd (club); I wore the black one and thought I was cute I was sitting at the bar when a guy came in [dressed to the nines]; he walked close to where I was sitting; he was looking at me real crazy! Then he walked up to me and said: "that's my coat!" I said: "No it's not." He said: "Yes it is...I was staying over at the hotel on Broadway and someone broke in my car and stole my stuff." He said: "that coat was specially made, it has some initials engraved in the lining;" sure enough he was right. I told him that I needed to get MM. We went to the gambling house where he was; the guy looked at MM and said: "that's one of them also." They talked; MM told him that he paid $1000.00 for the coats and that he would give them back when he got his money back. The guy was a big time hustler out of New York; he gave MM the money, and so we took the coats off, then I went home and got the rest of the guy's coats and gave them to him.

We became associates; he had some really potent dope; the kind you could cut at least 8 times. I started cutting his stuff (to make more money out of it). As bad as I felt about my life, I still didn't stop dealing; I continued to do my thing; the more money I made for the pushers the more money I made me and MM.

I didn't like JC but I was with him just to keep getting the "good stuff." I made him believe that I was his woman (which of course) was the wrong thing to do. He found out that I was still with MM and I guess he thought that I was playing him, because I was not having sex with him. I didn't see it that way (because I gave him his money).

One day my friend (the one who hitchhiked to Junction City with me) was at my house visiting me; some other friends stopped by while we were talking so we were all just hanging out when one of my visitors looked out the window and saw JC's, car; someone said: "that man is out there!" Everyone scattered!!! I went to the front hoping to head him off...he was standing at the door, I looked at him like I had swallowed the canary. He said: "come outside I want to talk to you;" I asked my friend to come go with me and she said: "ok."

When we got outside he put a gun in my side and said you both get in the car. My friend said "B>>>> you're fixing to get us killed," JC "is going to kill us!" He was getting in the back seat, and telling us to get in and drive. I got in on the passenger side; I went in one door and out the other, I was running down the driveway screaming; my girlfriend yelled: "No you're not going off and leaving me!!" JC was coming after me, when all of a sudden, MM's, friends were coming round the corner; they both said: "why are you running like that?" I fearfully said: "that man has a gun! He's trying to shoot me!" They hollered: "STOP!" The man came around the corner and they stopped him. They asked him what the hell he thought he was doing messing with their friend's woman! (I think that really pissed JC off!) They said to him: "you knew that wasn't your woman in the first place! You need to go back where you came from." I was so glad to see them. JC left and MM's friends and I went back to my house and talked; I told them what happened. Boy! Some of the risks I took!!!

I was so far off into the drug world] that I felt there was no turning back, I had made my own drug connections. MM and I were buying and selling and he was getting high; he would only sniff it. I stayed in that apartment for another whole year then I moved; JC never came back to that apartment again. I moved into a house on East Murdock (over in the hood) I had to put bars on my windows.

I would go out of town and bring more and more drugs back into the state. One time, I went out of town to deal some drug, and I accidentally booked myself on the wrong return flight; I ended up in Oklahoma. I called my mother; her and my brother-in-law drove from Kansas, to Oklahoma to get me. I figured it was safer that way, who knows, I felt that I was being watched [paranoia was setting in]. Thinking back! I dragged my mother into a lot of stuff. I thank God that nothing happen to her, because of me. My mother knew what I was doing; I would always give her money and I made sure she had what she wanted (when I was selling that stuff). My father was a very different story.

When I returned to Wichita I saw the people I needed to see. I met up with one of JC's friends, although I didn't know at the time that he was his friend; I began to deal drugs with him (also). I had a habit of getting with the craziest people (drug dealers). I went to California to meet "the guy" and I started making money and giving it to him. I was messing with big quantities of [that stuff]. He liked to get high off cocaine; he would shoot it up, and it would make him weird. One time he shot me up; it scared me real bad because it made my heart beat so fast that I thought I was going to die! I didn't like that high at all!

I went back to Kansas with some more stuff (of his); I was cutting it in smaller pieces to make extra money (for myself). I was known for [playing] drug dealers (although I did not think I was playing them, because I would always give them the agreed amount of money). I just never would let MM go.

So one time I flew out to California and when I got to the hotel to meet "the guy" I walked into the hotel suite, and lo and behold, JC was there; I was by myself! I just knew I was getting ready to die! "The guy" took JC into the other room; a little later JC came out and left (he never said a word to me but I was really scared). "The guy" came over to me and told me that every dime I thought I had taken from him, that before I left California...I was going to make it all back! He had a rifle with a wooden handle on it (that he kept in his room) he hit me with it across my legs, and I hit the floor he beat me with that rifle all over my body except for my face. After he finished beating me, he raped me; I was so hurt and humiliated (it took me back to when I was raped the other time). I was in pain from being beaten and he had the nerve to make me have sex with him! I felt so cheap.

So then we got dressed and caught a plane to Fresno, California. We got a hotel room and he called two women to come over. He told them to take me down to the [hoe stroll] and to make sure that: I caught some tricks, and that they were to get the money from the trick before I went into the room; and they were to watch me all night. I thought I was never going to make it back home again. I didn't even have money to make a phone call! The pay phones were only a nickel back then (so you know I was in trouble).

They caught me my first trick; they introduced me as the new girl on the block, so the trick was eager to sleep with me; they already had rooms booked for that night. They took his money and

I went into the room with him; as soon as he shut the door I started to cry, I told him that I wasn't a prostitute and that I was forced to do what I was doing. He said, "I am getting out of here I don't want any part of this," I said: "Please don't go out there!" I asked him to please help me get away and he said: no at first, but when he saw I was really scared he asked me what I was going to do if they were waiting out there for me? I told him I was going to go out the window. He said lady: "we are on the second floor" and I told him: "I don't care I'd rather break my legs than allow them to turn me out like that." I showed him where I had been beaten; it must have looked real bad to him because of the way he looked at me.

I asked him to stay in the room long enough for me to get away. I don't know why, but I felt that when I jumped, I was going to be all right, so I raised the window and I prayed: "God help me!" Then I jumped! I landed on my feet, it was as if my fall was braced.

I started running and I never looked back. I was running down the highway crying and calling out to God. I was real scared that they were going to try and catch me so I tried to stay out of the view of oncoming cars; it was very dark. I had run quite a ways when I saw an all-night diner that was next to a truck stop (there were hotels around it). I went over there by a pay phone; I didn't have a penny to my name.

All of a sudden a very well dressed man drove up and parked his car; he walked over to me and asked me if I needed any help I told him no! I didn't know if he was one of them, or someone coming for me for them; he walked away. I was still just crying out to God for help, then the same man came out of the diner, he had gone in to order some food (to go); he said to me: "here's some money to use the phone;" I took it.

The man hadn't left and he heard all of my conversation. He walked back over to me and began to try and help me. My brother said: "Who is that?" I told him I did not know, I said: "It was a man that gave me the money to call you" my brother said: "let me talk to him" I said: "no! I don't know if he is with them" my brother said: "give him the phone." So, I did and they talked; the man gave me back the phone and my brother said: "go with him." The man made a phone call, and after that I went to his car and he took me to his house.

I was overwhelmed; I could not even find the words to describe what had just happen, ***BUT GOD!*** His wife opened the door, she was waiting for us; I guess that was who he had called. He had dropped her off at home, and then he went to get them something to eat (they had just come from church).

She took me into a guest room, and got me some fresh pajamas, and then she ran some water in their bath tub and put me in it. She bathed my wounds and prayed over me the whole time. I was crying so hard, not for what had happen to me, but I was thinking about how God had that set up for me. ***Even in the midst of my mess my God had me, His Grace and His Mercy covered me.*** They gave me a nice warm bed to sleep in, and she and her husband came into the room and they both prayed over me.

The next morning I called my brother and he asked me what I wanted to do: "come there or go home?" I said: "I want to go home." So he bought me a ticket from where he was and they took me to the airport and made sure I had enough money, then they put me on the plane after praying with me. I will never forget that couple as long as I live. I wish I knew how to find them I never got their names. **God sent a couple of His angels to rescue me**.

When I got home I was so messed up from the beating that I told people I fell down a ski slope Ha! I don't know a thing about skiing; I did not want to deal with anyone else with dope.

My brother called me and asked me how I got mixed up with those people so I told him the truth. He did not know that I was off into dealing, like that so I talked to him about it and he told me: "we can do this." He said he'd give me some money and that my cousin could get me a connection; he and my cousin started [hooking up].

I caught a plane out there about a month later. They had put the money up front for me to get some drugs. I took a friend out there with me to test the dope and she shot some and said it was good, so we bought it.

I got that stuff back to Wichita and realized we had been had; I tried to cut that stuff and it turned pure bunk! I had just bought a pound of goober dust! It was a substance that smelled and looked just like heroin I was so hurt and mad! They had invested 10,000 dollars on that mess. I guess that was God's way of not letting my brother get money. I called my oldest brother in California (I was crying); I told him what had happened and he asked me where I was: I told involved in that life, although I could not help but feel stupid; I still felt real bad about the money he lost. This is what happens when greed sets in; it was like I just couldn't get enough. I was putting my life and others around me in harm's way.

The next few pages will assist in overcoming the spirit of Greed and Guilt.

Greed and some things greed can do

Sometimes our plans can lead us down a destructive lifestyle path when God is left out of the blueprint. Drugs was the life I chose. God never intended for me to be in the underworld. But I chose it because I thought that it could get me where I wanted to be (materially) at the time. The money was very good. It was fast and easy (I thought).

Very often we want things that appear to be easy; it's all good until we get caught--and caught up in the hype. We live in a society that is constantly in a state of wanting. Oh, it's not just the drug life. Greed is in every facet of society! People are always saying, "I don't have enough." We can trust God to give us what is ours. Proverbs 30:8 says, "Remove far from me vanity and lies; give me neither poverty nor riches; feed me with food convenient for me." Getting things by illegal means is not of God.

An ungrateful heart and eyes that always want more can bring us to a deadly end. God wants us to live for Him and have all the things in life that we need according to His riches. *Philippians 4:11, 12 say's: "Not that I speak in respect of want; for I have learned, in whatsoever state I am, therefore to be content. V12. I know both how to be abased, and I know how to abound everywhere and in all things I am instructed both to be full and to be hungry, both to abound and to suffer need."* Paul learned to be content with whatever he had. He knew all he had to do was draw on Christ's power for strength. We have to learn to rely on God's promise to help us. Paul saw his life, from God's point of view. And we can too. The Apostle Paul was grateful for everything God had given him. We can trust God to keep His promises.

1. Genesis 14:12, "And they took Lot, Abram's brother's son, who dwelt in Sodom, and his goods, and departed." Lots greediness led him into sinful surroundings. It cost him his freedom and his enjoyment. Prosperity can cost us if our motives are not right. It can actually enslave us if our motives are not in line with God.

2. Numbers 22:20-23, " And God came unto Balaam at night, and said unto him, If the men come to call thee rise up, and go with them; but yet the word which I shall say unto thee, that shalt thou do. V21, "And Balaam rose up in the morning, and saddled his ass, and went with the princes of Moab. V22, And God's anger was kindled because he went: and the angel of the LORD stood in the way for an adversary against him. Now he was riding upon his ass, and his two servants were with him. V23, "And the ass saw the angel of the LORD standing in the way, and his sword drawn in his hand: and the ass turned aside out of the way, and went into the field: and Balaam smote the ass, to turn her into the way."

Balaam went with Balak's messenger, but God was angry by Balaam's greedy attitude. Balaam greediness blinded him from seeing what God was trying to do for him. He looked at what the king was offering him instead of seeing God. Sometimes we see our way of getting blessed instead of seeing what God has for us so we do what we see and end up in trouble.

3. It could cause us to lose everything in our lives that we thought we had. 2 Chronicles 10:16-19 talks about Rehoboam who lost everything because of greed and power. He did not need more

money because he had already inherited the richest kingdom in the world! He was king he did not need control! He was motivated by selfishness rather than reason and it cost him everything.

We must love God and strive to be who He wants each of us to become. We cannot be greedy and do things that will hurt or destroy our brothers and sisters. My greed almost cost me my own life. It did cost a few people that I love their life's worth and freedom. I carried a lot of guilt because of what I did.

The Holy Spirit did not let me rest (I lived in spiritual bondage). I am sorry for what I did to all of the people whose lives were affected by my drug dealing, in the past. Being truly sorry will produces true repentance leading to salvation.

Chapter 5

Busted To Parallax

This was around the time when I had begun to get tired. It had gotten to the point where not even making the money was pleasing to me anymore; it was just a routine. I was going through the motions, trying to make it from day to day. Seems like all the people that I cared about were on that stuff. I was feeling low I began to feel like one of the worst people on this earth. God had begun to deal with me. I felt more and more like I was destroying people's lives; dope is as deadly as poison, it only takes longer to die; Heroin is a downer; Cocaine is an upper, they are both killers! But people just kept coming, they were like scavengers looking for poppy & coca to ease their pain! I couldn't understand why they squandered their money on dope until [Things turned] and God allowed me to experience that stuff for 6 months (for six months I got high off of it myself (I felt like crap). I had actually thought that addicts [wanted] to keep doing drugs, but! I found out the hard way what it really means to be hooked.

Life was beginning to be like: What, the hell am I doing! I was getting very disgusted with myself but I felt that I was so far into that life that I could not turn back. I didn't like that "high" at all. I remember a guy who [said] he liked me; he was always giving me dope to keep me getting high. Using his drugs meant that I didn't have to mess with mine.

I did not want to crave drugs anymore; one day someone told me about the Methadone Clinic. I thought that I needed it to help me kick the habit, but, it was worse than the heroin! Methadone was for people who had been on drugs for years (I lied to get in the program). It's funny you know [some of the things we do to get what we want] I didn't know that Methadone would be harder to get out of your system than some of the other stuff.

[Time passed]

I was still doing my thing (selling drugs). MM and I were still together; a lot of the dope dealers were beginning to get busted.

There was a guy who everyone knew was working for the [narks] (as we called them); he would buy drugs and then report the dealers to the police. Every drug dealer in Wichita was getting busted. They got one woman at the airport; the cops had a doctor there waiting for her when she got off the plane. Back then, women would put dope up into their vaginas; isn't that something!

They had nark agents that would hide in bushes, or they would hide in the trunks of cars. There was one we called dirty >>>>! He was crazy; he would do whatever it took to get you! Many people had cases, it was no joke! They hadn't caught me yet! But they busted into the other house where MM was staying; they didn't find anything there. Like a fool, I went to California on a Monday to picked up some Heroin, and strawberry and pineapple Cocaine.

I returned to Wichita that Wednesday. When I got to the Wichita Airport the narcotic agents were waiting for me. My mother came to the airport to pick me up; she knew them by sight. It was sad that I had my mother involved in my mess. Anyway, she told me that they were waiting for me, I told her to leave because I didn't want them to take her to jail for being with me (that would have been all she wrote), the church would have had a field day with that! I had $4100 on me I gave her four thousand dollars and kept a hundred I told her to go. After she left I prayed that they would not stop her. "I had to think fast."

This is what I did: I took the balloon of heroin that I had on me, and put it in my mouth. But, before I left California, I had overnight expressed the drugs I was transporting back to Wichita. I guess the cops thought I'd be foolish enough to bring that stuff back with me on the flight even after that woman got busted at the airport (that time) and after all the busting they were doing all over town! I knew how to elude the police.

After my mother left my presence they could not stop her because they did not have a warrant for her. I told her what to do if anything happened to me. All of them including some of dirties

>>>>> right hand narks, were there; [dirty] really hated MM.

I walked down to where they were; I went right up to the agents; they looked at me like I was crazy I said: "How yawl doing today?" They walked away from me, so I began to follow them. They did not know what to do, so they went into the gift shop; I went in behind them and stood beside the one that was looking at some books (a lady agent), and she walked away. So, I went in the coffee shop and sat down, and ordered something to eat (I still had that spoon of dope in my mouth). I knew how to do whatever I needed to do to throw them off track. After I ate I got up and went over to them and asked them if they wanted me! They said nothing; they did not know whether to stop me or not, so I told them I was going outside to get a cab. I said: "This is your last chance." I started walking towards the baggage claim area to pick up my suitcase and then I walked towards the door I was really scared! But I did not let it show.

They always had cabs in front of the airport so I went to a cab, and I turned around and said: "I am getting ready to go, do yawl want me?" They still didn't say anything to me; but they talked amongst themselves. I got in the cab and we pulled off, I looked through the back window at them and waved good bye. You know I had to be nuts to do what I did and get away with it!

When I got home I told some people what had happened. We took the spoon of dope (that I had on the plane) and cut it. I had some people who were at the house [test it] including one of the white girls that I talked about earlier (she was not with "the brother" anymore), she had married someone else.

Over time she and I became very good friends. I even walked her down the aisle at her wedding: isn't that something! She and her new husband were on that stuff; she had gotten to where she liked the cocaine more than she liked him.

The next day my package (of drugs) arrived; I picked it up, and took it over to my mother's house (she did not know it was there). I didn't tell her what was going on just in case something [went down] I was very careful not to let anyone know about it, other than MM.

The following Thursday, I met with two of my friends and I gave them some of the cocaine, they both had bought drugs from me (in the past). I was always giving away drugs whenever MM was not around.

(Tragedy happened about a month before that, when one of my friend's mothers house "caught fire," her mother was burned real bad because she went in and out of that house ***to save all of the kids who were trapped inside. I've always had respect and love for my friend's parents as I stated earlier. It was hurting me that tragedy struck their family). Anyway, I had placed some dope on the dresser and went to the restroom; when I came out it was gone. My friends were in the room getting high, I said: "where is my stuff?" Neither one of them had an answer, they both tried to make me think that I took it and put it somewhere. They tried to play me!

One had a syringe and was getting ready to shoot the dope in her arm, and she could not [get it]; she asked me if I would hit her arm for her! I took that syringe and pushed it out onto the floor. I was so mad at them because I had just [given] them some dope! I couldn't understand why they stole from me; That hurt me more than losing the dope (I didn't care about that)! I thought they were my friends! I had to realize that, that stuff was a total controller I [really] began to get weary of pushing it. I prayed: "My God! What am I doing?"

The friend, whose mother had been badly burned came to me and said that if she did not tell me that she took my stuff (but, I know they both did it) that, her mother would die (her mother was in the burn unit of the hospital at the time). I was so mad at her for even saying something like that (and it didn't make any sense); her mother ended up dying anyway.

That Friday night the white girl, her husband, another couple, my cousin and MM and I, were hanging out at the house. We had just made some balloons to sell. MM was walking around with some of the cocaine on a tray just walking and talking. My cousin stayed awhile and then he left after he bought some of the strawberry cocaine (I had put his dope purchase in a pink piece of paper, folded like a small envelope and I let him out the door). About two to three minutes later the police tried to break the door down we had bars on all the windows, they had our house surrounded. I ran and grabbed the tray from MM and blew the cocaine off of it then I grabbed the balloons and I ran into the back room and got in the closet; there was a hole in the closet where you could go up into a small room that was about 4 feet wide. I tried to get rid of the balloons (I had ten of them). One of the cops was looking in the window, he said to me: "get out of that closet because I see you" he could not come through the window because of the bars, but they finally knocked down the door and they ran to the back where I was. I had put all of those balloons in my mouth.

They brought me out of the back, and told the lady [nark] to take me to the bathroom and search me the cop said: "I saw her with something." They were the same ones that was at the airport (that time); the lady said: "We got your smart a>> you aren't so cocky now!"

I had $2400.00 in my bra she tried to take my money and I grabbed it back from her. I said: "this isn't dope money" (It really wasn't!) she and I started to squabble, and one of the balloons fell on the floor I said: "Damn!" After that, she took me out and said: "Cuff her, and take her out of here!"

One of our cohorts tried to flush a syringe down the stool and the cops caught him. They had rammed shacked that house something awful and they hand cuffed everyone and all of us were on our way to jail. They had me sitting outside on the ground for about 30 minutes before they put me in the car; I still had the rest of those balloons on me.

I was very small back then, and after I got in the back of the police car, I put my legs through those cuffs and put them in front of me. I took my mouth and pulled the top of my blouse open, and I dropped those balloons in my bra I had to really think fast; they had already searched me in the house.

I knew when I got down to the police station that I was going to be in a holdover cell for a while before they took me anywhere else. They did not put me in a cell; they put me in a room and handcuffed me to a table they left one hand free and that was a mistake (on their part). I got rid of those balloons right in that room; I got on the floor and I pushed them down a hole that was against the wall. As I was putting the last one down the hole, an agent came in and caught me on the floor; he ran over to me, and shouted: "What are you doing?" He pulled me back to see if I had anything, but it was too late I said to myself: "Praise God." Yes! In the middle of all that I had the [nerve] to praise the LORD. The cop didn't see anything so he put me back in my chair then he asked me: "What did you do?" And I said: "Nothing, I just wanted to get on the floor." He didn't buy it, but anyway he had to accept my explanation.

Then another detective came in the room attempting to intimidate me; they wanted me to turn on MM. They told me how he was using me, and that he didn't give a damn about me, they said that they had been watching him a long time. I told them I didn't know what they were talking about. The cops had been trying to bust me for about eleven years but this was the first time I'd been arrested for drugs (outside of that thing in California, which was not my case so they couldn't make the charges stick). I had some misdemeanors, but nothing big.

They took me to be booked and I saw everyone else that they had arrested from the house. Now! This really blew my mind, there was a guy standing at the booking desk, a very BIG fellow, [that they called a snitch]. He was standing there like that was his job; he said to me: "I would have called and told you that they were coming, but I didn't have you-all's phone number." This man had no shame in his game!

By the time they finished booking me, my bond was being posted; the guy that liked me who had been giving me dope had posted my bail. He took me to my mom's house, where I had some money stashed so that I could go back and get everybody else out (they all got out).

When MM walked out the door, they arrested him again (on some bull crap); the police said they had another warrant for him, so I got him out again. They released him and then they arrested him again; they were just messing with him, trying to make us spend a lot of money [and we did] that third time we were able to just leave quietly. I told MM that the police was trying to turn me against him.

The cops had a pound of heroin written in the search warrant. Someone had tipped them off (that was the amount of heroin that I had gone to California to get). Thank God! I was relieved, I was glad that I hadn't brought it back on the plane with me. So, they! Planted some weed, pills and a gun in MM's closet, in one of his jacket pockets.

My cousin had set us up!!! When he walked out that door (at the house), they should have brought him right back in to be arrested with the rest of us but they let him go. The reason I knew he did it, was because the cops had that pink little envelope that I had put the strawberry cocaine in, for him. He was so bad on that stuff that I believe they gave him the rest of the dope, so he could plant it in there.

Anyway, they took everything we had in the form of money, cars and anything that they thought was bought with drug money. We had a Lincoln that was in his father's name that they couldn't take (we were able to keep that car). So we had to regroup for what was ahead.

We started going to court and we both ended up with public defenders. They had taken all of our money, even what was in the banks. We talked to the lawyers that the court had appointed for our arraignment, they turned out to be good; so, MM hired them because, they would prepare a better defense for us if we paid [them] instead of them being paid by the state (MM had some money put away somewhere).

By the time all of our cohorts (that got busted with us) were ready to go to court the nark's informant had gotten busted, so the police had to drop all charges against them. I heard that the nark-informant had stolen the dope evidence from the room they were holding it in.

Our case was still pending; at our arraignment they presented more stuff than what we had in our house as I said before, they had planted stuff that wasn't even ours; the weed wasn't with the evidence, so someone had to have taken it, I guess they smoked it themselves. Those were some dirty cops back then and I believe there are still some today, they just haven't gotten caught.

I didn't want to end up in prison and there was a program that everyone was talking about called: the Parallax Program (for addicts); I asked my lawyer to sign me up for it. I wasn't the drug addict that they thought I was, but, I told them that I shot two hundred dollars a day, I think they knew I was lying! I didn't carry myself like a junkie; neither did I look like one, but I stuck to the lie.

I was taking methadone, but I was on a very low dosage. The women at the clinic knew that I was lying about being an addict I think for my own safety they helped me.

Anyway, I took the whole blame for that case because MM was facing a lot of time because of the firearm that the police had planted in his things (a convicted felon automatically receives five times the years of their original sentence, if they are caught with a firearm). The house was in my name and that's why they tried to get me to drop a dime on him.

Before I got in the program I talked to the director who was a very cool person I really respected him; he had me talk to an intake worker: An intake worker would write down your information to decide if you would benefit from the program, they said they'd get back with me and my lawyer. Everything had to be submitted to the courts.

During that time there began to be more distance between MM and me. I was out one night and I met these guys I think it was at the: Bouncing Bucket (maybe it was the Inn Crowd), but wherever it was I ended up going with them to one of the guy's sister's house; I stayed out all night because I was going to be sentenced the next day.

I was talking to one of the guys until day break (the other fellows had women in their rooms); this guy and I just sat in the living room and talked all night. I told him about what was happening to me. He was a very nice person; when morning came, they took me home. He had given me his number to call him (if I needed anything).

That same day I went to court and they sentenced me to Parallax I was given two weeks to turn myself in. For the next two weeks I got to know him; he was a few years my junior (DG-Detail Guy).

I started seeing him a lot during the two weeks; we spent most of our time together; sometimes we'd go to one of his friend's house. I think they thought they were players and at least one of them was married. They all had diverse women, including the one that I was spending my time with. We would hang out at his friend's sister's house; she was the sister of the girl who was supposed to be DG's girlfriend, and her brother was one of DG's friends (who was with him the night I met him). He told me that he and the girl had broken up; so, her friends and relatives wasn't mad about our relationship, he was very nice to me.

My two weeks was up and DG took me to turn myself in. After I got settled, the first thing I had to do was to go to Detox (for two weeks, that was the routine). You have to be examined by the doctor; they put you in detox to kick any addictions that you have. They listed me as having a big habit and on methadone, so I was on a twenty-four hour watch. The nurse on duty said that people on methadone will have convulsions and all kinds of things. They said: It Is the hardest habit to kick. Well the first night, all I did in there was read my Bible. Through all of this I felt I was still connected to God. Prayers were still being sent up for me (I thank God for always having praying people to enter my life and circle around me).

So as the week went on, they saw that I never got sick, I never went through withdrawals, or even had pain, even though, some drugs was built up in my body; I should have felt something! But God knew that the life that I was in I didn't want. They thought that I was getting something [brought in] for me; they called me the "High Class Junkie."

We were allowed to have our own clothes; I was glad because I still loved to dress; I loved my clothes and I always believed in looking your best. (It makes you feel good on the outside.)

After they saw that I was alright, I went out into the mix of all the other people that were there, it was a CO-ED treatment center the men were on one floor, and the women were on the other.

There were many people there that I already knew I had sold drugs to a lot of them in the past. I was talked about among the staff and everyone else. I became friends with some of the staff, especially the nurse who watched me (during detox). I began talking about God to everyone; God was really working in my spirit; putting me on the right track. I became the person in there who prayed for everyone.

While I was there, the [city] came over with warrants for me every other week; the warrants would come and the director would go to court with me. I believe that God was clearing all the stuff up that I had on my record. They came over once again, and the director said with a smile on his face, she will be OK, God is going with her.

After a while I got on level 3 and I was able to go out and get a job. MM got set free; his lawyer had beaten his case.

As time passed my newfound friend would come and pick me up and take me where I needed to go; the rules required that we catch the bus; but everyone would always have someone waiting around the corner, or down the street, to give them a ride (but I think they knew that).

I got a job at a place called Rainbow United, which was a school for special needs children. I liked working with those kids because they had some amazing gifts.

One day DG came up there to take me to lunch; I got in his car; all of a sudden this car pulled up like the police. This older woman jumped out and said: "Is this who you been spending my damn money on?" He pushed her back and told her she'd better get on...she was going crazy! I told him to go on with her, because I did not need that stuff in front of my job. I did not want those people to see that, and call the program on me. Whatever he said to her, she left. I asked him who that was and he told me some far out story. We went to lunch, and he went on to tell me how much he liked me, and he was sorry that had happened; he said to me that, it would not happen again.

So that evening after I got off work, about an hour or so later, I got a phone call; I guess she found out who I was, and where I was staying and called the program. She could not get me in trouble (with them), so she thought she could intimidate me over the phone she tried to talk real crazy to me; I told her: "Let me tell you something, you are acting like a fool over a man;" and I told her "I don't have time to be dealing with your old a>>you need to talk to him and leave me the hell alone! You're the fool if you give him your money, and you know what he is doing with it. I know that you are older than me and I respect my elders, but I'm not going to let you talk to me any kind of way." I hung up the phone and then called him I told him: "I don't have time for this drama with this woman so if you are with her, leave me alone," He said, "NO! Please I will take care of her."

I went upstairs and played cards with some people then all of a sudden (out of the blue) a girl that I had known vaguely from the drug world was released from the two week detoxification process she walked over to where I was sitting and she said: "Look at you! You always thought that you were better than everybody else, even now you think that you are all of that." I asked her, "What are you talking about?" She hauled off and hit me in my head! I jumped up and grabbed her around her throat, and I tried to choke the life out of her; they had to pull me off of her I wasn't bothering her she had some chip on her shoulder. I guess she'd been walking around with revulsion for me, for years! They put her in lock up. She had been on that dope really bad and I felt pity for her. I said: "God what was that all about!" Drugs had messed with a lot of people's minds.

I saw and realized (more and more) what I had done, by selling that stuff. She was in lock-up for two weeks. After she got out she just sat back and watched me; she never said anything to me for a long time. I went on with my life, praying and asking God to help me and change me because I really didn't want that kind of life anymore.

One day the girl approached me; she apologized for the way she acted; she said: "after being around you, you are nothing like I thought; I judged you for what I thought I saw, and for what other people said;" so we became friends and I began to minister to her. I wanted to help, and reach out to every person that ever got strung out because of the drugs that I brought into the city.

[Time Passed]

I served my time there and got out I was on [reporting probation] I had to give urine samples every week. I kept dating DG we would go out, and people would wonder who he was and where I met him, and where he came from! He was not the average person that ran in our circle. MM, didn't like the fact that I had moved on without him.

DG and I would be out, and people couldn't figure out why I was with someone who appeared to be a square. That older woman was going crazy over him I asked him, "What did you do to her?" She would sit behind us at the club and just watch us all night; so I really had to watch my back. He didn't let her get near me he kept telling her to leave us alone and that he was through with her. I guess it was hard for her to accept that.

After a while, he learned about me and the full degree of what I was known for; people were telling him that he was out of his league; they would say: 'Man, you can't handle that woman.' Anyway, I ended up back in the drug trap (selling small amounts of drugs).

DG, knew how to detail cars, he worked for his cousin (or brother-in-law; I don't remember which one) at their detail shop. He had connections with a lot of rich people that had boats, private planes, and bars; he would detail their cars, boats, planes, or whatever they had. He taught me how to detail also, so I started working with him.

My father took an interest in him and started asking him about the detail business (my father was a business man). My father told him to find out how much it would cost to open a shop, and so we did. We found a building that used to be a service station on 21st

and Hillside it had two big garages; it was perfect. My father gave us the money to get the place started. He really tried to keep me from going back to the dope life.

Business was good; a plus was that it was a busy street and my father even got the hang of it; he was a man who loved to stay busy (I guess that is where I got it from). DG started buying and selling large amounts of weed he got from the people that owned this club he would go to sometime. The drug world slowly creep its way back into [my life] until it was in full force again. We would sell a little, and then DG became a user.

I started stealing again (but not like before) I had a friend who was a prosperous jewel thief. It seemed like trying to live an honest life wasn't fast enough for me, or something; I don't know; DG was hanging out with his ex-girlfriend's brothers getting high. I cannot really remember (exactly) when he became an out of control user.

He began to take money from the business. Addicts would come to the shop to hang out; they would get high and talk loud although it didn't stop him from doing his work, but! My father began to get worried. Car dealerships loved his work and so did other customers (he was very good at what he did).

My father had a feeling about what he was doing, so one day he checked the bank account (my father had a joint business account with DG) the account was so short, that my father came to us and asked what was going on. I really didn't know that DG was playing with the money (that way); it was a shock to me. I asked him, and he said that he didn't take the businesses money and that my father and I were turning against him; DG was reversing blame, and he was paranoid!!! He was smoking that rock. People say that rock is no joke! He was there!

We had gotten an apartment together. Sometimes I'd return home (after I did what I needed to do) and he would be gone, and sometimes he'd come home very late, or not at all, but when he did come home, he would get up and go outdoors saying: he was going for a walk. Sometimes he'd be gone for hours at a time I didn't think anything of it. He was very sneaky and cunning after he got that stuff in his system. He tried to say that I was the reason he was on the drugs, I said: "No! I wasn't, you chose that route yourself you were doing this long before I even knew that you had gotten on it." I told him: "Whoever you were with; it was your choice." It just baffles me how people always try to point the blame (for what they choose to do themselves), towards other people.

My father and I had a BIG!!! Falling-out about that business. I really-really hate that I allowed someone to come into my life and use my father (that way). I was fooled by that man but my father was smart enough to pull out of that business.

DG and I kept the business as long as we could. He was from Arkansas, the same place I'm originally from. We began to go to Arkansas a lot; his mother and his sisters lived there, and most of my people on both my parents side, were still there. I really liked going down there to visit. There's nothing like being out in the country.

One weekend we left from down in Arkansas and traveled to Dallas Texas I think one of DG's friends was from Dallas (but he had moved to Wichita because his sisters were there).

It was January of 1981; we were all (DG, me, two brothers and one of the brothers girlfriends) riding together. We were over at someone's house just hanging out (I guess the other brothers wife came where we were, because it was a relative's house). Anyway, a woman walked in the house and saw me and the other girl she said: "If another woman walks in here, your a>> was mine!" She was mad as heck!

That was a very bad day for all of us. After everything settled down we all got hungry and we ended up going to Denny's I ordered some French toast with a lot of whipped cream, lots of strawberries with maple syrup. That man's wife, looked at me, and said: "You're pregnant" I said: "No I'm not!" She said: "OK, you'll see." When we left Denny's someone lit a cigar; the smoke made me so sick that I started throwing up. [After she told me that] everything that I smelled made me sick I still didn't believe I was pregnant.

So anyway, the next day they bought some ribs, and I took

one of them and I got the urge to add some peanut butter, I then submerged barbecue sauce all over it I took the jar of peanut butter that was on the table (me, it, and that barbecue had a field day) everybody thought that I had lost my mind. That was soooooooo good to me!!! I thought to myself, well, there might be something to what she had said.

We left Arkansas and went back to Wichita and I just kept doing what I was doing, still trying to do those cars, and not even thinking about being pregnant. After all if you're pregnant you are supposed to stop your periods (and I would still have menstrual cycles). Spring had just arrived; it was kind of warm day when I started bleeding real bad. I ended up going to the emergency room. After I got there they took a urine specimen and some blood; after they checked it out, they told me I was pregnant and that I was threating a miscarriage. They said I was going into my fourth month I said: "What! I'm in my fourth month?" I told them that I was still having menstrual cycles, how could that be? They explained some things to me; they told me that I had to go on complete bed rest, if I wanted this baby. I was so out done that I didn't know what to do.

Things got bad between DG and me. I found out that he had impregnated his friend's sister, also. When he was having one of those long walking spells, well! He was around the corner in her bed!!! He was playing two houses back and forth; the older lady was just a plus; he was [jogging] the young girl around the other corner. The man I thought was so sweet was nothing but a male hoe! He had two children by "his friends sister" already; and she and I was pregnant at the same time; she had a baby girl, two weeks before my baby girl was born. This man got so bad on that dope it was unreal.

After I found out I was pregnant, I left the dope life completely I moved out of the apartment that he and I had shared, and moved into a smaller place then I went out looking for a job. I ended up getting a job at Cessna Aircraft (my ex-brother-in-law helped me get it) I worked there until I could no longer pack my tools; while I was still there, some of the guys would help me out a lot. Food kept making me sick (I had a very troubled pregnancy).

One Sunday DG came by; he took me to [a] church and I began to like it, so I kept going there. (He finally lost the shop and things got real bad between us; he ended up going back to the other girl. I was attending that church, and he and his other baby mama started coming there too; can you imagine how I felt? I didn't blame her. DG ran to her because, she had always been in the church, so he thought he would be safe with her. Well he ended up marrying her and they announced it in church I was so hurt but I did not let that stop my life I knew that it was time for me to let go. I kept on going to church and I began to really turn back to God. Sometimes MM's brother would attend church with me. MM was upset because he said my baby should have been his: Yes I agreed, it should have, but it was what it was, I knew it bothered him a lot and I really felt bad.

One Sunday (before I had my baby) I was sitting in church and the craziest thing happened; it was the first time I really saw that spirits really manifest themselves in people, for real! I was sitting at the end of the bench on the second row from the front. This other lady was sitting at the other end and all of a sudden she jumped up and pointed to the preacher. In a very strange voice, she said that he would: 'have to sit down, because her master was going to preach today.' She proceeded to run up on the pulpit, and they grabbed her and she started fighting all those men! She was very strong with that spirit, that spirit that was in her was not going to go away without a fight! It took several men to hold her. The congregation stopped and everyone began to pray. They got her out (and the service proceeded).

The pastor explained what had just happened I was so scared at the time...but I thank God for how He steps in. We have to understand how to deal with demon spirits, because they are real.

Well they brought her back in and she was crying. It was so amazing how God moved on her and she was so humble after that but I didn't want her to sit anywhere near me.

After service people were hugging each other: guess who came to me first? Her! I pulled away; because I didn't want her to hug me; I was big and pregnant and I didn't want that negative spirit around me. I was scared that it was going to get in me and my baby. She did not know what she had done so I began to pray for her, and I prayed that God would cover me from ever having to eye witness a demon spirit in Church again. I didn't want to go back to the church that I had been raised in because so much had happened in my life.

Time went by and DG was working in a detail shop down the street from where I lived. I would go down there to see him (just to let him know how my pregnancy was going), and I would bump into his wife. I should not have gone down there after the way he had treated me in the past. They ended up moving to Arkansas.

I was getting too big to go anywhere, I was huge! When I was 7 months pregnant, I looked like I was carrying twins. I ended up moving home with my mother.

I was going back and forth to the doctor; it seemed like every time I went, I had gained between 10 and 15 pounds. WOW!
My doctor told me I had to stop gaining weight I was getting too heavy for my feet to carry my body. My mother would cook a 9 inch peach cobbler and I would almost eat the whole thing, plus eating almost a half-gallon of butter brickle ice cream; all I was doing was eating, I think a lot of it was depression. I couldn't get in and out of the bathtub by myself [that was something] my stepfather had to help me get off the couch, out of the car, and anyplace we went.

One time I went fishing with him and my mother and I rolled down a hill; that was so funny to me they thought I was hurt, but I wasn't. I went in the store one time, and I saw some people that I knew; they walked right pass me without recognizing me (that is how different my looks and my body had changed) I looked like a big fat >>>woman, I gained 72 pounds carrying my baby.

I stayed in and out of the hospital my stepfather would always take me (every other week) I was having a lot of pain; my baby was hurting my insides. The last time I went to the hospital, they kept me for 2 days; they were going to send me back home but my spiritual mother was with us and she told her (the doctor): "you cannot send her home." My doctor said that it was just ligament pains I were having, and all I needed to do was go home and put some pillows behind my back and stay off my feet the doctor said that I would be all right. My spiritual mother said: "NO!" She told my doctor that I could not have that baby, and that the baby had been in me too long she told the doctor that God had showed her by the Spirit that I couldn't go into labor (because of something she said I can't remember the exact conversation she had with the doctor). The doctor told my spiritual mother that God put doctors on this earth, so let her do her job.

My mother was there and she said, "B>>>> if anything happens to my child because you think you know everything, I will whip your a>>"; my spiritual mother told my mother to calm down, that they were not going to go there. My spiritual mother told the doctor to just run some tests, and you will see what I am saying. The doctor agreed and ordered the test.

So they gave me an X-ray from below my stomach. Whatever she found, she told them to get the OR ready, and get her ready for surgery: "STAT"! They rushed me into emergency surgery! They were going so fast, that they almost cut my stomach before I was fully asleep I was in surgery for a long time. They said they had to cut through some things and move some things to get my baby out; her head was crushing against my pelvis! They said if I had gone into labor, it would have killed me and the baby. That doctor was so out done, that she kept apologizing over and over.

I had to stay in the hospital for 12 days my baby weighed 8 pounds and 13 ounces, "Big girl!" When I saw her for the first time she looked like a big fat white baby I said that is not my baby, and they said, I rolled over and went back to sleep: That's funny! It was July 11, 1981 and they took her out July 13, 1981 she was the joy of my life.

God has watched over me all of my life. My spiritual mother said it was for that baby to come here she said, "You and that baby have a great purpose here on earth." At that hospital after babies are born; they would give you and the baby's father a steak dinner (a steak of your choice) I had to have the dinner with my father (that was so awkward) Oh well.

I was still big after her birth I was a size 22, and my bra size I was 42DD, and my face and my nose, my God! I was a hot mess! I didn't want a shot to make my breast go down; neither did I want to breast feed, she was a greedy baby. I had never had any breast, and having a baby gave me some I wanted to lose a little, but not that much. Before I got pregnant I had been between sizes 7-10 (depending on where the cloths came from). I could not believe that a pregnancy could stretch a woman's body all the way up to a size 22 I thought my body would never return to my normal size.

(Remembering back my baby sister was pregnant at the same time; she had her baby 2 weeks before I had mine. We would do a lot of fun things together when we were pregnant. I remember us going on a picnic on the Fourth of July; it was very hot her baby had already been born we had a good time.)

After I got out of the hospital I began trying to get my life on the right track. I went back to church hoping to turn my life around. Hoping and Praying for God to make me a good mother for my daughter. I started visiting different churches trying to find out where I belonged. There were churches that needed to be closed.

[**Time passed**] My mother and stepfather decided to go to Arkansas and I wanted to take my daughter down there to see her father and her people; so I went with them. I always loved going to Arkansas. It was a pleasure just being there; we went to my grandmother's house (I still called it that even though she has passed away). My uncle and his daughter still lived there.

After we arrived I called my baby's father and he came and picked us up. So he saw her, and said; "She sure is light, are you sure this is my baby?" I was so mad at him for saying that, it made me go off on him. We went to his mother's house, so his family could see the baby and when his mother saw her she said: "Yes that is my grandbaby; she has his hands and that mole in the middle of her forehead just like his oldest sisters and she is as light as my daughter, even lighter" my baby looked just like his people he had 14 siblings.

I really liked his people; his mother was a beautiful person. He was a male whore as I said before, but for some reason I loved him I guess maybe it was because he was my baby's father he wasn't doing anything for me or her, plus he was on drugs, although he tried to hide it. My mother was upset because she did not want me to take the baby to see him at all. He and the woman he married were separated when I got there so I started back [like a fool messing with him again]. When my mother was getting ready to go back to Wichita, I ended up staying down there; she was so mad, I mean really mad! She talked about me so bad. I felt awful, but he told me, he was getting ready to divorce his wife and that he was going to change.

I ended up staying in a hotel until I found an apartment. I ended up moving to Texarkana Texas I lived right on the State line; Arkansas was right across the street. Things were OK for a moment: he would come and leave and stay gone for long periods of time. I already knew what he was doing so I would go over to my favorite aunt's house to visit. One of my cousins was hanging around my baby's daddy I think she was getting high with him. One of his sister's would come and pick me up to get me out of the apartment. I started trying to find a job, because he was not helping that much; his people would do more than he did. He had a rust orange Cadillac, and I would drive it sometime.

One day I had to take my daughter to get her shots; I went to the clinic and I ran into the woman he married; she and another lady were on the same elevator with me (I really felt bad about the whole situation). This man was a real piece of work; at the time I was blinded and refused to see his flaws. I know that his ex-wife and her friend were talking about me like nobody's business. I got into the car, and they were watching me but I acted as though they weren't even there. I went back home and told him that I saw her and he acted like it did not matter to him.

Things were not going well at all, and I started stealing things to sell to his sister's to make money in order to survive. I didn't like what I was doing; I was still going around the same mountain. I would have to hide my money, because he would steal it and try to make me think I had lost it then he would take the money and buy his dope; I began to realize how bad things really were. I would go over to my aunt's house, and she would try to talk some sense into to me she told me that when I get tired, she would send me home. I used to go to church with her. Looking back I can say that God has always had a hold on me I would talk to the LORD, even when I felt that I was not worthy to call HIS name. God knew that in my heart I wanted to be better. As I said before they really worshipped in those little churches in Arkansas. The power of the Holy Spirit was in those country churches all I needed to do was stay in them, but I didn't.

One day I went home to get some money I had put away to buy the baby some cloth diapers; that's what they were using back then (Pampers had only recently begun to be sold in the grocery stores) my mother and all the country people would rather put diapers on the babies than those pampers. Anyway I thought I had hidden the money in a safe place where he couldn't find it, but, he found it I started crying and I was ready to leave. When he got home I don't really remember what happened but we got into a big fight I hit him and ran out the door; he chased me and I fell, he was getting ready to beat me, but he stopped.

I went back in the house and got the baby, and then I left. I called my aunt and told her I was ready to go home. My cousin picked me up and I went to my Aunt Ruby's house in Texarkana, Arkansas I was there a couple of days before she bought my bus ticket, and she talked to me real good. She was my mother's oldest sister, she was a woman full of wisdom; a God fearing woman that I talked about at the beginning of my book I loved hearing her talk). She said: "Baby, that man was not for you" "His lifestyle is not what God has for you." She went on to tell me that there are many fish in the sea, good ones that are not tainted she said, throw that one back and throw your hook back in and allow God to put the one He has for you, on that hook don't settle for any kind of fish.

I cried and I called him and told him that I was gone he said: "You are going to leave, just like that?" I said: "yes" he wanted to talk, but I did not want to see him anymore. I felt that if I saw him, I would have never left. I got on the bus, my baby and I, and I cried most of the way home, but I never looked back.

I was glad to get home, and my mother was glad too she was happier about the baby; my mother would take care of those babies. It didn't matter what happened in our lives, as I said before my mother would fuss and curse us out, but! She would never let us or our kids go without. From when we were kids (as I said earlier in my book), mama was there for us no matter what.

Addictions and CO-Dependency: Whether it is drugs, or bad habits, or even being controlled by people and or obstacles around you. We all have had some type of habit, or even been controlled by something or someone, even if we are in our own way. The next page talks about Addictions & Co-dependency.

Addictions/Co-Dependency

An addiction is a controlling behavior that you feel you have but can't stop. It is anything that controls your life. I felt that I was an addicted drug dealer who was also in an addictive relationship that kept me in bondage. We can be addicted to all kinds of things. For some it is:

Drugs: We become addicted and it destroys your mind, body and your families.

Alcohol: Also destroys your mind, body and self-worth, and families.

1. ***Food: Destroys our health if we don't eat right and we become overweight or obese. Also developing all kinds of health problems.***
2. ***Activities; always feeling that you have to be doing something. Never at peace unless you are.***
3. ***Work: Work-a-holic, always working, never at home enjoying the family God has given you. It sometimes***

4. ***destroys families and a happy home.***
5. ***Shopping: Always buying things that you don't need.***
6. ***Getting into debt, running up credit cards and taking money from where it is needed.***
7. ***Unhealthy relationship: Living with an abusive mate.***
8. ***Settling because you don't want to be alone.***

We can't allow our confession to God to be that something or someone is taking first place in our lives over Him. Saying, God, I love this or that more than I love You. Things that we become addicted to become priority in our lives. It only leads us to a path of destruction. God wants us to face the facts and look at ourselves honestly. We can't escape the realities of life. We can't heal unless we allow God to take control of [everything] in our lives. We do a lot of destructive things in order to escape truth. We need to establish good boundaries in our lives, and allow ourselves to be led by the Holy Spirit through God's Word.

Chapter 6

Jail to Prison

I returned to Wichita, and everything was fine I was happy to be back home with my mother. I was going to church and being a good mom to my young daughter.

One day I ran into the white girl (that I talked about earlier) I went over to her house; she had, had a baby of her own (her daughter was almost a year old and mine was 3 months old). She and the guy she married were still together and they lived in an apartment complex over on Woodlawn; so, I started going over there to visit (they were still getting high). They were getting drugs from a man that we knew who used to work at a Club called the INN Crowd he was also their neighbor. I went over to his apartment and he asked me if I wanted to get back on my feet? He wanted me to [deal] drugs with her (since she and I were close friends). I did not want to get back involved with the drugs; but, I had taken some over to her house for him. [Without that personal relationship with Christ see how the enemy can keep creeping back in!]

I had only been back home for about 2 weeks! One day she wanted me to go to this store with her because she wanted to make some money to buy some dope. I really felt in my heart that I didn't want to go. I said: I'll go with you, but, I'm not going to steal anything. God was really talking to me that day all I had to do was listen.

My ex-brother-in-law came over there (the one that was married to my sister that was under me) to see the baby. If I'm remembering correctly, he and my sister lived in those same apartments; but anyway, my friend's husband was watching the kids, so I went with her. All the time we were riding, I could not shake the feeling (I was having), [that] I was going to jail that day. Every store she went in, I stayed in the car, except the last two they were stores that had some of the prettiest boots and western outfits; I got a red and blue outfit with a pair of red western boots (out of the first store); when I went to the car, I was so scared, she came out with a lot of stuff; she was on a mission she had a habit that had to be dealt with. I did not realize how bad her drug habit was until I saw how she was stealing. She used to be a dancer, and she ran some of the massage parlors for the guy she used to be with, she was really turned out!

We left from there and went to the other store near Andover. Andover was a little town outside of Wichita. We walked in the store, and I stayed up front while she went in the back she started stuffing things under her coat. She came walking toward the front and the clerks were following her I said to her: "you need to take that stuff out" you could see the fringe that was on a coat she was stealing, hanging from under her coat, but she said she was not going to take that stuff out. They said STOP HER! We ran to the car and jumped in, and she took off like a jet.

I was so scared I started taking the tags off the stuff that we had in the car. We were going down the street at about 80 mph when a highway patrol passed us, and he turned around in the middle of the street he was stopping us because we were going so fast. I kept telling her to slow down, but she was high on that cocaine, and all she could think about was selling that stuff so she could get some more dope.

The highway patrol tuned his lights [on us] she pulled over and he asked her why she was going so fast (I forgot what he said he clocked her at)? But as he was getting ready to write her a ticket, a call came on his radio saying to look out for a green Cadillac with a white male, white female, and one black female. He saw that, that was us, and he came back to the car with his gun drawn and said: "Get out of the car." I knew from that second on that I was not going to see my baby for a long time.

I had been close enough to God to know [when] HE was talking, but! I didn't listen I allowed my flesh to make the wrong choice. My heart was hurting real bad (back then).

They took us back to the store for the people to identify us.

The lady said that I was not in there stealing, that I was just standing around in the front of the store, looking. The cop said she still was with her.

They found a lot of [loot] in the car that I had torn the tags off. They could not prove where the merchandise came from, so we did not get charged with those items. They took us to Eldorado county jail and they booked us in. I was so mad at myself, but it was too late; it was payback time. Things happen, and we say, I should have, or I wish I had listened, regretting ever having done what we did.

I had escaped prison for so long. I thank God for saving me from myself, because I was headed back to that same way of life.
I was hesitant but eventually if I had stayed free I would have been back there again selling drugs.

They booked us; she was charged with grand larceny and my charge was accessory. They put a five thousand dollar bond on me and a seven thousand five hundred dollar bond on her. The man that was with us was one of her former tricks. I called my ex-bother-in-law (that use to be married to my oldest sister) to bond me out. They said that I could not bond out; because I had a probation hold on me; I was so hurt.

The guy she used to be with before she got married (they were still connected) made a cash bond for her, and then she got the man out and I was stuck in jail! I thought that it was not fair that she got out and I didn't. I went to court that next morning on the charges and they said I had a violation on my probation. I went back to my cell and I cried all that day. I finally called my mother, and she went and got my baby.

(God warned me over and over again) and yet I had the nerve to get mad at God I said: "God why did I have to leave my baby!" I tried to bargain with God I was asking HIM to just give me another chance. God warned me, He had given me a chance but I made a choice, so now I have to deal with it.

My journey had just begun and I felt really bad (for myself) I guess I was feeling sorry that I got caught. After that day I did not cry anymore. I said OK, God; you got my full attention now.

He reminded me of what I had asked Him to do. You wanted me to make you a good mother and that's what I'm getting ready to do.

While I was waiting to go to court for the case; I began to fast. At first, I would just fast from morning to evening; at dinner time I would pray, read my Bible and just talk to God. I was in a cell all by myself and I would sing and praise God all the time.

There was a trustee who would come to my cell and talk to me he would worry when I was fasting (he'd tell me to quit starving myself), I told him I was not doing that. God had begun to give me a peace with what had happened and why. The fast was making everything very clear to me. Some ministers came to the jail from a church out of El-Dorado, they would come to my cell to minister to me, but God allowed me to minister to them, also.

One night I was lying in my bed and God told me to open the Bible to ***Jeremiah 1: 5-10. It said: "Before I formed thee in the belly I knew thee; and before thou camest forth out of the womb I sanctified thee, and I ordained thee a prophet unto the nations, V6. Then said, I Ah, Lord God! Behold I cannot speak: for I am a child. V7. But the Lord said unto me, Say not, I am a child: for thou shalt go to all that I shall send thee, and whatsoever I command thee thou shalt speak. V8. Be not afraid of their faces: for I am with thee to deliver thee, saith the Lord. V9. Then the Lord put forth His hand, and touched my mouth. And the Lord said unto me, Behold, I have put My words in thy mouth. V10. See, I have this day set thee over the nations and over the kingdom, to root out, and to pull down, and to destroy, and throw down, to build, and to plant."***

It was such a peace and a joy in that cell! God was getting [ready to mold me] into my purpose I knew that to even try and fight this case was a waste of time. I began to understand how God grieved when I was selling those drugs.

My cell became the place for me to stop and think and renew my faith in God. HE reminded me how His grace and mercy had always been within my reach God had protected me all of my life; there were times I knew I should have been dead. All of that began to come back to my memory, so that I could see the unconditional love that HE had always had for me. Being bound for prison was saving my life. He said by rights I should have been dead or in prison for life. I began to praise God in that cell to where that cell became my prayer closet. I began to walk in God's favor in the El-Dorado county jail I never really understood God's favor, until I went to jail. I did not learn in church what I learned in that cell.

The jailers would love to hear me sing, they would turn on the intercom just to hear me. They would all bring me food when they came on duty. I still got to eat hamburgers and have pop and stuff that you normally don't get in jail. The folks from the church brought me food [That's God]!! HE let me know in the midst of it all, that HE was still there.

Time went on I got closer to God I wanted to receive the Baptism of the Holy Spirit.

The trustee would come by the cell with a book cart; one day he asked me if I saw a book that I wanted to read? I chose two: "Please Make Me Cry," and the other was: "Jump and I'll Catch You." That night I prayed to receive the Baptism of the Holy Spirit after I finished praying, instead of reading my Bible, I read: "Jump and I'll catch you." That book was totally amazing; it helped me to understand what it means to be totally dependent on God (who we cannot see). That book helped me understand that all I had to do to receive the Baptism of the Holy Spirit was to [truly believe in my heart]; Believe and Receive, and the Holy Spirit would Seal me until the day of our redemption.

"Jump and I'll Catch You," is a book about a man and his daughter the storm came and destroyed their home and nothing was left standing but the corner in which the little girl was in. Her father was thrown into a hole a few feet away, he heard his daughter crying but her mother had gotten killed; they were all in the house when the storm hit. Her father called out to her; he told her to start walking towards the sound of his voice she said, "But daddy, I can't see you." He said to just keep walking until my voice is louder to you so she kept walking and crying, saying, Daddy, I can't see you, where are you? When she got close enough that he saw her, he said, "I'm down here; now come over to the hole, because I can't come up, but you jump, and I will catch you." She said, "No daddy, I still can't see you." He said, "I can see you just trust daddy and jump, I will catch you." So she trusted what her father said and she went to the hole and she jumped by faith, believing that her father would catch her safely in his arms. That made me trust that God's gift of the Holy Spirit was mine for the asking that was an amazing story.

That is what God wants for us to have, that childlike faith we need to totally trust in the Him our God always has a way of escape for those of us who depend on Him. So that night, I went to the Lord and prayed for the baptism of the Holy Spirit; that prayer was different than any prayer I had ever prayed, the jail cell seemed like it had lit up! I had an amazing encounter with God that night then I began to pray in tongues, that night it just flowed out of me! I felt such a peace in that jail that I knew from that time on that I was going to be alright. I was so excited with my prayer language! The trustee came by that next morning and he was looking at me he was such a nice person, the guards and all of the trustees and workers were nice. I knew that God was getting ready to deal with me. After reading Jeremiah again, the word became life to me in my spirit man. I really realized what God was doing, after that I said, "OK, God, Your will be done."

The other book I began reading was, "Please Make Me Cry" it was about a young woman that was into drugs and prostitution she had a very hard life (actually the book was very similar to my life) I could relate to her in a lot of ways. I learned many things through reading about her experience; it helped me to deal with the journey that I was on. I knew in my heart that God had a plan for my life (all the prayers that had been prayed for me, and over me). I knew that God was not going to let all those prayers go unheard. The people that were praying for me I knew they could get a prayer through to God. I read that book in a few days it was a thick book too! It was so good that I could not put it down; besides, it was not like I was going anywhere.

Days went by and it seemed like no one was getting arrested

in that town I was the only woman in that jail. Then one night I was sound asleep; a loud noise woke me up, it was a woman screaming at the top of her lungs: "Let me the hell out of here!" She was cursing up a storm; I mean she had a very nasty mouth. I went to the bars of the cell, and I called for one of the guards to come in there; I asked him what was going on. He said: "She's keeping everybody up!" He told me that she was arrested for DUI and they had to put her in the drunk tank.

They could not do anything with her; she was trying to fight with them to let her go. They wanted her to sleep it off so they could deal with her better. I told them to let her come in there with me. They said, No, because she will have you up all night. I said, "She's doing that anyway, and everybody else also!" He said, "Are you sure?" I told him, "Yes, I'm sure." So he went, to the tank and got her; they handcuffed her to bring her back there where I was and she was still cursing.

After they put her in the cell with me, I asked her what was wrong? All of a sudden, she got real quiet. The presence of God in that cell calmed her spirit. She came over and sat on my bunk, and then she began telling me that they stopped her, claiming she was weaving on the road. She was explaining to me that she had been driving on that road for 11 years (she was on her way home from work, and she had never gotten stopped before). She said that they told her she was drunk. I said, "Well maybe it was for the best that they stopped you" I told her it may have saved her life and some other people too. She said, "How could that be?" I told her: "God saw what was ahead," you could have had a wreck, run off the road, or you could have hit someone or caused a bad accident and God looks after us even when we don't look after ourselves, all they want you to do is sleep it off. I assured her that she would go home in the morning; she was very intoxicated. She laid her head on my lap, and I began to pray over her, then I sang a song and she fell asleep.

The guards were so amazed at what had happened that they thanked me for calming her down. I told them that it was not me it was God. One of the guards said, she won't remember anything in the morning. I got in another bunk and went to sleep.

The next morning after breakfast they came and got her and she went to court, and I said bye to her. She left, but after she saw the judge, she had them bring her back in there to tell me she will never forget what I did for her; she remembered everything that God did in that cell that night. She told me she was going to write and keep in touch with me. I told her what I was there for and that I was going to prison. She did just what she said she would do, she kept in touch with me and she kept her word. God allowed her to come through there just to show Himself to her. That divine appointment changed her life; it was a blessing to me it also showed the guards who God really is. They used to say things to me about how I talk.

Time went by, and I went to court to be sentenced, plus I still had to face parole violation in Wichita [the drug case]. God even gave me favor with the judge I was talked about a lot in that small jail everyone knew me, or knew of me. The judge told me that what I had done carries its own sentence (when your probation is violated it is automatic time, on the previous charge). The judge said she would run this new sentence concurrent with whatever Wichita gives me for the parole violation (if Wichita would go for it). I had a two 2 to 20 year sentence. I was facing no more than forty, but no less than four years, your time depends on you. I went back to my cell I was a little shaken by what she had said; (immediately) a calmness came over me and I knew that God would get me through this.

I stayed on my course of praying and fasting, growing closer and closer to Him. A week later another woman came through there (she was an older woman in her sixties); they called her granny she looked a lot older than she was; she looked to have had a very hard life (you could tell she had been something else) she came in for forgery. She told me she went cross country writing checks, and till tapping. I had learned till tapping; but I did not write about it in my book.

Granny was on her way to prison that was just a stop off place for her for a week until they could transport her. She did not like talking about God at all. I told her she needed to change her life. She told me she had spent most of her life in and out of prison. I asked her if she was tired! She said it was too late now? She asked me: "what can I do at my age? "I replied there are still something's that you can do to better and change your life I began to minister to her; whether it got through or not I don't know, I did what God told me to do.

One day she got a bad headache God told me to lay hands on her head and pray for her I said, "God what if I pray for her and nothing happens?" God was teaching me obedience I really didn't want to do that, because she was already skeptical, but out of obedience I did it I said I was going to trust God to do what he said. I told her I wanted to pray with her she said OK. She was looking at me while I was praying with her; I asked God to prove Himself to her that day, and He did. Her headache went away, just as I was praying, Praise the Lord!!! She was so amazed at that and I thank God for His marvelous act. I gave Him the entire honor and the glory! She began to believe in God a little after that. The next day they came and got her she said, "I'll see you when you get to Lansing prison." [That was another divine appointment.]

God was just revealing Himself to me more and more. Although I had been in church as I was growing up, I never experienced God the way I did in that El-Dorado County Jail.

I was beginning to get restless I told the LORD that I had been there long enough, I asked Him to please let me move on so I could start my time. I still had to go to Wichita to face my parole violation. Lo and behold the next day they told me that I would be leaving that afternoon I was glad because I had not seen daylight for a while (I had spent Christmas and New Years in that cell).

I left the jail in January, I think it was the middle of the month. A prison Van transported me to the County Jail in Wichita; I don't know why I was in such a hurry (that Wichita jail was no joke!!!) It was nothing like the one in El-Dorado. The El-Dorado jail was a palace compared to the Sedgwick County Jailhouse).

When I got there I went upstairs to be booked and then I was taken to the women's floor. I heard the women talking loud and silly, I walked around and they all started shouting my name. They had assigned me to North-1 cellblock, that was where the black women were, and I did not want to be part of the drama. I said: God, all the progress that I've made I don't want to hear or smell: the cursing, and the cigarette smoke (I needed peace in my spirit). They did not have the keys to North-1, so they put me in the hold-over cell until the guard came back to let me in. During all this, it came time for them to change shifts so I had to stay where I was until they finished.

God did an amazing thing; He heard and answered my prayer. After they changed shifts, the guard coming on duty said, sign her to South-1 (across from North-1) I didn't know why they did that, but I was glad. When they took me to the cell, the women were shouting, "Why y'all putting her over there? You belong over here with us!" I said (to myself) I think not! After I got to the cell, I walked in looking for an empty bed (those beds were so thin, it was a shame the way we had to sleep). It was all white girls in South-1 except for one. God had put me where He could use me the most. There were women in that cellblock who had committed heinous crimes: like murder; one woman had burnt her baby; another raped her daughter with a pop bottle and broke it in her, and one of them killed her stepfather because he had been raping her; she was full of hate and hurt; all of the women in South-1 were very bitter (they were some very sick offenders), they needed deliverance. On the surface, my crime appeared to be nothing compared to theirs. I said, "God how do I approach this?" I began to really reach for answers.

One day some women came to minister to us from a church that I was familiar with (one of the ladies was the aunt of one of the girls I ran around with back in the day). They all were "Strong women of God." They had prayer and bible study with us. Everyone in the cellblock came to the table. The jail had something like a dayroom where we could sit, chat, eat or just watch TV; it also had a walkway around the bars like a catwalk; that's where the guards would make their rounds (at night) that was also where the church ladies had to stand until the guard let them in the room (to join us). I will never forget the wisdom they imparted to me that day. (The ladies brought a gift for each woman.) When they got ready to leave, they asked me to pray, so I did. The Spirit of God led me to pray in my prayer language and as I prayed God began to reveal to me that I was to be a light in the cellblock. One of the ladies said she knew that, that was what God wanted me to do; she said that God was going to use me in that jail (she interpreted what I had prayed). Another lady told me to memorize some scriptures, because: you never know when you'll need them, and a bible may not always be available (in other words: hide the Word in your heart). The ladies from the church also prayed (with us) and then they left. "God is so good."

I began to talk to the women in my cellblock. The one who killed her stepfather was a hard person to talk to, but I was not going to give up on her. One of my cellmates had heart problems and so, she would stay in bed all the time they would take her back and forth to the hospital; she'd be away for a day or two at a time. I started a bible study group and we began our studies in Acts. (I don't know why I went to the Book of Acts, unless it was because of what I had experienced when I prayed in the spirit the day the church ladies came.) I wanted to learn more about devotional and diverse prayer language (and as I was sharing with my inmates they also wanted to learn more). It was very calm and peaceful in our cell. The women across from us were loud and out of control, I am thankful to God that I was not placed in that cage. I prayed for the women in North-1, that God would give them the same peace that He had blessed me with.

They called me out of my cell the next day and asked me if I wanted to be a trustee; I said yes. It was good for me to be able to get out of that closed up cell; I was out of the [block] most of the day. I would pick up the dirty laundry from each cell, and take it to the laundry area to be washed. I would push the book cart from cell-to-cell to distribute reading material; I also helped serve lunch. In the afternoons, I would go back in my cell and we would have our bible studies.

I always looked forward to the church ladies coming to share the love of Christ with us. My fellow inmates would ask me to pray with them before they went to court. I saw a lot of women come and go. I'd be sad when they would leave but, I was always glad to see them return to their families.

Finally, they let the woman with the bad heart out of jail; and the one who killed her stepfather turned out to be a very sweet person; she had been hurting so bad (for what she had been through) that she used that [tough girl exterior] to cover up who she really was (they returned her back to the State where she had killed her stepfather). God broke through to the hearts of a lot of those women. The inmate who raped her daughter (with the pop bottle) had psychological problems (dah!!!); they sent her to Learned, Kansas (it's a hospital for people who are mentally ill).

Finally it was my day to go to court I had prayed and gave the situation to God. I already knew I was going to prison; it was just a matter of how much time I would be [doing]. I went before the same judge who had sent me to Parallax. When I faced him this time he talked to me like he was disappointed in me for having violated my probation; he had my file pulled from El-Dorado and he read the El-Dorado judge's recommendation. He said he would honor her request to run my sentences concurrently; he said he felt that if I did the time I would not be back; he suggested that it was my associates who had influenced me; he said he thought that prison would change me for the better.

I accepted what was given to me and I knew that the amount of time I would spend in prison would depend on my behavior; I deserved more time but [**God's grace and mercy**] saved me.

My cellmates were waiting to see what happen to me; not a single person felt that I should be serving any time. I told them that what has happened to me was for my own good; and that God allowed [it] in order to save my life. I talked about my past (a lot) and about how God has covered me (even in jail).

I began to study the fascinating life of Paul. His life stuck out for me more than anyone else's other than Jesus' I began to read the Bible about the things that Paul and others did and how what they accomplished, was for God's Glory. I was there another week, and I said to God! It is time to move on.

I, was on the next bus to Lansing. There was a woman on the prison bus with me (she had been in the cell that I didn't want to go to). When I looked at her I couldn't understand why she was headed to prison. This woman was very quiet; she was one of the nicest people you could ever meet; she didn't appear to have ever committed a crime in her life. (I was shocked at her crime! You just never know.) It was just the two of us women and about 12 men. She and I were chained together; it reminded me of the prison buses you see on TV; it took me back to when I went to San Aretha in California, and I took the ride on that prison bus.

It was a 3 hour ride to where we were going; they dropped us off first; the men's destination was about a block away (where they had to check in).

Lansing had become Co-ed we got to the gate and I was looking around; I said to myself, I am really here. (My sister had been there a few times so they knew her. I had been up there in the past to visit her but, I never thought that I would one day be incarcerated myself.)

They checked us in and we had to go to the infirmary, it was part of the orientation process (for health reasons); they also sprayed us with something that smelled like Black Flag roach spray. We had to stay in isolation for two weeks before we could go out into the population. There were some male and female prisoners on the other side of the fence (in minimum security). I would get in my bed and read my Bible. There was a guard who would always look in my window but she didn't say very much to me. I could tell that she was once "in church," but I think: working there (at the prison might have) weakened her faith. (They say she liked women), she always seemed to want to ask me about the bible. Finally it was time for me to go into "population."

As soon as I came to the surface this guy came up to me because he had heard a lot about me; he thought he would try and catch me (in prison). I was not thinking about a relationship in prison. He was with this white girl (his prison girlfriend) who got mad when she saw him talking to me. Little did she know I did not give a darn about any man in that prison!

When I got to the chow hall that evening (for the first time) there were so many Wichita people there and I knew half of them. I had gotten so close to the Lord that I did not want to hang around anyone. (The male inmates had clicks there, and I did not care what they thought of me.) I was in the recreation room and I heard that white girl talking about me she was telling somebody that; that B>>> think she is going to get him, I'll kick her a>>. I came around where she was and I said to her: 'First of all I could care less about that Negro he came to me, plus! If he cared so much about you I couldn't have gotten even a conversation out of him; I came to do my time and go home Y'all have set up house here so be my guest, because I do not give a damn.' She went on and left me alone. I did not feel like having conflicts with anyone I wanted to keep my peace (with God), so I stayed clear of everybody.

Later that day [that] guard came to me and we began to talk; she said she that she had previously been in the church and that she was stressed because of her job (working in a prison is no picnic). I told her that I would keep her in my prayers.

A week later God moved me. I was transferred to a prison called Candy Land, in Topeka, Kansas; it was like a college campus in a residential neighborhood it was nice! The same woman, who rode the prison bus to Lansing with me, went with me to Candy Land. They called our living quarter's: "dorms;" they were Co-ed also. They put me in J-Dorm it was outside the gate, actually on the street (in a residential area).

After my evaluation, they put me on minimum custody. They told me that throughout the time I had been serving, that all reports from one place to the other (about me) were excellent. I kept myself out of trouble and [I did not care what people thought of me] all I wanted to do was to get back home to my daughter.

Once I got to Topeka I finally got to have my first visitor; I had only seen my baby one time while I was in the county jail, in Wichita. She was so funny they told me some great stories about her I had filled out the visitation form in Lansing, but I left before they got up there for a visit. Topeka was quite a ways to drive for a short visit, but my mother and my stepfather brought my baby to see me. I'm glad that I wasn't in the County Jail type setting because I wouldn't want my baby to see me from behind bars. My sister under me and her husband kept my baby girl a lot; they spent time with her and they would send me pictures, they were crazy about my daughter I knew she was well taken care of.

I had problems with the guards when I first got there. One of the guards told me that she was frantic when they heard that a sister of a woman that gave them hell was coming (my sister under me was well known in the prison system). She gave them hell! They said (after a while) that they couldn't believe that we were related. My sister was a hell cat she would do crazy stuff, and she spoke her mind; whatever she had to say she would say it. She's the one I was in California with; we went through a lot together (back in the day). One of the female guards said that my sister snatched her wig off her head one time. They really did not like my sister. Candy Land appeared to be a nice place (better than Lansing).

[Time passed] and I got adjusted to being there; we had two beds in our dorm rooms; I just happened to get a roommate who liked women (there was a lot of that going on up there); I said: I really didn't know why because it was Co-ed, so, why not have a man if you just couldn't contain yourself! My roommate had a woman that was very jealous of whoever was around her I told her that she didn't have to worry about me at all.

That place was something; they had more drugs and alcohol in there than what was on the street! They'd have COUNT every hour; so everyone would have to be in their dorm unless you were assigned someplace else. They had a recreation room, and a gym you could hang out in, and they had a beauty shop where you could get your hair done. That place was just like a little town of its own. They had a school you could go to for vocational training, or if you still needed your GED you could get it there; that's where I got my diploma. (Dropping out of High school in the 11th grade was very stupid, but I did.)

After I got my GED I enrolled in a Sales Management Course I got so involved in school that I didn't have the time to do other things that were available to me on campus.

I still had all the weight (on me) that I had after my baby was born (I was a size 18 to 20 when I got locked up). You could not lose any weight in jail, because all you did was eat and recline in your spare time; you never got any exercise. So I started walking the track everyday. There was an older inmate who was really fit; a group of us would meet her in the rec room (of our dorm), and we would do forty sit ups every night. It was hard at first, but we were determined (to get in shape) and she was persistent in helping us to get there.

I got on the **soft ball team**, it was fun. We would go to Lansing and play the women there, and sometimes they would come to Topeka and play us. There were even dances in prison; I tell you the truth, it really was a little city within itself. The drug distribution and use was really bad in prison and the inmates would make their own alcohol (they used all kinds of stuff up there). I got a little bold. My sister would bring weed to me on visiting day. You could stick that stuff up in you and they couldn't find it; the guards would ask you to bend over, but they would barely search you. Some of the guards would even bring that stuff in (themselves) for certain people. I did that twice, and never did it again. You could sell a joint for $8.00 and you could make almost $100.00 off one bag of weed; people would have money put on their [personal inmate pushers books].

One weekend they had a drug raid; featuring dogs and everything! It was a real bust! In prison!!! They found drugs and syringes; they found a suppository in my drawer! That violation could get you a class one felony; they would not allow you have a douche bottle I don't know what they thought you would do with it! (I had gone to medical and they gave me the suppository.) I didn't want to use it until I took a shower that night. You are supposed to use it right away (but I didn't).

There was a guard that really did not like me; it wasn't because of anything I did, it was because [none of them] liked my sister.

And then there was my singing! They didn't like the fact that I was always walking around singing (singing has been part of me all my life). They truly could not understand how I could be so happy, and be locked up.

Every morning we had to get up at 5 AM and be at breakfast at 6 AM I had to walk through CONTROL to get to the chow hall. They would be looking so mad and unhappy and I would cheerfully say: "Good morning, how are you ladies on this wonderful morning?" They would look at me and turn their heads I'd ask them: what they had to be so unhappy about: "You got your freedom! You ought to make the best of it." Some mornings they would go behind the booth to keep from speaking to me. I would wait until they thought I was gone and I would say: "I thought I missed you I just wanted to say hello." OH my God, they would be so mad you could see it all over their faces; so they were trying to find a reason to write me up. I already had favor with the warden; he was MM's cousin. Boy, that warden was fine, too! I did not like seeing him; he was one of the good cousins in MM's family.

[Back to the bust] that suppository gave them a reason to write me up, they gave me a "Class One Felony." That's like a drug felony on the streets; I said, "Come on, that was not that serious." They were grasping at straws! Lots of people got caught with serious drugs in their rooms. I wrote a letter to the Judge, I said you sent me here to be rehabilitated! I told him there's more going on in here than on the streets! He did not respond to my letter.

Time passed, and I had to have a hearing on the write-up that said: I was harboring medication. They presented the evidence and the Warden looked at them and asked: "where's the medication, she was harboring?" He said, "I know that this is not what you wrote her up for!" He was very embarrassed for me. He said: "if y'all don't get this s>>> out of here," those were his exact words. He asked them: what can you do with this, outside of what it is for? They tried to tell him that I was supposed to use it right away, and I explained to the Warden that I was going to use it when I took a shower, but after I got back to the dorm they had COUNT and after that...the raid. He apologized (for them), they looked very stupid; he told me that I could leave. He dismissed that funny style charge, so they were really out to get me (after that).

God continued to watch over me. I didn't want to get involved with drugs or anything (else) that would cause me to get off track, again. I wanted to stay on the course that God had me on. The last of the weed that I had stashed I flushed down the toilet (I wouldn't give it to anyone). One of the girls that I knew from the streets of Wichita was there and I was familiar with a lot of the women out of Kansas City, but I stayed on course, trying to stay free from all distractions.

[Timed passed] They decided to put on a talent show and there were a lot of people trying out for it, so I signed up, also. These girls and I were going to sing Aretha Franklin's song: "Giving Him Something He can feel;" I was singing the lead. One of the girls did not like that, so she talked the others into quitting a day before the talent show. They had that planned all along and I said to myself, that's OK I can do this by myself.

So the night of the talent show, I was so nervous, I did not want to go out there. My counselor was sitting in the audience (she was always amazed at me I felt that she genuinely liked me). So I went out there and I gave it all I had, and Guess what? I won!!! When they called my name, I went up there like I was this big TV star. My counselor came up to me, she had the most surprising look on her face, she said wow! "You are full of surprises Ms. Lady," she said: "that was amazing!" It was an unforgettable night.

The next day I was moved to another level (I forgot how the levels went). I was in school and doing very well; so good that I became the class instructor. My teacher was very impressed with my work. God was showing me who He really was in my life; His Favor surrounded me.

I was praying a lot for people out in the yard (people would come over and listen to me speak about God). We would have church on Wednesday nights and people would come in from the outside to worship with us. We had a chaplain who was just there because it was his job, IMO, he could care less about the people's spiritual needs; he even tried to get me written up (he accused me of trying to form a cult). He was mad because people came to me for prayer instead of him.

He called me into his office one day and asked me what I was doing? God anointed my mouth that day to speak the word to that man, he could not help but back off me; God protected me in a way that I didn't understand (I was never taught this). I was learning with the help and power of the Holy Ghost (my teacher-my comforter) I left his office and went back to campus.

The following Wednesday the church people came again, and this time the Pastor and his wife were with them (they were a beautiful couple). I'd never heard of this happening before but they were able to take me off campus (to their church). They were having a program, and after the program a reception. That was nobody but God!!! He can make things happen in such a way that you know man had no part in it.

I had great times serving God locked up! God was molding me to be pleasing to Him. Sometimes God puts us in a place for a long and difficult time of testing. Jesus went into the wilderness for forty days to be tested; what makes us any better? I brought all of this on myself, but I thank God for His grace and mercy that saw me through it.

[Time passed] I continued working out: walking, doing sit-ups and playing soft ball; plus I was working in the kitchen. The wages were 45 cents a day, which was something like 9 dollars a month. The food was pretty good because they had some good cooks in the kitchen. I started talking to and hanging out with a fellow inmate (after the girlfriend he had there was released from prison). He worked out a lot in the gym and he would walk the track with me; he seemed like a pretty nice guy. There was a car shop in the prison and some of the male inmates worked as mechanics on all of the city workers vehicles; they had put some mattresses in the back and they would take turns going back there to have sex. The women had boyfriends (except for those who had other women). There was a woman there who tried to "hookup" with me; she would try to buy me stuff; I told her that I did not like women, and that there were too many men on the campus to have sex with if that was what I wanted. She left me alone after she saw that I was not playing; some of the women thought they were in paradise; they acted just like men on the prowl.

[Time passed] I finished my course and received a diploma in General Sales Management (General Sales Manager); I completed 782 hours in that class; I was very grateful for that. I put in a request to go to [work release]; my counselor said it would be a while, because there was a waiting list, I said OK. I prayed about it, and I asked God to open the door if it was His will for me to have a job. Two weeks went by and nothing happened; then one day my counselor called me into her office, she said: "I have some good news; you are next to go to work release" I screamed!!! I was so very happy, I said: "I thought you said it would be a while," she said: "I guess your God heard your prayer;" then she informed me that I would be leaving in 2 weeks. God was manifesting Himself to them and to me. So I told my guy friend. I knew I had to really be careful, because any little slip could set me back. They were trying to find something to write me up on, but I knew God had me covered.

We had a soft ball game that weekend. The women from Lansing came over to play us (I could bat, and run real good, but I could not catch a ball). We were ahead, most of the game, and we won! Everybody was jumping up and down, really happy because the women from Lansing thought they were tough. I threw my glove up in the air, and when it came down it hit a girl (by accident). She came over to me and took that glove and hit me cross my face so hard I froze!! It hurt so bad I grabbed my face. Everybody came running over there, they thought it was getting ready to be a fight but I looked at her and walked away. An old roommate of mine out of Wichita said: "B>>>> you gonna let that girl hit you like that, and you not do anything?"

The girl that hit me was constantly trying to bait me into a fight. All I could think of was I am leaving in two weeks so I could not afford a setback. Fighting was lock down time, and also time added to your sentence. I started walking towards my dorm; everybody was walking and shouting, trying to get me to fight that girl. She thought I was scared of her, but my friend knew I wasn't. If it would have been another time and place, I would have beaten the hell out of that woman.

The coach told me to keep walking and when you get up there both of you go to Control. So we both went in the warden's office I did not have to say a word the coach told the whole story and they sent me to my dorm; she got one month lock down, and 6 months added to her sentence.

I wanted my freedom more than anything else and what I did, really proved it. It took a lot for me not to hit that woman. Everybody saw that what I did, was not about being afraid; I was not going to prove nothing to anyone, but God, I did not care what people thought.

That Monday one of the guard's mothers was in a car wreck and she died. The guard was gone for most of my remaining time; she came back two days before I was scheduled to leave. She was really having a hard time. I kept watching her that day, and God told me to go pray with her, so I went into the office (where she was); she was one of the main ones who hated my sister.

I started ministering to her; she told me that her mother had a heart attack while she was driving, and that's what caused the wreck. She said: the doctors told her that her mother: "didn't know what hit her." We were in there alone for about an hour. She was so blessed by what God had given me to say to her. She told me that she was really surprised by my life after learning who my sister was. She said you two are as different as night and day, although the two of you look alike; then she thanked me for sharing with her.

After our conversation she got called to Control and they told her that what she did was not professional, so they suspended her for a week. She came back in there to get her stuff, and she told me it was worth it. She said I hate to see you go, but I wish you well (the day came for me to leave, and most of the guards said the same thing). ***God had a plan for my life even in prison: it was a wary pilgrims journey but I made it through.***

That Wednesday, they sent me into the work-release program. The Work Release Center was in the building that once was Parallax; (Parallax had moved to another location).

When I arrived, I saw many men and woman that I had sold drugs to in the past. The first night you are given a 30 minute walk outside the center. It was so nice to be back in Wichita. I walked to the gas station around the corner with a friend she'd been there for a while. (She smoked weed a lot.) While we were walking she lit up a joint and I ended up smoking some with her. I only took two puffs. I never really had a high tolerance for weed; just a little would make me high; after I took a hit I got scared and regretted what I had done. I was so nervous when we got back.

I had to go see my intake counselor to check in; he looked at me and asked me if I enjoyed my walk. I thought he knew that I had smoked some weed but he didn't. I went to my room and asked God to forgive me for doing that, and I asked Him to help to be strong. I said to myself I have come too far to allow myself to be that stupid. I stayed in my room for the rest of the night.

Around three o'clock in the morning, I was awakened!!! I had an awesome experience: I observed a very tall and bright peaceful being over me, and I was not afraid. God assured me [that night] that He would always be with me. He said: "I will never leave you nor forsake you" I just rested in His presence, I won't forget that night.

The next morning I started my life in the work release program we had four levels to get through. (I arrived there in December (1982) and I was scheduled to meet the parole board the following July 1, 1983.) I was hoping that I would be able to go home on a pass to see my baby (I was so glad when that happened). (She would be turning two years old in July, and I prayed that I would be out by my birthday and hers.)

After being there for a month, I was at the level that allowed me to go out and look for a job. I would walk down town (it was about 8 blocks from the center). I went into a store call Lewins (a very expensive clothing store); they needed a seamstress and I could sew; after I filled out the application I had an interview with the head seamstress; she was impressed with me. Surprisingly, she hired me! But, after she called me (at the number I gave her), she realized that I was a convict; she told them to tell me that she was sorry but she forgot that they had already hired somebody. I knew she was lying. I said: "OK LORD, I don't want to have any more problems like this; God, you know my lifestyle has changed, please don't allow people to keep looking at me based on what I did in the past!"

So I set out again the next day I went to the Broadview Hotel (it was a very old establishment). I talked to the banquet manager, and he said they needed some banquet servers; he hired me. I told him right off who I was and where I was staying; I said: "if you have a problem with that, let me know right now" he said he didn't, and he asked me when I could start? I told him that I could start whenever he needed me; so, he said that I could start work Friday morning; he told me to wear black pants and a white top.

I left there and went back to the work release center; I told my counselor that I had been hired and so they had to verified my employment; but, it was all good! I could not wait to start working. The pay was $4.50 an hour plus 15% gratuities. I was determined to stay strong and not be tempted by greed (again). This was a big drop in pay compared to the money I used to make in the drug world. But! I was resolute to change my life and I knew that God would help me to do it. Dressed in my black and white outfit I arrived at work that Friday morning (on time; as a matter of fact I got there early). I didn't know we were going to serve the Fourth National Bank Banquet. The party was for two thousand! I said wow! We had to set all of those tables I knew I could do it, this was right up my alley! They had managers assigned to each station and there were 4 stations; I was on the first table, it was going to be a very busy that night I walked around getting things together (everybody was rushing).

The banquet was scheduled to start at 5 PM and we were ready. The kitchen had all of the plates ready to be placed on the tables; the salads and the desert were already out front. There were 30 workers on each station. When it was time to serve the plates we all got in line, grabbing them and carrying them out (I could carry 5 plates at a time). They had it organized to where people would carry the trays and someone would follow behind them, but it was much easier for me to do it that way. I was moving by the grace of God; when I finished I helped the other stations. I started floating wherever I was needed. Everything went well. Cleaning up the mess afterwards, wasn't as exciting, but we did it! It was about one o'clock in the morning before I got back to the center I was so tired, I just checked in and went straight to bed.

The next day I had to talk to the counselor that the center assigned for me; I wished I had gotten this other guy because he was real cool! When I went back to work the day after that we had more banquets, but they were not as big as the first one. (My boss scheduled me a lot.) I had worked for about two weeks when he called me into the office; I didn't know what he could have wanted, I thought: what did I do? The boss asked me how I liked working there, I replied: it was good. He told me that he had been watching me, and he liked the way I handled things; he told me I served with grace (isn't that something he said grace). He said the way I handled that Fourth National Bank Dinner was amazing. I told him that: "if I do something I want to do it well." (That was the way I was taught.) My father told me that if I was going to do something, do it with excellence; he said if you don't like what you are doing, why do it? I always remembered that. God is so good!!

After the boss finished raving about how much he liked my work he offered me the Banquet Supervisor position, I was shocked! (There was a girl who had been employed there for 5 years waiting in line for that job. I didn't want to cut her out, but I said: "that would be great!") God just came in and moved me all the way up from that $4.50 an hour that I was earning, while waiting and trusting God to open doors. God knew that I did not want to go back to my old life. ***God said in His word that He will never see His righteous forsaken.*** I was so excited; I went to salary, and that was good. We had to pay rent at the work release center; they would take our pay checks and put them into a savings coffer and they'd deduct our portion of the rent based on our income and give us $25.00 for the week (unless we needed more for something important). The amount they saved for us would stay in the account until we were released from the program; I guess that was good. I was overjoyed that I had been promoted in such a short period time but I still felt bad for the girl who was passed over; she was very angry about it. She talked really crazy to them but they did not fire her because she had been there for so long. I became her boss. I had 25 girls working under me, it was great. I did all the scheduling for each dinner, I watched the ladies and I knew who would fit where. I did not sit back and give orders; I would schedule myself too, and help where I was needed I loved working with the staff, and they really liked me the managers were also pleased with my performance.

I was not at the center very much (that was good for me). One day the center had a shake down and they took a UA from everybody. People wanted me to sell them my urine, isn't that something! They knew that I had not been doing any drugs but! I wouldn't do their urine test for them; I told them that I was not going to get in trouble for doing something like that. Everyone's UA was dirty except for mine and one of the guys (the whole center had been smoking weed; their privileges were revoked, the only place they could go was, back and forth to work). The two of us could leave the center on passes (as usual). Finally the others were taken off restriction.

[Time passed] It would soon be time for me to meet the Board and I was getting scared; why! I don't know, because God had already shown me time and time again that He would never leave me nor forsake me I had to shake those thoughts because I knew they were ungodly. I talked to the counselor (that I admired) and he said: "You have been a model inmate throughout your time; I've read your file and you'll make it."

I had been spending time with this guy; we had been going on passes together; stupid me! One night I decided to sleep with him and after that (one time), I was so ashamed of myself that I couldn't stay focused. I'm so thankful to God that He has always reminded me of who I am in Him. I would always feel conviction whenever I did something that was not pleasing to God. I told the guy that I couldn't do that anymore. Sometimes you might think you've been delivered from a weakness and later you find yourself still frail in certain areas.

As days went by I started to feel sick (a lot) I didn't know what was wrong; my girlfriend told me that I should see a doctor so I made an appointment outside the work release program. I had an idea what was wrong (because I was having morning sickness). I said, "Oh my God!" I went to the doctor, they took a urine test and it came back positive; I was pregnant! I said: "LORD! What am I going to do!!!" I told my friend and she said you know that if they find out, they will send you back (I had about a month left in that place); I just couldn't go back! So I took a chance; I went to the counselor (who was real cool with everyone) and I told him that I was pregnant, I also let him know that I was going to have an abortion. He asked me how I was going to do that because they had my money? He told me that he would make up a good reason to take the money out of my account. (I did not tell "the guy," but I didn't want a baby.)

I felt bad for doing what I was getting ready to do; I knew that it was against God's will but I didn't want to go back to prison. They probably would not have known, but I did not want to take that chance, in case I didn't make the board, so I had the abortion. I felt bad a long time after that, but it was done (that child would be 28 or 29 years old now).

The day came to meet the board. (I asked God's forgiveness for the things I had done to disrespect Him; I believe that He forgave me because His mercy is renewed every morning.) I got dressed and went down stairs, to face the board. They asked me why I felt I was ready to go home? I answered them, and then they told me about the good reports they had about me. They said they felt that I was ready, so they gave me a release date of July 8th, three days before my birthday. I was going home and I would be there for my daughter's birthday to enjoy it with her on July 13th

I could not ask for a better birthday present. I praised God all the way back to my room.

(Everybody was waiting to hear what happened.) I thanked God! ***I said God we made it. God helped me to do my time, and not allow the time to do me, Glory to Your Holy Name.*** On July 8th 1983, I was released. I praise God for all He allowed me to go through while I was in prison, it taught me to be patient. The next few sectors teaches us about spiritual imprisonment.

Reaching Beyond the Bars/System

Prison is one of Satan's domains, it assists in keeping God's people in bondage. Prison can change you (for the better or for the worst) and it can totally destroy you (if you let it). I chose to allow God to help me change my life. It was a time of transitioning for me. Prison helped me to develop a real and true relationship with Christ.

God prepared me to be a living testimony for Him. (Isaiah 61:1-3 was an enlightenment for me, after all the mess I had gone through.) V1. "The Spirit of the Lord is upon me; because the LORD hath anointed me to preach the good tidings unto the meek; he hath sent me to bind up the broken hearted, to proclaim liberty to the captives, and the opening of the prison to them that are bound. V2. To proclaim the acceptable year of the LORD, and the day of vengeance of our God; to comfort all that mourn; V3. To appoint unto them that mourn in Zion, to give unto them beauty for ashes, the oil of joy for mourning, the garment of praise for the spirit of heaviness that they might be called trees of righteousness, the planting of the LORD, that He might be glorified."

God used a lot of people that were put in prison. Let's look at a few. Paul was imprisoned because of his faith: Acts 16:23, 24. Joseph was thrown into prison by his master in Egypt, and there he met some men who had been servants in the kings place. See: Gen 39:20. John the Baptist was beheaded in prison. (Matthew14:3-12) Jeremiah was put in a dungeon. See Jeremiah 37:16. Even though my imprisonment was justified, God used me for [His good] right there on those prison grounds. Prison is not only where people are physically detained, it can also restrain our minds. The prison system has a way of making a person feel degraded and your true identity is fuddled. Joseph could have fallen into deep despair, but, instead he decided to do his best in every task he was given. His diligence and his positive attitude got him promoted (he became second only to the Pharaoh). God sees our circumstances and [it is] His will to turn them and will reverse all odds against us if we trust Him.

Chapter 7

Freedom

I was free! This was wonderful I was glad to get out of the system to begin rebuilding my life. I still had the job at the Broadview Hotel. I had saved around $800.00 but it wasn't enough to get a place of my own and get my furniture out of storage, so I moved in with my mother and her husband (where my baby had been the whole time). My mother and stepfather had been my baby's guardians while I was away. My mother had her own way of raising my daughter; our methods were completely different; she loved taking care of babies: And Feeding Them. Food was how she showed love. My daughter was a little butter ball. They would be up at all hours of the night eating snacks. (My mother had been used to me giving her things when I was dealing drugs. In the past I never let her go without; anything she wanted I got it for her). My sister and her husband had generously helped her to take care of my baby; they provided clothing and other things that she needed (I am grateful to them).

My mother really acted irrational, towards my stepfather. She would pick fights with him (as I said before, my mother had a mouth on her I was used to the way she was) but, I refused to take her side (or any side) in their arguments, although she wanted me to be in her [amen] corner.

Before daybreak that morning, my mother told me to get up and make my baby some oatmeal. I told her that my baby didn't need to be eating (like that) at all times of the night. I really didn't want to get into a confrontation with her; I tried to stay prayerful and keep my focus on the Lord, but that night it didn't happen. She got so mad at me that she started to, CURSE ME OUT!!! I told her that I was going to change my baby's (bad) eating habits and she said: "YOU CAN GET OUT OF MY HOUSE." I didn't argue with my mother, I didn't believe in that; so I got my belongings and placed them on the porch along with my daughter I called my father and He picked us up. My father said that it was OK to stay with him (but his wife and her kids were there, and they really didn't have enough room for us all); so I told him to take us to a hotel. We drove down on Broadway and I got a room off of Pawnee and Broadway. I didn't like it, but that was all I could afford it was part of Wichita's [streets] where there was a lot of prostitution and other vices. They lived in those hotels all up and down Broadway. Lord! Please don't leave me, was my prayer.

My ultimate tests came after I was physically freed, I had trusted God in prison, but things were different in the real world. I didn't have a car and I still had to get to work. I called a lady that had been friends of our family for many years; she used to babysit my younger sisters while my mother worked. I asked her if she would watch my daughter for me and she said yes. Now, all I had to do was get her there (I had to be on the job at 6:00 am).

I walked to the store to buy food and we settled into our temporary home. I never stopped reading the Word and praying to God to help me get where I needed to be at peace and stress free; but it was hard. I couldn't believe that this was what my freedom brought.

We got up the next morning and I dressed and fed my daughter, then I got dressed. We caught the bus over to the lady's house, then I caught the bus to work; (this was our daily routine)

[Time passed] After the guy (Crazy) from the Work Release Program (who had impregnated me) was freed himself; we got back together. He had a good job so we got an apartment (way out, south of the city) together. He got my furniture out of storage and my life of sin [began again] I was not into drugs, but I was fornicating.

He bought a new red Volkswagen (it was cute); now I always had a ride to and from work (no more bus transfers). Crazy, had a son that his mother was keeping for him and she began to help me with my daughter. She didn't like the fact that we were living together without being married (his mother was a minister and a choir director). She was a God fearing woman; she told us that nothing good would come from what we were doing. I knew in my heart that what she said was true but, I felt bad enough (by the situation) without her always bringing it up to me. She said: "y'all need to get married" (I had lots of respect for her).

My mother had some other friends who were truly women of God and they would always talk to me; one of them was the lady who was with me at the hospital when I was pregnant with my daughter, she convinced the doctor that I was in immediate need of prenatal care; and she was one of the ladies who would spend time at Crazy's mother's house. They began to invite me to their prayer groups; these women stayed on me like white on rice and I loved the fact that they cared so much. I was having a hard time trying to stay focused, but my past hindered me from moving forward. Many times I made an effort to do what was right, but, after you're convicted of a felony, you are thought of as the scum of the earth. [Those women held my arms up] regardless of my past.

Crazy had gotten to the point where he would drink a lot and he would come home very violent. His mother would get mad at him because I'd tell her what he was doing (his father was unhappy with his behavior also). He had a good upbringing but he still had issues. His sister was the exact opposite; but he had a brother who was in trouble all the time (like him). Their sister was married to a preacher; a guy I knew from back in the day; he totally changed his life; now, he pastor's a church in Dallas, Texas.

My troubled relationship continued for months. He started hanging around a guy I used to date back in the [tarp] days; he would come over and they would do things together and I was getting very tired of it. I couldn't afford to move, so I dealt with it in spite of the way I felt. I kept praying to God to get me out of that relationship; but, we know that God won't help us out of something that we are willingly wallowing in. I knew that what I was doing was wrong; God won't force us against our own selfish will. I needed to make the choice to leave but I was really scared of him, he had started to fight me, and tell me that I was never going to have anyone else but him. Alcohol really made him his name sake...CRAZY.

I began helping out at an alteration shop with a friend of a mine and her mom. She was putting together a fashion show for a group called: the Men of all Seasons. It was a big group of guys that were very well known [They were SOMEBODY in Wichita]. So my friend's mother got a professional model to teach us how to perform. This was going to be a big fashion show and I was happy being part of it and being around good people; I had fun training for it.

The event was being held at the: Century II Convention Center, in downtown Wichita. The Big Event sold out (dinner, dancing and a fashion show). The day came and I was so nervous. My friend's mother was in charge of the fashion show. I looked out there and saw all of those people; my friend and I got into her mother's gin and we fixed ourselves a drink. I wasn't a big drinker; so it did not take much for me!

Well, it was time for the show, "Haw" and we modeled our butts off! I went out there like I was the only one in the room I was tipsy, and my fear went away; my friend did likewise; she was a very tall and slender (pretty) woman with a great personality; I liked her whole family (I loved her mother and she loved me). It is a blessing when you meet people like their family. It was a very, very nice fashion show.

When it was time for the grand finale all the models had to walk around the whole floor (off stage) and that was a big floor. As I walked around, they told us to stop and pose I stopped in front of a table where a man was sitting, and I said: "Damn! That man is fine!" He was an older guy; he had some of the nicest green eyes I'd ever seen; I got very nervous standing there in front of him. Our eyes met and he stared at me the whole time, I stood there.

When it was time to move I walked on around; when I got back stage I told my friend about him. I told her that I wanted to say something to him, but that boob boyfriend of mine was there. So, I went out front to see if I could get another glimpse of the man and there he was: standing close to where Crazy was. I walked over in that direction and Crazy told me that he would knock my eyes out of my head; I was so mad (CRAZY was watching my every move). I really wanted to get away from him; he was spoiling my whole night. The man looked at me and he walked away after he saw how Crazy was acting. Crazy was drunk and very rude I was glad when it was time to leave, we argued all night long.

This was on a Friday night the next day was Halloween. Yes! Back then I was [still] celebrating Halloween, because I didn't know any better. Anyway they had a dress up dance at BJ's steak house. That Saturday night I dressed as a Black leopard. I wore a body suit and some high heel boots; I had a tail, the ears, and the cape. I had a body back then (smile) I was looking good. When I entered the room, everyone noticed (my dope selling days were over but I still knew lots of people from that world). A fine way for a child of God to appear in public, huh?

I had gone all the way south again (metaphorically speaking); the decisions that I was making were [far from the will of God]. I sat at the bar and ordered a club soda with a lime and a splash of cherry juice (that was my drink along with nabs); every once in a while I would order a gin and grapefruit juice, but I would have that [one] drink all night as I revealed before I really didn't drink very much.

At the other side of the bar sat that green eyed man OG (Old Guy), that I had seen at the fashion show. When he saw me, he moved to my end of the bar and sat next to me. I was praying that Crazy wouldn't walk in. The first thing OG said to me was: "why such a pretty face looking so down?" I don't know why I opened up to him the way I did, but I began to tell him everything I was going through I even told him that I was recently released from prison. He asked me why I didn't get away from the guy? I told him that I didn't have the means or the resources to move: He asked me; what if I did, would I move? I told him, yes. We talked for a while and then we danced most of the night. Near the end of evening he told me that he would help me move. I looked at him and said: "you don't know me, why are you willing to do that?" He said: "you look like a nice lady who fell on her luck and you deserve a break

and I want to give it to you with no strings attached." I was shocked! He said: "Besides I like you and you seem to be a very nice person" He asked me: "can you find a place on Monday?"
I said: "I will try." He gave me his number and I gave him mine, he told me to call him when I find a place to move. (I thought he was playing, just to get with me that night, but he never approached me in that way at all.) The night ended and I really hated to go home and have to face Crazy; I said, "Lord, I hope this man is for real" (if not it was a good dream).

Sunday Morning I got up and went to church; you couldn't keep me out of church (back then); I would leave church and go home to hell all the time.

Monday, I didn't have to work, so my daughter and I got up, and I called some friends and they took me apartment hunting. I found an apartment that was far from where I was staying with Crazy. I called OG and he asked me how much money I would need and I told him. He came and gave me the first and last month's rent, the deposit and he paid to move my things;
I wanted my things out of that apartment before Crazy returned from work and I didn't want him to have any idea where me and my daughter went. We pulled it off; I was overjoyed!

OG came over to visit us (after we settled in) and he bought us some groceries (everything was good). I needed transportation so after a few months he helped me buy a car; I really liked him; he didn't try to put pressure on me to doing anything. He worked at an oil refinery; I heard that he owned some oil wells. He confided in me about his life, and after a while we began to date.

[Time passed] I started working for Mrs. Quinn a white lady that my mother introduced me to; she was a wonderful woman. I told her all about my past, and she expressed compassion for me; she said: "that is not you anymore I can see who you are as a person;" she and her husband took me under their (collective) wing I was blessed!

My hours at the Hotel began to decrease; they had built another big hotel downtown and that was where all the business was going, so I went to the Wichita Country Club and applied for a

job there; they wouldn't hire me because I was a felon. One day while I was working at Mrs. Quinn's house I told her about the country club not hiring me because of my past and she told me to go back out there on Monday, so I did, and they hired me.
The manager said to me: 'the Quinn's really like you; they have a lot of faith in your ability to do a good job.' The Quinn's were Legacies at the Country Club. The club management always tried to make sure that their members were happy (and besides that, the Quinn's knew that I was a good worker). The Country Club became a big part of my life. They paid very well and if you worked one of the parties, OH my! You made a big tip! I loved working out there among all those wealthy people; if they liked you they would do anything for you. I would get off work and meet OG at a club down on 21st to play cards or just hang out.

One weekend OG and I were on the dance floor and Crazy walked in; he hit me as hard as he could cross my face; OG got real mad; he said: "Why don't you hit me, you little punk?" Crazy's father was in the club; he was steaming! He told his son to get the hell out of there acting like a fool embarrassing him. His father pushed Crazy out the door and all the while he was shouting at me: "I'll get you!" He was REALLY CRAZY! (I was always anxious when I was alone for fear he'd popup out of nowhere).

That night he was waiting around the corner when the club closed. OG walked me to my car and we kissed goodnight I started driving home (I lived straight out 21st off of Somerset). I saw through my rear-view mirror that Crazy was following me, so I turned off and kept driving because I didn't want him to know where I lived. He started driving faster and it became a chase I was crying because I didn't know what he might do to me. He started running his car into my car trying to run me off the road I knew that he didn't care (because he was wrecking his own car). My tires busted on the passenger side but I did not stop I kept on going. I went all the way down to the city building where the police station was; I drove up to the door and I jumped out of the car I was running and screaming! Some cops were walking inside I ran up to them hawling: "he's trying to kill me!!! He just tried to run me off the road!" Crazy ran in there behind me and the police wrestled him down and then they handcuffed him. He was still hollering: "I'll be out; I am going to get you." I called his parents and told them what had happened. His father said that he was going to let him stay in there for a while. I was so shook up...that I called my mother; she came and got me.

My life seemed to be spinning more and more out of control I didn't know what in the world I was going to do? When I told OG what had happen he came over and gave me a gun for protection. I didn't like guns, but I was not going to let Crazy hurt me. My baby didn't need to be around him at all I see why his parents had his son, I said: "THIS man IS CRAZY!" I didn't see him for a long time, but when I went to work or anywhere, I'd always look to see if he was near me (he would always tried to find out where I was staying). I filed a restraining order against him so that if he came near me he'd be arrested.

About a month later I got off work one night and went straight home; I dressed for bed, then all of a sudden I heard someone on my balcony (I lived on the third floor). Crazy had jumped or climbed up there (he had followed me home). He took the rod iron chair that was on my patio and broke the glass out of the patio doors; the sound of the shattered glass was deafening! I grabbed the phone and I got under the bed; I tried to call the police, but Crazy pulled the cord out the wall. He beat me real bad and then he raped me; he made me have sex with him until I bled I was bloody and my face was messed up. After all that he had the nerve to lie beside me and fall asleep. I went to the kitchen and got a butcher knife and I stabbed him I didn't care where the knife went. I think it went in his leg but I didn't stab him hard enough to do any real damage. I called the police, and his parents. The police arrived, and then the ambulance came. When his father got there, he told them to: "take his a>> out of his face," I was mortified. I stopped crying but I was still very angry!!! At that time, I wished that I had killed him!!! The police didn't take me to jail for what I did.

I went to the hospital, and they [treated and released] me.

Crazy went to jail. I felt desecrated. That took me back to the other two times I had been raped; I cried out to God, I was tired of what my life had become outside prison. I had made so many bad decisions. I was really being tested and I was failing every one of them. I had regressed (right back to some of my old conduct). I was carrying my own cross. I talked to Crazy's mother and she said that both of her sons was a wasted F>>> They both apologized to me about their son.

I kept seeing OG, we were finally having peace in our relationship because Crazy was out of the picture. I introduced my cousin to OG's friend and the four of us began to hang out together. My cousin and I had a birthday party for the two of us at my house, down by the pool; our birthdays were literally one day apart (she and I were the same age). OG and his friend barbecued some ribs; he was one of the best cooks...his Mexican cornbread, oh my God, was the bomb!! It was a nice party until my nephew arrived and jumped in the pool. I got splashed! I was so mad!!! I really loved that pantsuit; "it will dry so I kept it on." I went into the house to get the baked beans, and when I picked up the pan the beans spilled down my leg (that suit was messed up) so I just changed clothes and went back down to the pool to enjoy myself. I exhaled; it was time to relax.

[Time passed] and everything was good with OG and me. (About 8 months into our affair I found out that he was a married man.) Most of the time when we were playing cards (at the club), his wife would also be there playing cards. I didn't even know, Wasn't that something! OG told me that he and his wife lived separate lives and that she was in a relationship outside their marriage. I never thought he was with anyone else because when he'd get off of work at 3:00 o'clock in the morning he would come over to my house; he was never at home. It was still wrong, but I was with him and I really liked him. He didn't pressure me for sex, but I wanted to give him some, that's sad because I knew better I should have been ashamed of myself. He was married and I had no right to want him the way I did, but he had been so wonderful to me that I felt he was mine. (I don't know what was going on in his relationship with his wife.) I had thought to myself that if he were my husband I wouldn't want another woman to be with him; I don't know why their marriage was open and their vows were broken. Anyway our affair continued.

I desperately wanted to stop committing fornication and being the object of his adultery because it went against everything that God wanted to accomplish for my life I was pulling back like the stubborn mule tries to do when he doesn't want to pull his load. I still prayed; I even started to pray for something that wasn't mine to have. A woman is not supposed to [covet] someone else's husband but it did not feel like he was married. Everyone thought that he was my husband it was him and me for many years; my life became part of his.

Concerning the [crazy] guy that had caused me so much trouble (when he wasn't in jail); I put up with him much too long. I have to stop at this point to confess: I ended up getting pregnant by him twice. When we were together I was committing fornication; killing babies and conducting myself as an infidel. I had 2 abortions! I said God: "I'm so messed up!" But I did not want his kids. I really wanted to be pleasing to God but I couldn't do it by myself and that was what I was trying to do.

[Time passed] The day I was to get off parole (it had been two years and I hadn't been in any legal trouble). My mother and I went to pick up my release papers at my parole officer's workplace. He was upset when we got there because he had to hand me a warrant for my arrest! HUH you have got to be kidding!
I was shocked! I just started crying (me and my mother both). I asked him for what? He explained, but I didn't know what [the hell] he was talking about. When the police arrived at his office to pick me up, I said: "God why?" I knew I hadn't done anything (that I could think of). The police took me over to the jail and booked me for [assault and grand theft] I was placed on a five thousand dollar bond. I had my rent money on me that day, because I had planned on paying it when I left the parole office. I called a bondsman and made bail.

I went to work at the Country Club that night but I could not function. They put me in the dining room because it was slow; they knew something was wrong with me because I'd been crying and my eyes were swollen. I went out on the patio; I could not stop crying). My coworker (friend) saw how upset I was; she saw the Quinn's as they entered the dining room; Mrs. Quinn inquired about me and my friend let her know that I was on the patio crying.
Mrs. Quinn found me and asked me what was wrong! I told her what had happened; she said she knew I didn't do that, she went and got her husband; she told him: "Carolin needs our help." I went to her house the next day and her husband called the best criminal lawyer he knew; he was one of the highest paid attorneys in the state. When I went to his office, he said: "those Quinn's love you."

The case was pending for about a year; during the trial, just before the jury was to go out they [caught my sister], yes my sister. My lawyer had the jail bring her into court. (She had used my name.) Back then she and I looked a lot alike. I ended up being acquitted. [But all the hell I had to go through.] They tried to get me to charge my sister for using my name, I wouldn't. I just wanted to get on with my life. After all that! I was finally released from parole.

I decided to leave the Church that I'd been going to, because of drama. I couldn't grow [spiritually] in that environment. There were many problems [from the top to the bottom]; one of the preachers took a special liking to me (he had a very sweet wife). Some of the leaders were misusing funds; there was an ongoing family feud; the secretary had a fight with the pastor's wife, and to top it all off, the pastor had a child with a young woman! [I was too through.] I realized from my experience with the Lord in prison that, you can't give what you don't have. That pastor needed prayer; we all have faults (even men of God) we all have to pray for one another.

I began to attend a Pentecostal church. It was good and full of the spirit (I thought). I continued to have a sexual relationship with the married man; I didn't feel good about myself, but I did not let him go. I met a girl at the new church that had my same last name. We became good friends, and started to hang out together; she was in a complicated relationship also. We would get dressed up and go to clubs and then we'd go to church on Sunday (or anytime there was a revival). I joined the church choir (I would join the choir at whatever church I attended). One church had a good choir; a very large choir. The Bishop was a powerful man; I loved his preaching and there were some very powerful women of God attending that church. After a while I started seeing a lot going on in that church.

One night I was on 13th street; I was talking to a guy about catering an event for them. The event (fashion show) was to take place in that club. Some of the girls from the choir were in the fashion show; one of the church mothers came in there with one of her daughters to get some food (from the restaurant portion of the club) The girls were there practicing for the fashion show. Well, that Saturday at choir rehearsal, the (same) church mother stood up in rehearsal and said: 'there are some people in here that have a lot of nerves because I saw them in a club.' She was the president of the choir. I spoke up and said: "How do you know they were in there?" You See, she didn't see me that night, because I was in another area, talking to the guy. She said: "what business is it of yours?" I said again: "How do you know they were in there?" I said: "If you had not been in there yourself, you would not have seen them." She said, "I just went in there to order some food." I said: "But you went in there and if it was so bad for them to be in that place, then you should have gone somewhere else to get your food, so that makes you no better than them. For whatever reason you were in there, the point is if you had not been in there yourself you would not have seen them. We can't judge anyone that way." She left me alone. I don't like people trying to make themselves out to be better than everybody else. ***The job of the older woman is to teach the younger women.***

I went to church (this is strange) that same woman ran up to the pulpit and told a man that he was a devil, and he needed to get out of that pulpit. The man had been in prison, but he had returned into society, and turned his life around; he was a Preacher (the Bishop of the church had ordained him). I didn't understand this woman; she was trying to judge everybody; this church was very different to me. My friend was a member there and she told people we that were sisters (we had the same last name). She and I would hang out together at church (I ended up leaving the choir). I started just attending the Sunday morning service and YPWW on Sunday evenings. There was a member there (a guy I'd know from the streets) who was married to the Bishop's daughter, he used to try to talk to me back in the day but I wouldn't have anything to do with him because he was a pimp. So when I saw him with his wife, I said to myself how did he manage that? I mean to get married to her, but she used to be a pistol herself. God had changed her life also. His mother was a powerhouse (she was really anointed of God). They didn't let women preach in the pulpit there nor could you wear pants they said that it was a sin. (I did not understand that either).

Sometimes I would go to their daily morning prayer meetings. One morning at the prayer meeting; a young lady came in; she was wearing pants, "the prayer warriors" jumped up and grabbed her; they told her that she couldn't wear pants (in there). The young lady was really in a bad way. I was so baffled at what they did to her that I forgot about praying for a second; the way they treated that young lady was not beneficial, in my opinion. They took her out of the prayer room, and when they brought her back, she had a sheet or something wrapped around her. My focus was gone! I asked God: "What does wearing pants have to do with prayer and needing answers when you're going through trials?" I really needed to talk to someone, I didn't like wearing pants, but if I did, I felt that it should be my choice. I don't think God cares about that as much as what's in your heart.

I began to get more and more unsettled about that church, it had become nothing more than a fashion show (who was wearing the better suit and hats) Oh my God! You could see all kinds of hats in those churches. People took pride in what they looked like on the outside but, spiritually they were unclean (it was sad). The Bishop's wife passed away (I am not sure exactly when); women went after that man like vultures. You would have thought that they were on the bachelor show! It was kind of funny they would be shouting and parading around trying to win the pastors hand (I'm sure that some of them were perpetrating whammies). There was this one woman who would shout, she would do it so cute, if her hat was about to fall off she would stop and straighten it back up and go back to shouting. They would talk about her on the radio, they would say, "OK Sister >>>. >>> here's your song, now get your shout on" it was funny to me.

I had started working for the hotel again; they had changed the name to: the Ramada Inn at Broadview. They asked me to be the Banquet Manager. (I went back to the hotel job because after working at the Country Club for about 3 years they started laying people off, I was one of them. I don't remember why they had to cut back, but I remember the good times, and I still miss those big bonuses. They only kept the people who had been there for many years; it was OK because I was still working for Mrs. Quinn, plus I was catering parties, and OG always made sure that I had what I wanted.)

I began to move a lot. My white girlfriend was still around, she had slowed down quite a bit by then; we would go out together sometimes. I was a church girl, and a club girl (I was straddling the fence like crazy) I would be lying if I said I wasn't having fun; but at the same time I felt guilty.

My oldest sister had gone to prison, she was there for about 2 years. She had been married since she was a teenager to one of the best men in the world. My sister started hanging out with drug addicts and picking up their habits; her life began to spiral out of control; she and her husband broke up (they have two daughters together). I was told that my baby's daddy was getting high with her and supplying her with dope.

After she got out of prison she came to stay with me. She took care of my daughter when I was working (which helped me a lot). I worked very long hours at the hotel (sometime I would leave the house at 5 AM, and not get home until around 1 AM).

My sister was a wonderful person she was really trying to get her life back on track, but the guy she was messing around with was a stone dope addict (they had a son together). My mother took care of her son while she was in prison. I told you how my mother fussed all the time! Well, my oldest sister and my mother didn't see eye to eye on a lot of things; that's why she ended up staying with me.

One day I let her drive me to work, and she didn't come back to pick me up I was upset with her because I did not want her to get involved with the bad guy again I was scared that she would turn back to drugs. She had some lame excuse to explain why she didn't pick me from work (she was still looking well, so I didn't think she was doing drugs again).

One night I returned from work around 12:30 AM and she was sitting on the porch; I asked her what was wrong. She said: "You came out of prison and got yourself together and your life has really changed; I can't find a job or anything, and mama won't ever let me live down, what I've done." (My mother hated that her marriage ended; she really liked her husband; everybody did.) Anyway, I could hire people at the hotel but they would not let me hire her I was kind of upset about that because I had a felony and they gave me a chance. My sister went on to say that she was tired of living off me. I told her she was not living off me! I said: "You are a blessing to me to be taking care of my daughter, sending her to school and being here for her, that's helping me not to have to find a babysitter; so what you're doing is a blessing, and you are not a burden at all." She had thought that because she did not have a job, and was not giving me any money that I did not want her there. I said you can stay here as long as you need to; I knew how it felt to come out of prison and have your past follow you. I told her to trust in God; that it was the LORD who helped me to get where I am I could not have done it myself. Even in the midst of my mess, He is still looking out for me. I said to her, don't worry about what mama or anyone else says about you; just do what you can for yourself and your kids.

Her ex-husband had the girls; she and her little boy both lived with us (it was all good). After we talked, I told her I was going to bed because I had to get up and leave at 5:30 AM, because there was going to be a breakfast event at the hotel at 7:00. It was about 1:30 AM and she said: "I don't see how you do it" I said: "God, that's who keeps me going." So we went to bed.

At around 6:00 AM I was getting ready for work (I had over slept), all of a sudden she screamed: "MY HEAD!" I went in the room where she was and I said to her: "that's all of the stress you're under" I told her to stop worrying so much. I took a Motrin out of my purse and gave it to her but she was really different; something was wrong! I called my mother and I said: something was wrong with her. My mother said she was on her way; she told me to call 911; I did and they said they'd send an ambulance. I think my mother had a feeling that something was haywire because she got there before the ambulance, and she lived across town (on the North side) I lived on the South side.

By the time the ambulance got there she was like stiff and she never opened her eyes again. My mother and stepfather followed the ambulance to the hospital, and I got the kids off to school and then I called the hotel and told them that I would be there later to make out the schedule, and to call in a replacement to finish whatever was needed to set up the breakfast I told them I had to get to the hospital. When I got there, I went to the emergency room where my mother was, and I asked her what was going on. She said she did not know; so I went to talk to the doctors who were working on her; one of then came out of the room and said something had erupted in the back of her brain. I was like, "What does that mean?" He said, "We're going to have to put a tube in her head so it can drain." I told my mother what they told me. My mother and I stayed at that hospital from then on. I asked him if I could see her and he said yes; but first he asked me if she had been getting high. I told him No! He said that some kind of drug she took set it off. So I went in and pulled out her arm and I saw some fresh needle marks; I got really mad; I didn't express my anger to her. I started telling her that she was going to be all right. I began to rub her head, that seemed to make her feel better, but she still would not open her eyes I told her I would be back. I went home and looked through her stuff I found a syringe in her bag. I was hurt and mad at the same time I was mad at that dope-head she was messing with, I knew that he started her back on that stuff.

I started screaming I was walking around the house and YELLING "why?" I asked God, "why did this happen to her?" She wanted so much to get her life back together. [I never mentioned it before], but about a couple of years before she went to jail, she had a heart attack, over at mama's house. My stepfather beat her in the chest and brought her back she was mad because she said: where she was going was peaceful; she said she wished he would not have done that (brought her back); the paramedics said he saved her life; they took her to the hospital and she made a full recover.

I had sent the kids on to school that morning so I had to get them from the bus stop that afternoon and I took them over to my baby sister's house. We called and told everyone what was going on. When I got back they had already put the tube in her head.

My mother was just <out of it> it was hurting her real bad, so I called my aunts and some of my mother's friends and they came to the hospital to be with us. After a while there were many of us in the intensive care waiting room, so they gave us a room where we could console one another in private. I did not want to leave at all I had convinced myself that as long as I was there she would be all right. I would go in and pray and sing to her.

Her ex-husband came (he really loved her a lot) he didn't get into another relationship for a long time after their breakup. He came in the room and told her that when she got better he was going to take her home and take care of her. We were telling her that she was going to be all right, but she kept shaking her head [no] he said: "yes you are;" still she never opened her eyes. She was in intensive care and they were monitoring her real close (we were up there all that night).

The next day the doctor said that the fluid was draining real good, and the day after that they removed the tube. I decided to go home and freshen up. While I was gone they called to tell me to come back to the hospital that she had taken a turn for the worst (just that fast) I hurried back to the hospital; when I got there they had put cold ice packs over her whole body. They injected ice water into her veins (I'd never heard of such a thing). Her temperature went up to 107 degrees and during that time, she had a massive heart attack. (I felt like they killed her; I was so mad at them for what they were doing to my sister.)

All of a sudden her bowels moved (I felt that she had died right then) she was still on the machine. The doctor came out and said: "there's nothing else we can do; why don't you think about donating her organs." My brother lit into that doctor. He said, "Yawl done killed my sister and she's not even cold yet and you want her organs?" I had never seen my brother that angry. Her daughter was getting ready to graduate that following week (and she was pregnant). Through all of that heartbreak, she was able to graduate (and, she had to listen to us telling her to go after those doctors; she had a legal right to file a complaint). They moved my sister to the tenth floor (my mother was not ready to let her go); she was on life support and she was deteriorating, but, I just kept talking to her (although I knew she was brain dead). My mother would go see her and then she would go home and cry (she cried all the time).

One day, I was waiting for the hospital elevator and next to me was a little booklet (on top of the newspaper stand) that said: "this is your life." It was very strange because the pamphlet was about two sisters; one was in heaven [talking down off a cloud] to the one that was still on earth, she was telling her that she was all right up there. She said it is beautiful up here! That was so odd to me but it was telling us to let her go. When I got to her room I looked at her and she was getting dark around the eyes and all that stuff around her mouth so I cleaned it off and I called my mother and said: "mama it is time to let her go." I said: "she is not coming back mama let her go out looking the way she was, this machine is breathing for her and when we turn it off she will stop breathing." So she said: "you think that's best," I said: "yes" so she said: "tell them to turn it off." I called the nurse in and I told her while my mother was on the phone, to turn off the machine; so they did. Her breathing went on for about ten minutes and then it stopped. They covered her up I knew that was really final I cried and sat there just looking at her. I called Jackson Mortuary and told them to come pick her up then I called her daughter and the rest of them and told them she was dead. They marked her death on June 2, 1988, but she really died on May 24th 1988.

I left, and went to my mother's house and started making the arrangements for her funeral. She did not have any insurance because her ex-husband had dropped her off of his when he found out she had married that man; I did not even know that myself. Anyway I thought the family would get together and help pay for the funeral. Everybody backed out from wanting to give any money I was so out done that I didn't even know what to say. I could not believe what I was hearing! My mother was in no position to give, so she put on a program at church, with the Christ Way Singers (she was part of that group) they raised $450.00. I asked every sibling to at least give something. They gave me all the reasons why they did not have the money, and that I did and so I was the one that should do it. Her ex-husband gave me some money, and our half-sister in Florida paid for a casket and had it shipped to Wichita, but I had to pay for the pick-up.

My sister up under me said, "Let's bury her in a Dashiki" I told her, that was not the way she lived and we were not going to bury her that way; so she said she was not going to give anything. The hospital had shaved her head, so I went and got a wig just like her hair (she had long hair) so, the whole funeral rested upon me. I had to pay for the [open and closing) I bought the plot and vault (I had to pay $5000.00). I was going through a lot. I maxed out my credit cards. The lady that I was working for was so mad at my family. She said: "You should not have to do all of this!" She said:

"I will not help you bury your sister, but I will pay all of your bills up." I had a new car at the time. OG was so out done with my family, although he did what he could but with reluctance. The people who owned the mortuary were angry also. I went there and dressed her I [did] her make-up and made her look pretty (I was at the mortuary a lot). They made a mistake on the obituary and I sat down and wrote the names one-by-one; the mortuary people said: "why don't you go home and get some rest before you pass out." I told them: "I want everything to be done."

I carefully watched people come through to [view her body] because people were lifting up her wig I did not want anyone to touch her. Well the day of the funeral was here I got to the church early to make sure she was looking OK, and she was, I was still hurting by what my family did.

The funeral started and the family walked in; I was numb during the whole service. When it was time to view the body they opened the casket and everybody started crying I got up and walked out. I said those bastards did not even want to help bury her and now they are putting on a show. This girl that I have always known came out to where I was; she said: "are you all right?" I told her how I felt, and she said: "you did what you could do and God will bless you for it."

So I went back in the church and I viewed her body and then we all proceeded out. We went to the cemetery and said our final goodbyes. I felt bad for what I had said about my family and I asked God to forgive me I was really trying to be strong for everybody. I was torn on the inside, but I never let it show. The mortician asked me if I wanted anything off of her body before they put her in the ground. I told them no. So they locked the casket and gave me the key (I did not know that, that was the procedure) we went back to the church and had dinner and went home. People were in and out of my house all the time. My sister up under me ended up buying her head stone

Things finally settled down and I was glad that it was over. I had been off work for so long, but they kept my job for me. I went back to work the following Friday because they had lots of big banquets booked. They had 200 in one room, 150 in another room and they had 200 in the third ballroom and 80 upstairs. I had scheduled 25 girls for that day only 12 showed up. They'd had a party at the club the night before, and half of them went to it and got drunk, and they all called in. I was not in the mood for this. I had not even grieved my sister's passing. I was tired and my mind was not ready for what the employees had done. So I said: I have to work with what I have.

The manager had a lot of faith in me; and the [corporate office] loved me (they came down when we served Senator Dole's dinner, just to see who I was. They were very nervous and the manager told them: "she's got this." It went off without a hitch). That's why they were glad when I came back to work they knew what I could do. I had to pull this thing together with what I had, I was so mad; I didn't even think to pray.

We would make fruit trays (on the big old serving trays) we would fix them up and make them look pretty. I knew the right people to assign to serve and work the bar. I also did the entire inventory for everything that went out for each banquet. I knew it was wrong, but when I signed out a bottle of liquor for them, I would sign out one for me. I had two ladies that worked the bar and I would tell them to keep the money they made for the extra bottles I signed out and we would split it at the end of the night. That was an awful thing for me to do, I know! But I did it.

It was time for two of the banquets to start I had fifteen minutes to get everything into this one room. I told my two servers to go get the fruit tray and bring it out on a cart (the trays were too heavy to carry without a cart). I was running around like a chicken with its head cut off; it was like a mad house.

Meanwhile, in the back of the work area...here come these two young girls trying to carry this big tray of fruit; they were trying to show off in front of the security guard; they dropped the tray and I screamed!! Then I started shouting at them, and telling them they should not have tried to do that; I said some other things that does not bear repeating. We only had a few minutes to get the tray back together. So, I took off running into the pantry; there was water and salad stuff covering the floor when I went to turn around (with a hand-full of fruit) I slipped on that stuff; my feet went up in the air, and the fruit flew one way and I went another I came down so hard, that I fell on my right arm and wrist. Everyone came running to help me up, except the chef, he stood back and watched. When I got up I was hurting, but I kept going, I guess I was so numb from my sister's death and I was so tired that I did not realize how badly I was hurt. I saw all of the banquets through but at the end of the night my arm was swollen.

I went to the hospital and they said it was broken but not bad they put a sling on my arm and sent me home. (My arm and wrist hurt very badly) so I called my employer and they sent me to the company doctor. They tried to say (at first) that I got the injury somewhere else, because I did not go to the doctor as soon as it happened (I did stop to fill out an accident report I'm glad I did.) That chef that stood back and watched it all, said: he didn't see a thing. I thank God for the five people who came forth. The hotels company doctor took some X-rays and he put me in a cast.

They did not want to pay me workman's comp either I filed a claim, but they denied it. I went over to the Mrs. Quinn's house and I told her what had happened. She called her husband into the room and I told him the story and he called one of his attorney buddies and asked him to take my case. Mr. Quinn was a retired corporate attorney from Cessna (that's why he knew so many attorneys). I wasn't going to do anything at first, but my employer did a 180 when I go hurt. (They loved me at first, and now I wasn't anything but scum). I went and talked to the lawyer and he took my case (to help me get workman's comp, and to make them to pay my medical bills and all I had to go through). We had to go to court; the company really tried to fight my complaint.

I had gotten so behind in my bills it was unreal. (Mrs. Quinn paid the ones before, so I didn't expect her to keep paying them.) I started backing off of OG because I was trying to get on track with the Lord I did not want to ask him for help. I had twelve credit cards, stupid huh! Who in their right mind needed that many cards? I was going to school at WSU (I had gotten a student loan). I also had a car loan and a loan at the Credit Union. I had been doing quite well, before my sister passed away. I always kept my bills paid and I was taking care of things, for myself. OG had helped me get on my feet, and I just did not want to leave him (high and dry), but my conscience was eating me up. The lawyer started the process and I wanted him to fight on behalf of both shifts. I had worked as a first and second shift banquet manager (I was working under two different people). They did not have anyone to work for the 2nd shift, so I had been filling in for weeks. I felt that I was entitled to both considerations.

After about eight weeks we won the workman's compensation part of the case and they had to send me a check for all my back pay. They did not like me very much (right about then), but that was OK. They had used me, and worked me like a dog; I thought they were obligated to pay me. I gave them hour after hour of my time (sometimes 16 hours a day) and they had the nerve to think they were going to get by without paying me what they owed me. They didn't even want to pay my medical expenses; so their doctor did not examine me properly. They gave me minimal medical attention to save their dollars. I was not going to sue them, but, because of the way they treated me, I said to hell with them, I'm going to go after them with everything I've got. After their doctor put a cast on my arm and wrist I did not go back to work. My lawyer fixed it so that they could not fire me.

The cast came off and I was sent to physical therapy for 6 weeks. The whole time I was going to therapy my wrist would really hurt. They tried to say I was just making it up; they wanted me to be released by their doctor to go back to work. So I went back to work, but, they had to put me in the sales office because I wasn't able to do any lifting. They had some Corporate Trackers that was 5 years behind that they wanted me to catch up on: That was a hot mess! They should have been ashamed of themselves; a hotel getting that far behind like that! All the writing was hurting my wrist really bad, so I told them that I was in pain.

They sent me back to the company doctor and he could not figure it out. He shot some dye into my wrist and he was shocked by what he found. [Remind you] they thought I had been playing; he found two torn ligaments and an artery that was pierced I had to have surgery and the company had to restart my workman's comp. They really did not like me [it had begun to cost them]. They should have treated me properly from the beginning, but they wanted to be cheap and it cost them. (Those Corporate Trackers still had to wait.) So, the doctor performed the surgery; he had to fuse my wrist and put it back in a cast. After another 4 months of therapy I went back to work, again. The company then assigned a rehabilitation counselor to come to the job and watch me work. I told the counselor that I needed to go back to the doctor, but of course my lawyer had to [stay on their case] until they allowed me see a physician. Their company doctor said that he needed to put some screws in my arm and reset the fusion; I was laid up for eight months this time, and I had to go through more therapy and, I had to learn to use my left hand (I was going through a lot); I began to develop tendentious in my left arm and wrist, it really was a challenge to use my left hand. After all that, they put me back in the sales office.

It was still hurting me to write and do a lot of things so, what did they do? They put me in the front office! They tried putting me on the PBX switch board but that was even worse punching all those buttons. To top it off, they wanted me to wear a uniform that had buttons all the way up the back and the skirt had buttons up the side (that outfit was very tacky to me). (I'd always been a nice dresser and they used to get mad when I would come to work dressed up. One of them asked me how I could dress like that on what they were paying me (I was only working 5 hours a day). She said: "I have never seen you wear the same thing twice." I said: "My white mother takes good care of me," I smiled and it made her mad. If you could have seen the expression on her face.)

I called the rehabilitation counselor and told her I was still hurting. She went to the company, and they refused to let me go back to the doctor, my lawyer told me he would get a hearing set to go back before the judge; a hearing was scheduled.

The day we went to court the judge said that the only way I could see another doctor was to pay for it myself; He said, if a new doctor finds something wrong with what they [didn't do] then he would order them to pay for it; I told him I did not want to go to any doctor they knew. The judge gave me a choice of two doctors; he said I could go to a clinic in: Tulsa, Oklahoma, or the one in Overland Park, Kansas. I chose Overland Park, because I used to live in Kansas City and Overland Park was only 30 minutes away from KC.

My lawyer called and scheduled an appointment with the doctor and my father drove me (two and a half hour drive) there. I handed the doctor my medical records and after he read the reports he decided to run some tests. We waited in the consultation room, until the doctor returned with the test results; he said that he found "something very interesting." The Companies former surgeon had fused my wrist without repairing the ligaments. The doctor said that he would have to re-break my wrist so that he could (actually) repair the ligaments and refuse my wrist. I was upset because, all of that could have been prevented. The doctor wrote the report and I took it back to the lawyer.

My lawyer scheduled another hearing with the judge (who had ordered the examination). Before it was time for the hearing, the hotel's lawyer told my attorney that he was going to resign from the case because: the company was playing dirty. Wasn't that something; people are a trip! The things people will do to save a buck; the health and wellbeing of a human isn't important to [them] unless, that person is making them some money. The judge looked at the report and ruled that the company pay the doctor, and my travel expenses (past, present and future), and that also included any overnight hotel costs. (God was still watching over me.) Glory!

We made the doctor's appointment and my treatment started. My father took me to have the surgery; they gave me a block (that was the worst pain I had ever felt in my life). Getting a <u>shot</u> in the pit of your under arm is no joke (I felt the tug in my arm when they were operating but no pain). After the surgery I had tubes and, an IV running out of my arm for 6 weeks; boy!!! When the numbness wore off, man, I was in so much pain. I had taken so many pills it wasn't funny! I had pills for the tendentious and for inflammation and for pain and my medication was mailed to me. I had to go back to Overland once a week for 6 weeks. Then the doctor removed the tubes and the IV, and then he put my arm in a cast. After that I had to visit him every 2 weeks because he wanted to make sure things were healing correctly. After all that, I had to go to therapy for 6 months (to work on both arms) then [on to] occupational therapy; I had to learn to use my hand and wrist, again. Following that, they sent me to a rehabilitation school, to see what I could do and not do and (I was restricted from writing).

[Time passed] and it was time to go back to court. Everything that could be done for me was finished. We went to court to settle the case; the judge said: "I will not give you a big settlement, but..." he ordered the company to continue paying my doctor bills and he ordered them to keep me as an employee or pay for my disability. So they gave me 27,000.00 dollars because my hospital bills were so big.

I returned to work; and after I got there they tried everything in their power to make me quit. They had to have someone with me all the time in case I got tired they would have to help me do my job, you know they were hot!! While I was going through all this; one of my cousins passed away. I had to get a work excuse to attend the funeral and that same week my aunt also died, I was supposed to request [another excuse] to attend her funeral but I didn't, so when I returned to work, the hotel had hired a new cocky manager (he thought he was all that and then some) he asked me: "why I was there?" And I said: "I came back to work." He said: "you quit!" And I said: "no I did not!" He said: "you just can't leave and be gone and come back and expect to have a job." I told him: "you know I did not do that." Well! It was my word against his.

I went back to see my lawyer and he said that if I did not have a copy of the request slip, I did not have a just cause. I got played like a big dog!!! They probably gave the hotel manager a raise. This was the end of a long five year process.

I was going through a lot; I mean a whole lot. I tried to sue the company doctor for the wrong he had done, but the statute of limitation had expired (by 2 weeks). I had not been thinking about that so, here I was with a disability, which kept me from doing what I loved to do (waitress and serving parties), so I started finding people to take care of, plus I was still working for Mrs. Quinn.

I started booking parties (on my own) and I would find people who I knew could do the work, to help me (so that I would not have to strain my arms). My doctor said to me; "you could make just as much money with your mouth as you did with your hands." He told me: "when you talked to me I listened to how you explain things and how you delegated tasks, why don't you just become your own boss?"

I thought about it and that's how I got the catering service started. My mother and a friend of mine would do all the cooking (he was a real good cook). I had friends who knew how to tend bar, and others who could serve; everything was going fine. I was praying a lot (over my arms and my health in general).

Many things happened to me during that time frame. I was in three car accidents and I fell through a porch; I had so many medical issues (I should not have been moving around the way I was); but God, helped me through it all; I'm thankful that He did not give up on me. My life seemed to be one hurtle after other I ended up filing for disability. There's so much more to my life than I could ever express. Coming home from prison was challenging I was tried and tested; God was drawing me [back] to Him. I had women of God who stuck with me to keep me encouraged through it all. I cannot thank God enough for sending them into my life. They were solid like little rocks. My mother prayed and fussed at the same time, but I knew she loved us. As I talked about from the beginning of my book, my father would always speak the word to his children.

He was a faithful man of God. I was so hurt by what my sister did to me (I was arrested because of her deceptions a few times). I could not understand how she could use me that way. Still to this day I don't understand it but I love her anyway. We have to be content with our lives. The next few pages will teach us about being tested and making the right decision

Change & Transitioning Back in to Life after Prison

The uncertainty of change could be hard and scary; it can also be uncomfortable, especially after you have lived a life of crime for so long and then going to prison and adjusting to a [prison life style]. When you finally come through all that and you are free to change your life, you freeze in your tracks. Transitioning from one situation to another can be fearful because of the unknown. But when we allow God to bring us into the adjustment, we can depend on Him because He knows and cares; it's [all good]. Whatever changes we encounter we can speak Romans 8:28 (KJV) "And we know that all things work together for good to them that love God, to them who are the called according to His purpose." That is the key: "to His purpose." All things work together for good (Salvation) even our groans (our hills and valley's).

When we respond to His call, we will serve His purpose. Sometimes we make it hard on ourselves when we don't put our trust in God. Change should be positive. It took prison (a time out period) to make me begin to change (for the better). Your groans (hopefully) will be less dramatic than mine. Allow God to change and transition your life. Change is a gift from the LORD. God has a plan for all our lives. 2 Corinthians 4:7-9 "But we have this treasure in earthen vessels; that the Excellency of the power may be of God, and not of us." V8. "We are troubled on every side, yet not distressed; we are perplexed, but not in despair;" V9. "Persecuted, but not forsaken; cast down, but not destroyed." Our responsibility is to let people see God in us. Let Him change us and stop trying to do it ourselves.

Testing of your Faith

The [real test] is not the way we act; it is the way we react to the daily trials and troubles of life that we experience. God exposes what's in our hearts through testing. It is [our] spiritual mirror. God wants to lead us away from the world's way of living, in order to bring us to His Way. Again: He exposes our hearts. Let's look at Psalm 139: 23, 24, It says, "Search me, O God, and know my heart; try me and know my thoughts;" V24. "And see if there is any wicked ways in me, and lead me in the way everlasting." David asked God to show him any sin [in him]. David wanted to be exposed (the king wanted God to test his thoughts). This will allow God to reveal to us everything we need to change. Tests come through things that happen in our lives in order to show us our own hearts so that we can appreciate the grace that God has given us. During the times of testing, God shows us our hearts, our thoughts, our attitudes and our emotions. We need to be aware of them.

God has a unique plan for each of our lives, but [sometimes] we have to endure heartache in order to become the person God has created us to be. We have to be tried and tested. Yield to God by obeying and trusting [in] Him.

Making right Decisions

We all have to make decisions. God will direct us in every decision we make when we trust Him to lead and guide our every step. We can make right decisions by:

1. Studying God's Word. 2. Listening to the Holy Spirit

God has given us a daily map to follow, all we have to do is use everything that we have been given. When making decisions we should ask ourselves, why am I making this decision? Will this glorify God, or is this for self? Will this help or encourage someone else, or is it just for me? Will I reach my goal? Will it hurt anyone? There lots of questions you have to ask yourself. It is important that we listen to God. Find things that will benefit the Kingdom of God. Make decisions that will have positive goals. God will direct our steps as we seek Him in prayer

IT WAS GOD'S GRACE AND MERCY

Chapter 8

My Personal Relationship with Christ

My life seemed to have been on a roller-coaster. I had to start making some positive decisions for myself, and for my daughters sake. I got back in the church really heavy, asking God to help me to leave that man alone.

I had met another guy at the club and I still had not been delivered from going out to party I would still go out and then turn around and go to church. I would be in the club feeling really bad. I began to talk to people about God and my life. I met a guy who was from a good family (GF), who was a [disc jockey] for different clubs.

I would go to the clubs with him sometimes and sit behind him to keep him company. He took me to meet his parents (he came from a well-to-do family) and they took a liking to me; they were all really good people and I liked them. I started accompanying him to family dinners and other family functions and I always had a good time. They were a very close family; his father and mother were very fond of me. His father thought that his son had met his match with me; his dad was sick when I met them, but I don't think anyone knew how ill he really was (he had cancer but he would have big fun with his family).

I really loved their closeness. All of their extended family would come (both local and from out-of-town) to whatever special occasion they were celebrating. An uncle of theirs was famous around the world. I would attend church with his mom sometimes. During that time period, the fashion show lady (who owned Perfect Fit Alterations) was having show's all over town (in clubs and other places; they were big events). She was a beautiful lady. (I loved my friend's moms and they loved me: as I mentioned before. I was always drawn to my friend's moms and they were drawn to me, also; my friends used to say that their mamas thought I was such a good girl and they would say: "they really just didn't know you." We should always respect our elders. The love of God makes us love, honor and respect one another.)

About two months into my relationship with GF, his father was hospitalized and later released; they gave an anniversary party for his parents at one of the Centers; family came in from everywhere. GF's father and mother did one the most beautiful ballroom dances I'd ever seen; they danced with such poise, he told his wife: "this will be our last dance." I don't think she understood just what he meant (I might be wrong) but that was a wonderful night I'll never forget it.

The next night he was sitting in the living room on the floor, many family members were there; he made a statement saying: "They will have to have my funeral at the Century 11." They thought he was just joking around, but I felt he knew he was going to die. That next week they took him to the hospital in Halstead Kansas (it was a couple of hours away) and we went up there to see him; he was sitting up in his bed, very peacefully. I remember him telling his wife how much he loved her; he died the next day (it was very sad). They had been together for many years. He [did] have a big funeral.

I stayed close to his mother. During the funeral a girl came up to GF (that he'd known in the past), she bent down and hugged his mother (the whole family was having a hard time handling his death). GF was very close to his mother (all of them were) he stayed by his mother's side; he was the one who had always been there for her, his siblings lived in other states. I did not see him a lot after that unless I went over there. GF stayed at his mother's side and they grieved together. As time passed things got better for them (time heals).

We had a fashion show at the Civic Center one night (GF played for it), and on another occasion there was a fashion show at the Zanza Bar on 13th street and he was there sitting at a table with a group of women (one of them, was the woman who had hugged his mother at the funeral). I was sitting at the bar watching him. After I finished modeling, he came over and talked to me; I forgot what he said, but I remember that he did not want me to know that he was with that lady. The women at their table were looking at me strangely (you could tell that they were related to one another because of their looks). I kind of felt that he was a PLAYER based on what his father had said (that time). Some evenings (back then) I would be over to his parent's house waiting for him to return, and he'd finally show up late into the night). So anyway: the time he was disc jockeying, at the Civic Center (for the fashion show) the lady from the funeral was sitting behind him; she was the same woman sitting with him at the Zanza Bar.

After the fashion show was finished I went over to his table and asked him: what the hell he thought he was doing! GF told me that she was just a friend and he had given her a ticket for the fashion show and that she sat with him because she did not know anyone (I knew that his story was bogus). When she heard us arguing about her, she go up and left. After that, I said to myself: "this man is no good." I didn't have transportation because my car broke down, so I was driving GF's parent's car I drove it for a long time (I took care of it like it was mine) the tags on the front said, Mrs. C. I began to feel more and more convicted when I went to clubs. God never stopped loving me I felt that He was still drawing me Him, but I was not surrendering my all to Him.

One night I went to the club (where GF was going to be playing) with a friend; we were sitting in the parking lot and he drove up. He came over to the car and I introduced him to my friend; after he left she said: "That's a pretty black MF. Girl, he's tall and broad and built." She said, "I like the way he looks;" it was funny the way she said it. So anyway we went into the club and I sat where GF was sitting. OG walked in and saw me (he watched me all night). Later I got ready to leave so I told GF that I'd see him later; my girlfriend and I walked outside and OG came running behind me; he said: "so that's who you left me for." I told him that did not want anybody else's husband. I told him that I loved him but I had to let him go (He actually cried that night) I felt really bad, but I had to say it. The next day was Sunday so of course I went to church; the preacher's message convicted me.

I was still battling: good and bad, right and wrong. The guy that I knew from the streets (who married the Bishops daughter) lost his wife; they gave her one of the biggest funerals (and I thought that GF's father's funeral was big)! Everybody from the church world, and the street world was at the service I felt bad for him he really loved her. I feel that she was the one that he changed his life for. They had a shop together I believe that she was the one who encouraged SG (Shop Guy), to make clocks, and other beautiful items. He would be at church really being faithful to God after his wife passed away. Their whole family went there, except his oldest brother (he had a church of his own).

One night the Church had a revival; the guest speaker had been on a thirty day fast (with just water to sustain him). They had posters of him that announced his coming (he had been kind of a big guy, but he had lost a lot of weight I guess it was from fasting). Anyway, me and my play sister went to the meeting we were chatting about people.

That first night he was speaking into people's lives; I said to myself: I hope he doesn't call me out and say anything to me. I was the 2nd or 3rd person he called. He said: "Young lady back there! "Stand up!" Everybody including me was looking around. There were so many people in that church that you didn't know who he was talking to. He said: "The one with the dark blue sweater on, and you have some black beads on around your neck and they are long." I looked down at my sweater. He said: "Yes, you, the one who is looking down." I pointed at myself and he said: "yes come here." So I walked towards him I was praying that he would not say anything that would embarrass me. He said: "I see you standing in a place where there is a lot of green around you I see you walking around saying it was your fault. God told me to tell you that your sister's death was not your fault to quit blaming yourself." I started crying like nobody's business; he said: "What happened, it happened; God told me to tell you that what you want to do, go for it." He said: "he will be with you all the way." At that time, I'd never said anything to anyone about it, but, I wanted to help people coming out of prison. I did not want anyone else to go through what my sister had to go through trying to get a job with a felony conviction, and trying to be accepted for who they are trying to become, instead of what they did in the past. God favored me and I wanted everyone to know that they could be favored also. The speaker said some other things but by that time I came unglued and I began to shout all over that church. He made me one of his prayer partners for the week of that revival. My life took a whole change from that night on. God revealed to me that night that I was really ready to come back to Him. (He never leaves us, we leave Him.) The first night after I went up to him the preacher told me to go lay my hands on a certain woman's stomach, so I walked over to her and laid my hands on her stomach; she started screaming and shouting. God's amazing!

It was a very powerful service (that night). After he finished prophesying to people and praying, they had testimony service. The woman that I had laid my hands on, got up and testified about a pain she was having in her stomach. She said, "As soon as you laid your hands on my stomach, it was like a fire that went through me, and then the pain left." She said, "I was healed as soon as you touched me." I started crying and rejoicing with her; God had used me that night. I really felt blessed that God would use a person like me after all the bad things I had done. God took me back to the El-Dorado County Jail, where He had given me that scripture in Jeremiah, I began to praise God. God had been waiting on me He's not going to force Himself on anyone. Well, service went on until 1:30 AM; that was something that I had never ever experienced before.

That next weekend they were having the: Black Arts Festival. I went there with some friends, and I saw SG; he was there with his clocks (and the other things that he and his wife had made). He had a booth at the festival I went over to say hello, he seemed really stressed, there was a girl with him; she attended that church also. She tried to act as though they were a couple; it didn't make any difference to me I just wanted to tell him how sorry I was for his loss. I think it had been only a month since his wife passed away. I don't feel that anyone is emotionally ready to move on that soon. Women were like predators on him. He told that girl to quit making people think they were together. Anyway, I asked him how he was doing and he replied, "I'm dealing." I was telling him how beautiful the clocks were. They were made from different kinds of tree wood and some were made from the roots of the tree (the artwork was beautiful). It was a nice day and all the people were walking around looking at different things. The event took place in the: Wichita State University parking lot. The Black Arts Festival was something BIG in Wichita back in the day, not so much now. I ended up staying there with him for the rest of the day. He was telling me how he and his wife had made the clocks; they were made from pieces of wood that you couldn't find in Kansas.

The day ended and we packed up his truck, and he asked me if I want to go to dinner with him; I said yes. I followed him to his house and he got his car (and we drove to dinner together).

We began to talk about the past (I knew of him when he was on the streets) he really had changed his life; I was impressed with the person he had become (I think I mention this before, but I had known of him for many years). He used to try and [catch me] when I was of the world, but my life, was selling drugs and he had been a pimp (he had dancers and women who worked the streets). His life totally changed; he and his wife had done very well together, and they had a beautiful home. He was going through a lot with her kids; to me it was so unnecessary. She had grown children that gave him a lot of hell about her stuff.

He was the type of person that did not put too much value on holding on to things. He told them they could have whatever they wanted (out of the house). She had some beautiful things; she was one of the best dressed women I had ever seen; outside me (smile) I really admired her (God had molded her into a wonderful woman). She reminded me of who I wanted to be.

She would go down to the streets where all the drunks, dope heads, and homeless people were, and tell them about the Lord, she was fearless. She was older than SG, but they were good together (from what I saw). I would hang out with him and we would go to dinner a lot; he loved to eat out. I would go to his house and just listen to him pour out his heart about their life together; he would open up to me. Some nights he even cried I was just there for him as a friend. Her family did not come around him very often.

He invited me to attend his brother's church one Sunday; his family thought that he was still worldly. He had moments where he would get angry very easily. That Sunday his brother spoke into my life, he was a prophet what he spoke to me, was right on. I really did not like to hear people speak in my life because I always thought they would say something that would embarrass me, but I realized God is not like that. His brother's wife was an awesome first lady of the church (to me). After church she walked up to us and he introduced me to them; she took a liking to me and I liked her. She told me that when she saw me walk in the door, that God said: "Get her, she's worth saving." People of God were being put into my path. I liked that church, so I went back again.

SG started dating a girl that one of his friends brought over to meet him. Of course he was still grieving for his wife but as time passed he began to get better (although there were times when he wanted to talk about his beloved). We remained friends and I was happy to be the shoulder he could lean on. I helped him with his business; we leased a large one room building (plus a bath room). The woman he was dating had a problem with the part I was playing in his life, but he did not care, he told her that she would have to accept me. I had been there for him when he was going through the hardest time in his life. He told her, either you will help us, or get out of the way. We went to Home Depot and bought some wood and he began to section it off. He built a corner office for me to work in, he was very good at building things, repairing things and he was very neat and organized. We painted the store and had the sign made and the sign was made to reflect him and her, we kept her dream alive.

One afternoon the newspaper came and interviewed us. The article was on the front page of the paper (I managed the store). His lady friend tried everything she could think of to run me off (she and her friend). They would come into the store and she would be walking around [like she was all of that] he would tell them not come down there unless they were going to help. I began making centerpieces to make the place look nice I was good at making things. We fixed up the store (it looked beautiful).

My relationship with God was growing stronger. I started attending his brother's church I really liked the way they worshiped (there). His brother's wife came down to the store one day and invited me over for lunch; I accepted her invitation. She was going through some real serious health problems but her faithfulness to God was awesome she did not let her circumstance bring her down I really admired her strength. As I became more involved with their church I joined the choir. (I had totally left GF alone because I wanted to get my spirit life under control. I still visited his mother because I loved and respected that family. I believed that God allowed us to meet so that I could meet his people. He was messing around with too many women for me, but we remained friends.)

Anyway, the Pastor's wife and I started hanging out together she was very pleasant to be around. The sister of GF's girlfriend was a member of that church, and she was the choir director (I remembered seeing her at GF's table in the Zanza Bar the night of the fashion show. She was very nice and she could really sing.) One Sunday, her sister came to church, I was sitting on the front row; I still had hindrances getting in my way both spiritual and financial. I never wanted to talk to anyone about it, but God knew. I wasn't making a profit on anything at the store (yet) because we were still trying to get it together. My business partner was spending all of his money up front; I knew that when things got better it would all change.

OG was still trying to get me back but I could not do it anymore. That Sunday the sermon was about adultery and it made me feel ashamed of what I had been doing. The sermon gave me the strength to say to OG: "Hey look, I want to live my life for God I can only be your friend in the Lord." I told him: "I wish I could apologize to your wife." She had stopped doing what she was doing and I felt that he should have stopped his cheating also. I told him

I loved God too much to continue to hurt him with my sin. He did not like it but he had to respect it. I felt that I was getting closer and closer to God.

[Now back to the girl] I looked around and I saw her sitting in the back row I had felt that someone was watching me. We both had a mutual friend who had told us both that we were good people and if we got to know one another that we would like each other. She came back to church the next Sunday; after service she walked up to me and said: "God said you need some help" I said, "No I don't" I did not want her of all people to know what I was going through. I said to myself she will never get to talk about me to anyone! She said: 'I work at Emergency Social Service' (or something like that) I can't remember her exact words; she also said: "if you change your mind here then;" and she handed me her card. Pride got in my way that day real bad.

I went home that night I had been praying for God's help, and He told me: "I sent you some help and you turned it down because of your pride." I still didn't want to call her (I wrestle with the idea all day Monday), but I knew that God was not going to do anything else until I let go of my pride. I became tuned into Him speaking to me, so the next day (Tuesday), I swallowed my pride, and I called her. She told me to come on down.

When I got there she formally introduced herself and I likewise (like we didn't already know who each other was) it was kind of funny! When we came face to face, we started talking, and got to know each other; we were laughing about lots of things. She was one of the nicest people that God allowed me to meet. She was as sweet as her sister. We started talking about GF; we could not help but laugh. I believed that our friendship was set up by God. She taught music, and she could also sing. There were four of those sisters and they were all powerful women of God. She turned out to be a blessing to me (our mutual friend had been right). While I was there, she took every bill that I had and pulled from every resource she had. The agency (usually) only paid a 200.00 dollar maximum, but she went over and above the call of duty. That's how God was working in my life, He was showing me who He was in my life. I didn't want to go back to that old existence (anymore). Well, I would see old dope dealers, and they would ask me if I wanted to make some money? I prayed, God help me not to ever go back to that life! We know that: God is a God who honors His word; and our duty is to honor Him.

Going to Church became very exciting; the praise and worship was awesome. She eventually took over the choir: we had one on the greatest choirs in the world. Everyone was spirit filled and anointed to sing praises to His name (our choir was very well known). Singing to the Glory of God was a blessing and we were not full of ourselves. I thank God for the people who were in my life during my transitional struggles.

One night I went down to a club on 9th street and all I did was minister to everyone who walked in the door; the owner of the club said: "Carolin, you stop trying to reform my customers; you can't come in here preaching!" I smiled and said: "That's OK, this is your club, I will not be back, but you're still my friend." So I left.

Another time I went down to the club on 13th when I went in, it was [felt different], the smoke smell was so bad (to me). There was another smell in there, I said: "my God!" He revealed to me that it had always been that way, but! I was so much into the world, that I couldn't [smell] the difference between a foul odor and a sweet savor. (The club became as a devils den.) Everyone seemed as though they were moving in slow motion. I saw evil of all kinds in that club. I left out of there that night and I [never again had a desire to go back]. I felt better and I really thank God for my life. I still had a lot to learn, but I was ready to grow in Him. ***He said in His word, that He would never leave me nor forsake me.*** God had begun to show me who I was [in Him].

I kept working, praying and keeping things in order. Women were always coming into the store trying to entice SG (they saw him as fresh meat). We stocked the shelves with goods that we purchased from Texas; everything was going well. One day a lady stopped by the store (there was something unique about her); she had a soothing spirit I can't really describe her glow. When she walked in the door I knew she was a woman of God. She had commented on how nice the store was set up and she said that she had seen our newspaper article. She complimented me on the statement that I gave to the press. She said that my business partner was looking around for another wife and [she's right in his face]. I said: "Yes, the one that was in the picture with him!" She said: "No baby, God sent you to be his wife, but he can't see it." I was stunned! I said: "We're good friends." she said: "I know, but you are what he needs; he has a great ministry [in him] if he just comes all the way, with God. God brought him a woman like you to help him fulfill his purpose I hope he does not miss it." After she said that she left. I looked out the window for her and it seemed like she [just] disappeared. I have never forgotten her (to this day). I did not tell SG or anyone else about the conversation; if it was to be, God was going to have to reveal it to him. SG had many women coming in and out of the store but I don't think he was having sex with any of them, I think the women saw him as a potential [good catch]. He appeared (on the surface) to a big flirt, but not a prowler he always treated me with respect.

I ran into a couple of guys that I knew from back in the day. No one (back then) had been taught to start at the bottom and take one step at a time until they reached respectability. All they saw was the shiny object in front of them. One of the guys (I had known him from a distance), was a beautiful dark-skinned (black) man; he would [accept] applications from women who "wanted to be with him." He used to tell me that when he settles down, he was going to make me his wife. Back then my life was all about the currency; I usually felt more comfortable sitting at a table full of men talking, than hanging out at the girls table. When I saw the two guys I told them about the store. One of them came in the store one evening and SG looked at him like he was nuts (they had known each other from the streets). The guy was wearing this black leather suit (he was looking good with his pretty black self) I got a little beside myself for a minute there, I said: "God stay with me." (I'd never had any kind of dealings with the man.) SG began to look him up and down, but he greeted him: he told him that his leather suit was nice and the guy thanked him; he asked me out to dinner. It was close to closing time so I accepted his invitation and we left the store. SG looked lost when I left with the guy.

When I returned to work the next day, SG was full of questions; I said, it was just dinner I told him that I didn't have to explain anything to him, I tried to tell him that nothing happened. I was trying to please God (at this point in my life). It was all just a matter of having dinner and a conversation with and old friend to reminisce. Sometimes talking about what used to be, is part of the healing process that pushes you forward. I haven't talked much about my connection with pimps (in my book) they were in and out of my life quickly their lifestyle and mine were totally different.

[Time Passed] The store was doing well, but there was always someone trying to ruin my friendship with SG, he had gotten pretty wild; I think he was trying to fill the emptiness of his wife's death. The woman he was dating would always come in and complain about stuff (mostly about me but I didn't care). I was at his house late one evening, we were in the basement making things for the store; his girlfriend was there, walking around thinking she was too cute to work. He told her to leave if she wasn't going to help!

She stormed out and he told her to never come back. That night he told me how he felt about me and we began a relationship. We became a couple and he joined his brother's church (where I attended). His sister-in-law did not think that I should date him because she knew that I was trying to stay focused on my life with the Lord, she and her husband were a blessing to me. I began to spend lots of time at his house and I drove his car all the time. He bought me gifts and he did repairs at my house. My daughter loved him and my mother thought he was the greatest thing that had happen to me.

I started to sleep with him; big mistake! I was not doing anything illegal, but I was sinning against God. I started to care a lot about him. I was afraid to take our relationship seriously because of all the women that were coming around; but he never disrespected me with any of them. He always let them know who I was, and as I stated he treated me with respect. Our lives became centered on each other.

He accepted my family and I accepted and respected his. He had some awesome sisters they were all women of God. I kept people around me who loved God. (My accidental friend [that I mentioned earlier] was a great choir director I met her whole family; they were lovely, talented people. Those were some singing sisters; all of them could blow! They had a great anointing on their lives.) I thank God for how he was bringing people into my life. I really had a personal relationship with the Lord, and yet I still messed up from time to time, but God's grace and mercy covered me. I was not where I should be, but, thank God I was not where I was before.

God is willing to forgive us our debts even as we forgive our debtors. He renews His mercy daily and because we have accepted Christ Jesus (to be our Savior-Redeemer and our Mediator to the FATHER). We are Sealed by the Holy Ghost until the day of our redemption; no one can unseal us (not even we ourselves). Our sins are already forgiven; thanks to the death burial and resurrection of Christ Jesus who offered His Own unblemished Blood to His Father to pay (in full) our sin debt (once and for all times); but! Although we are sealed and forgiven, it doesn't mean that we are exempt from the consequence of our actions. God's justice often allows consequences to reprimand sinful behavior even after a person has turned to Him in obedience, but His mercy continues to offer the protection of a gracious and forgiving Father. That's what he did for me. I know God Loves me! He gave me my Identity. The next 2 pages will touch on who God says we are.

Our Identity and Blessings God's Gift

Jesus became like us so that we could become one with Him. God made each of us a member of His family. Let's look at Ephesians

2:19, "Now, therefore ye are no more strangers and foreigners, but fellow citizens with the saints, and of the household of God." God the Son, lives in us and He shows Himself to those who see us. When we become born again we become a citizen in God's Kingdom. Ephesians 1:13, 14, "In whom ye also trusted, after that ye heard the word of truth, the gospel of salvation; in whom also after that ye believed, ye were sealed with the Holy Spirit of promise." V14. This is the earnest of our inheritance until the redemption of the purchased possession, unto the praise of his glory." A down payment has been made ("earnest") and the Holy Spirit seals us until the day Jesus will call us to join Him in His Glory (in heaven). We belong to Him and He guarantees us that He will do what He has promised He would do. God's power works in us and it transforms us. As God's children we cannot live any kind of way. Our sinful and selfish ways and desires have to go.

God says in his word that we are:

1. Holy, faultless. We were called and adopted Eph 1:4, 5.
2. We are a child in God's family 1John 3:1
3. God has given us new life; we are complete in Christ Ephesians 2:10
4. We are declared righteous in God's sight Romans 5:1
5. We are set free from evil desires Colossians 2:11
6. We are heirs and joint heirs with Christ Romans 8:16, 17
7. You and I are ambassadors for Christ and full of His goodness. 2Corinthians 5:20, 21.
8. We are forgiven of all our sins Ephesians 1:7
9. We are sealed by the power of the Holy Spirit Ephesians 1:13
10. You and I belong to Christ Ephesians 1:5, 6

There are many other scriptures (I could give) these verses show us who we really are in Christ. 2 Timothy 2:10 says, "Therefore I endure all things for the elect's sake, that they may also obtain the salvation which is in Christ Jesus with eternal glory." God is saying we are free to choose life or death, God has chosen us to be his "elect." We ought to be truly grateful that He has chosen us.

Hebrews 4:14-16 talks about nothing being hidden from God. Everything is out in the open. Everything is laid before him. Jesus (being the High Priest), can sympathize with all of our weaknesses. He knows by familiarity everything that we will face and go through. [And yet He never sinned.]

God's blessings are given to all of us who follow Christ. Our blessings are not measured by who you and I are, but, who God is. We have to be obedient to receive His blessings for our lives. God blessed Abraham in Genesis. Let's look at Genesis 12:2, it says "I will make you a great Nation; I will bless you." V3. "And I will bless those who bless you; and curse those who curse you; and in you all the families of the earth shall be blessed." That's awesome. We have our family, our health, and most of all we have God's word to teach us how we should live our lives. God loves us so much. 2 Peter 1: 2-4 says, "Grace and peace be multiplied to you in the knowledge of God and of Jesus our Lord," V3 As His divine power has given to us all things that pertain to life and godliness, through the knowledge of Him who called us by glory and virtue," V4. "by which have been given to us exceedingly great and precious promises, that through these you may be partakers of the divine nature, having escaped the corruption that is in the world through lust. "God the Son: is our seed of hope.

It was truly God's grace and mercy!

Chapter 9

The Call on My Life Knowing God's Will

My life had been one test after other I felt I was getting stronger; the Lord God was molding me into what He wanted me to become.

I had been moving from apartment to apartment and my daughter was growing up; I needed to have a solid foundation for both of us. My friend (the white girl) and I had lived close to one another for many years. Our daughters grew up together until they were in junior high school. I was still with SG and we were talking about getting married, and all was well at church.

We both participated in the curriculum offered (I took every course offered because I was enthusiastic to learn more and more about the Lord). Prison life got me focused on God and I learned a lot about the power of Holy Ghost (our teacher and comforter) while there. I was very eager to serve. The whole congregation loved making a joyful adoration and praise to the LORD.

Sunday morning and evening services were a privilege and a blessing to us all. The word and prophecies that were coming forth were awesome and I knew they were from God (I had been in a Baptist church all my life.) I went to a Pentecostal church for about 3 maybe 4 years, but none could top the Baptist churches back in Arkansas. Those churches were anointed; I keep stating that because they were something worth remembering. The people would shout with [Holy Ghost fire].

The church that I was attending was Non-Denominational. I had developed a love for God like I had never known before (rejoicing under the power of the Holy Spirit is an awesome experience). We all need to have a personal relationship with

Christ. At the Non-Denominational church I began to understand what I was called to do. All of the troubles, trials, and heartaches that I endured in the past I could now use to help others repent (turn around, start over). My season of discontentment was coming to an end (thank God).

I was really in love with SG; it was a different kind of love than what I had experienced in the past. He was such a gentleman, but he could also be hell. He would lash out at times, but he would also give you the shirt off his back.

One day one of my old 'friends' came out of the past [trouble]. (She was the one who used to live with me back in the day; she was there when I was robbed and when my house got burned down (she was there). I really feel she had something to do with that, and no one could tell me different). She came into the house and played like we were all of that SG liked the fact that she could make money. He remembered her from the strip clubs, and she used to dance in a club that he used to run. One weekend he disappeared! SG, his friend, his friends girlfriend and my long lost 'friend;' went to Dallas. I was at his house when they returned he brought me something back, thinking that would make it all right.

(They came back into town with lots of those fake designer purses; she'd take them to small towns when she went out prostituting.) SG began to get a taste of the fast life, again (from which he had been delivered). He would never be at the store anymore, nor did he come to church.

One Sunday I was at church and he had the nerve to walk in there with her. The pastor and the rest of his family really thought he was disrespectful; especially the pastor's wife; she saw the look on my face I could not function in service that day. I hate that I allowed my feelings for him to pull me away from all the progress I had made in my walk with the Lord. The pastor's wife would always minister to me (she just took me up under her wing). It got to the point that I backed out of the store. He had started getting high and he just turned all the way back into the world. I kept going to church. I thank God for those He put in my path I still had the women of God that He placed in my life when I left prison. I began to serve diligently in the church.

We had some powerful guest speakers come through there. I was [in charge of] the new members receptions; when people joined the church we would have a reception for them; everyone loved my cooking, especially the pastor and his wife. I would fix dinner for all the guest speakers that came to the pastor's home.

They had a conference coming up in Baton Rouge, Louisiana, and there were a lot of us that signed up to go. All the women who went were: myself and four of the women that I named in my [true friendship section]. The five of us drove there in a Suburban owned by one of the ladies; it was a very nice vehicle. The lady who owned the truck paid all of my expenses (I felt so bad) she was a blessing to me in so many ways. Well, we left that evening and we had a long ride ahead of us (I think it was a 12 hour drive; some of us took turns driving). We had a ball just the five of us. We were singing songs of worship on the road trip. Well, we got there that morning, and checked into the hotel we had a wonderful time just having fellowship together we bonded on the road; there was one lady that God had moved to Wichita just for that season (she took the trip with us also). Her husband was in the Air force, and we all knew that she would not be there forever she was an anointed woman of God I just loved her spirit. Lots of people referred to her as mother although she was not an old woman, but she was seasoned in the spirit.

Our pastor fellowshipped with us a lot but we always respected him, as pastor. Well we wanted to wash our car and get something to eat so we followed pastor; he knew where everything was because he had been going there to churches that he was associated with. He took us to the carwash and he actually helped us wash the car! That was a blessing to all of us.

That night we got ready for the first night of the conference; the name of the conference was, "Glory conference going to The Next Level." There were some awesome speakers there and we were having the experience of a lifetime, but the last night, Oh My God! There was a woman who was to speak that night (that was so different), we watched her during praises and worship. This woman of God I cannot describe what we saw, but the lady who owned the car (that the five of us drove there in) and I, were sitting together, we were feeling the same thing; they introduced the lady as an Apostle, the anointing was so strong on this woman that it filled the room like fire! That's the only way I can describe it. The first thing she said was, "I want all the pastors, bishops, and whoever has their own church to come forth" she said, "I want all of you to line up across the floor." We were very amazed at what was happening. She said, "Now, we are not going to another level, we are already there" she said "Now Faith" God said, "Believe it when you speak it now." She said a lot more, but this is what she said to them, she said: "I am going to be short, and to the point" and then she said: "God said give it to the head, and when they get it, they can give it to their congregation." She was cutting with every word she spoke and when she finished we were all weeping.

She went down the row, and she began laying her hands on those men and women of God, and they all began falling out under the anointing. Some of them she did not touch, the power was so strong they just went down. All in that hotel, people were going out under the power of God even the children. All of us were down before we knew it. When I got up I was so high in the spirit that I felt I was drunk. The anointing was so strong in there you could cut it with a knife! That's how thick it was I could not stop crying. I ended up going back to the Hotel room when service was over (and I continued to worship the Lord). That was an experience I will never forget.

On the way back to Wichita, it was so amazing how blessed all of us were, it changed all of our lives. The woman who owned the truck was given a prophetic visions from God one evening at my house; she was sitting down and all of a sudden she said, "Oh My God." I don't know what she saw, but she began to praise God and weep before Him.

God began to show me my calling. The words that man of God spoke over me at that Pentecostal church that night, after my sister died began to be revealed to me. I started speaking a lot more about my life. I would go to drug treatment centers and get permission from the directors so that we could have bible studies at each facility; everything began to come together. I was taking care of people, and I met a lady at my church that was so special; she loved helping everybody. She ended up needing help herself, so I offered to do whatever she needed.

I started volunteering at the Salvation Army (the sister of one of the guys that I knew from the streets worked there). I would go down there and minister to all the people that were coming in there who had gotten out of prison; or that were living on the streets and needed clothing or food. God would show me a person and what to pray; also the whole staff there loved me. When I did not come, they would ask her, where is our angel? God had me minister to everyone that came through there, including the staff. I was so honored because God was using me!

Then one day the lady at the church came to me and told me what I could help her with. She had a brother that needed to be taken care of so she hired me to take care of him, and through that union God also used me to draw her daughter (she was into everything in the streets; you name it, she did it and she was no joke) she was so appalled at me for how I talked to her. I wasn't going to say anything to her, but God told me to go back and do what He told me to do, "It is a blessing in obedience" when we do what God tells us to do right then, you will see deliverance take place.

The ladies daughter was standing there with [her woman]; yes, she had women on the streets she was worse than those male pimps. When I gave her what the Lord had said, she began to cry like nobody's business, then I left; to this day, she has a ministry that she is really helping people to be set free. She and her mother helps people coming out of prison, and the families of the people in prison, and their children. She even has favor with Governors, Senators, and anyone you need to get connected with; she gives women's conferences. People from everywhere knows this young woman; she calls me her spiritual mother I am a mentor to her (it is an honor to see the fruits of your labor), Praise God! I thank Him for giving me a spirit of obedience. It pays to listen to the voice of God.

One day she had an event that led me into going to troubled High Schools. She was trying to bring all treatment centers together with one another. She wanted them to see how it would benefit them if they would work together instead of being agains each other, trying to outdo one other; she asked me to come for support; she said you won't have to say anything, I just want you there. I said OK, but while I was getting ready, God spoke to me and told me that I was going to speak; I felt it in my spirit when she asked me.

I went and there were people there from all over the city (even some out of Kansas City). I listened to all of them speak, and after they finished talking, she called me up, I smiled and ***God said, "Don't hesitate, go."***

As I began to speak, an anointing came over me and as I yielded, God allowed my words to flow. After I finished speaking and the event was over, people came running up to me. A pastor said to me, we need you! One of the ladies from the women's facility said, we need someone like you. The people over at the jail were also asking for me. It was a set up by God! The pastor in charge of the young people was a woman; she was the clergy over the youth at her church. I knew of her; she was the mother of a guy that I knew from the streets. She said we need your boldness to help us with these young people. She would go to the Youth Resident Hall (a facility that detained troubled youth who were caught up in the court system). It was the same place I was sent to, when I was young; only in my day it was called: Friendly Gables. It was turned it into a co-ed residence for youth. They did their time there; they went to school and they could also receive counseling (the Pastor had church services there twice a month).

I would go with her to the youth center and also to the women's treatment center; half of the women from the treatment center began to attend our church.

Well God was using me in a way that was a blessing to a lot of people; Jeremiah 1:5-10 was coming to pass. The ex-girlfriend of the (YLW) young lesbian woman that I spoke about earlier, was in one of those centers (she was the one who was standing outside that day with YLW when the Holy Spirit of God, compelled me to pray for her. I told her that she had to come out of that spirit of being gay; I told her that she needs to become the woman God made her to be. She did not have any women clothes; so God told me to get in my closet and give some of my clothes away (I had so many). As I said somewhere in the book, I always loved clothes. With the store, and all the stuff he had bought me, I always had enough of everything (clothes that is) I was glad to give them the clothes and the ones that could fit my shoes, I gave them some of those also; it really felt good to be a blessing to them.

There were a lot of drug addicts and ex-convicts coming to our church; they were being blessed and the word was going forth in their lives. Some of them thought the pastor was too strong. I told them that they had to allow God to circumcise their life. They listened to me talk about how God had delivered me I told them there is a lot about ourselves that we will not like when God shows us ourselves. The pastor (at that church) was a prophet he would speak a lot into people's lives. Very often we are afraid of what God would have a prophet speak to us, I know I was, but God was leading me towards my true purpose in life. I was tried and tested and I came out still in my right mind (sound mind) I'm grateful to know that God is not through with me!!!

As Christians we are obligated to tell people where God has brought us from (confess our faults). We should not allow fear to take hold of us, because it will stop us from reaching our goal. Our lives should be about helping others. The lesbian lady really wanted to change her life, she had three sons, and I think her demeanor was bothering them (she dressed like a man). After a while all the women went different ways; I did my part I gave them the word. Some of them went to other churches. One of them started her own church (and some of the women followed her). There were those who went back to the streets I did not see some of them for a while. After they got out of the treatment centers they did not (even) come back to the bible study. ***A person has to make up their own mind. God gives us a choice and it is up to us.*** I kept praying for all those who God put in my path, and I stayed on my course.

They had a group at the church for the ladies; the pastor's wife was in charge of it and I helped her whenever she needed me. I did a lot of the cooking for most of the functions at the church. I would get someone to help me, but the pastor only wanted my seasoning on the food. The Ladies group met once a month; we would have different people speak (even me sometimes). We had fashion shows both local and out of town. We had a Hawaii Luau once and it was awesome. One of those sisters that God put in my life did praise dances; the two sisters and I did a praise dance on the program and I really enjoyed it.

I was still house hunting. One day I was at my ex-brother-in laws house, and he had some friends over that I used to go out partying with, back in the day (there's so much about my life, I can't express it all because if I did I'd be here typing for years (smile) I'm sharing the parts that might help someone else).

They had a men's group called the Vintage Club. The guys were nice (and their wives and girlfriends were also nice people we got along just fine). They were people who would have gatherings at each other's houses and have good clean fun: laughing, playing cards, dominos and barbecues. Anyway, one of them had a vacant house for rent (they offered it to me if I wanted it). It was a very nice house, the only thing I did not like was that it was in what we called the ghetto. I hadn't lived on that side of town since I got out of prison.

There was a lot going on over on that side of town but, the house was on a dead end street, I said it might not be so bad. It was a three bedroom house with a double driveway, a large garage, a full basement, and a big fenced in back yard, so I took it. The rent was only $500.00 dollars a month (with an option to buy). They told me that I could buy it whenever I was able (you can't beat that); the deposit was only $100.00. He and his wife had it painted, and all the carpet cleaned, so the first of the month I moved in. I was so glad to have a home for me and my daughter to live in, she liked it very much. We got settled in and I enrolled her in school. The yard needed a little work, so I got busy; I liked nice things that included a nice yard.

I was still going through a financial crunch, but with God's help I was pulling through. I went to some garage sales and found some nice things for my house (it had a lot more room than the apartments I had lived in).

I was gifted with using my hands so I would buy something old, and when I finished with it, it would look new I made curtains and everything. I could paint and make beautiful vases and I would take an old frame and varnish it to look new. The guy I was in the store with had taught me a lot about working with my hands I could even fix different things around the house without calling a man to do it for me (I had watched him a lot when I was with him).

The house came together real well and I ended up putting wall paper in the kitchen and the living room. I had a green thumb (I was really good at growing plants). I went gathered everything that I needed for the yard and I went to work. I got some of those big pots and I planted flowers in the front and I edged the grass (when the Lord and I got through the yard was beautiful; I had prayed over that yard; I asked God for His grace to help me beautify it.) People would say my yard was Praising God!

Even though I was having a hard time with my arms I withstood the pain that I was in; sometimes I'd work until I could no longer stand the pain. I didn't want to accept the fact that I had restrictions. People told me that I should be careful, because they could be watching you I really did not care and I was still fighting disability. I really made myself do a lot of the things that needed to be done I know that was crazy but I did what it took to get a job done. I would pray for God to help me, but I still would not use wisdom (I know that was foolish).

All of the neighbors started taking care of their yards. My neighbors said you make us get out and mow our yards, before you came we did not care, that was a blessing to hear. God said you go in and you change your atmosphere, and that's exactly what I did I prayed over that neighborhood; It really wasn't a bad area, everyone who lived over there were older people that had been there for years. The man to the left of me had a lot of dogs, but he kept them in a very tall fence. That dead end street became a very nice place. I would help people plant flowers, a lady on the left, asked for my help and helped her. I went in that neighborhood, and made some good friends.

Life was OK It wasn't where I knew I needed to be, but I kept striving to do better. I started giving family dinners (at my house), and almost every time it would become a big blow out. My sisters didn't like my new lifestyle. I haven't mentioned my sisters a lot because after I came <u>out of</u> the world, it was like they didn't like me anymore. I took my life with the Lord seriously, they use to also, but somewhere along the way they changed. I still had a lot of weaknesses that I was trying to overcome. I don't know what happened with me and my sister's. I would give my family anything they wanted if they needed it when I had it.

I started engaging in fornication with OG, again (he was one of my weaknesses). You think you are delivered from something and find out that you still have those same demons come back and bite you. I started going out (sometimes) on Sunday evening after church to the matinees. It did not feel the same going out any more I felt so guilty; my conscience was bothering me. I'm glad that I felt that way; God would not let me fit in anymore. I kept going to church I wouldn't stop. I left church and went out to clubs for three Sundays in a row; the next Sunday, when I went to church the pastor was preaching about adultery (again). I felt so convicted and ashamed that I held my head down the whole service. He was talking about someone in the church today was with someone's husband or someone's wife, I felt so cheap.

Sunday after church I called OG and asked him to meet me at the club. So that evening and I met him; I told him: "I could not do this anymore I know I said it before, but believe me this time I mean it!" So, as fast as it started back, God gave me His grace to help me end it, and this time I knew it was for good. God has a way of getting our attention. OG said I love you! He said he was going to leave his wife. I knew that was a lie, even though they both had, had separate lives in the past. They had been married 20 years when I met him I told him again that this is not pleasing to God. The same way you get something will be the same way you lose it. I did not want to be responsible for breaking up anyone's home. I wanted so much to be faithful to God. OG really did not want to do breakup with me but I had too. I walked away from OG, that was the end.

As I was about to leave the club I saw a friend and I stopped to say hello. As I turned to leave a guy I'd known (in passing) stopped me; his name was SB (Stock Broker) he asked me to dance I said yes; I don't know why I danced with him instead of going out the door (everybody said he was dangerous but I thought he was a nice person). OG was standing there watching us, I felt bad, but I had to break away.

SB had been with a girl that I knew back in the day; they were really out there on that stuff. She used to turn tricks from what I heard; but I did not know that for sure. I heard that he had been a dope dealer, and that she almost got him busted; anyway he had taken her to the country and shot her, and then he left her there to die; some people found her and called the police and the ambulance, she made it to the hospital and lived to tell the story. (I don't know what happen to him for doing that so I can't comment on it.)

He worked for a major company; he used to come over to my house and while he was there he'd watch the stock market channel. Like Wall Street, and I would see him make anywhere from $5,000 to $12,000 dollars in 30 minutes! That was a lot of money to me. I would hang out with, him just riding around and talking. People would see me with him and ask me: "what the hell are you doing with him" (even his brother asked me what I was doing with him)? His brothers, and his sister were nice people. His mother was a God fearing woman they say; she seemed like she was mean (in my opinion). The more I got to know her all she wanted was for us to be right with the Lord she knew all the women that God put in my life. They would all be together in prayer meetings, and things that pleased the Lord.

So as you can see God would not let me go; everywhere I turned there was a woman of God I was always being put in the path of people of God. The LORD was always reminding me of where He had brought me from.

One day I was at his mother's house; we were talking about the Lord; she said that she knew how crazy her son was. She told me to read Psalm 91 [over my house]. She said to read it over every door and every window and anoint it as I go, so I did. One of his brother's had just moved out of town and the other one lived in Texas. SB and his brother in Texas had a printing company, and he would travel back and forth up there.

He went to church with me one Sunday (when he was in town). We were not in a sexual relationship; I had made up my mind to really get to know a man and make sure that God had put him in my life to become my husband (SB was cool with that). I had a feeling that he had someone in Texas; he said he didn't but you never know.

That Sunday the pastor was preaching and God spoke a word to him for SB; the pastor came out of the pulpit and he walked over to him and said something. To this day I don't know what the pastor told him, but he looked real crazy afterwards (I do remember that). So after church, I introduced him to the pastor and he asked us to step into his office. He started talking to him about me. He said this is a mighty woman of God, and as her shepherd I am to look over the sheep that God put in my care. Then he said to him: "you are not for her;" I was shocked! He looked at me and said: "let's go." Pastor said, "No offense, brother, but God has a greater plan for her." SB didn't say anything at first, but then he made a comment: the choice is hers. So he got up and said he was ready to go. I told him I would be right there in a minute.

I asked pastor, did he have to be so bold; he said: God wants us to be bold and speak the truth. He said: I did not mean any harm but sister you have come too far to allow the enemy to set you back when God has showed me what is ahead for you if you stay with this man. I still felt bad for SB I had real high emotions back then. So SB asked me if I was going to listen to the pastor. I said, I will see if he was right about you, God will reveal it to me (that's my prayer). I kept dating him, but he never went back to church with me anymore.

One time he came back from Texas and asked me if I wanted to go to Minnesota with him? I said yes, I had never been to Minnesota before so I got packed and took my daughter over to my baby sister's house. She had four kids and my daughter liked going to her house, so we left the next day I didn't know it was so far.

He was a very fast driver. It started raining after we got to Kansas City, I just sat back enjoying the ride. He got tired and I offered to drive so we stopped and gassed up the car and then I got behind the wheel. It started raining so hard that I could not see at all; those big trucks were in front and they were shooting rain from under their trucks and that made it even worse. I was going about 30 miles per hour when he said pull over we will be forever getting there (I did not drive again). I don't like those big trucks, especially when I'm driving by beside me. After he took back the wheel I went to sleep; it was a long drive I thought we'd never get there.

We got there! It was a lovely place. SB said: we had reached the "Twin Cities" (Twin City region). It was in May, I remember the weather was real nice, and the next day it got real cold. I wanted to go to the Mall of America; people said that was the biggest Mall ever; so his brother's wife and I got up the next day and got dressed and he gave me some money to go shopping. I ended up buying a big coat (it got so cold there it wasn't even funny). We got to the mall and it was packed; that mall had everything.
When I saw the roller coaster, I was too through! I said, "An amusement park!" They had hotels and many restaurants (in the

mall) it was beautiful. We walked around taking pictures, and just enjoying it.

I was buying everything I wanted. We were getting ready to leave and I saw this hat in the window of one of the stores I really loved hats (I wore a lot of hats back then). So we walked in the store to see the price of the hat; the clerk told me it was $50.00 on sale (they were having a Memorial Day Sale). I had spent all the money I had. I didn't have enough money (left) to buy it. I asked them to hold it, and I'd come back to purchase it the next day (all we had to do was to remember where the store was you could really get lost in that Mall).

We finally made it to the car. When I got back to their house and I talked about that hat all night long. I asked SB for the money to buy it. I went back to get the hat the next day. After we got there we could not find the store I was looking for the window display with all the hats. We were right by the store and did not know it, because they had taken all the hats out of the window. I said: this has got to be the store (after looking for an hour); so we went in and I asked the lady about the hat, she said I still have it. I said I'll take it. When she rang it up she said $75.00 I said to her, the hat was $50.00 dollar yesterday! How are you going to stop the Memorial Day sale on Memorial day? I said: I'm from Kansas and I have to take that hat back. So I asked to talk to the manager, and she said she was the manager, so she decided to give me the hat for the $50.00 (I was happy). I ended up wearing that hat two times and I gave it away. I wanted the hat because I knew that SB would buy it; I call that selfish!

We went back to Wichita and he stayed there for a while. He would stay with his mother when he was in town, but he would be at my house during the day. I didn't want any man staying all night around my daughter because she had gotten older and I always wanted to respect her. I went on a lot of trips with this man. One time he came into town and he was at my house when I got home. My daughter told me that he was acting weird. She said she had seen some white stuff in some paper in the bathroom. He was in my room; I went in there and he was very paranoid I asked him what was wrong with him. He said nothing, but I had looked down and I saw some foil on the floor kind of pushed up under my bed. People had said he was smoking "that pipe," but I did not believe them because he was always well dressed and groomed he didn't even look like he got high. That shows you that looks can be deceiving. I confronted him with that. My daughter did not like him and I did not want him around her. That alone should have made me leave him alone (right then). That explains why he was like he was; people that used that stuff care more about [that] then sex. I was glad because I did not want to do anything anyway, but, he wasn't respecting me, he just liked that pipe, so that made it easy for him. I kept on seeing him like a dummy. I think he liked being around me because everybody knew both of us and he knew what type of person I was.

Well, he ended up taking me, my mama, and my daughter to Arkansas. My daughter was 11 years old at the time and her people hadn't seen her since she was a baby. I decided to take her to see them. My mother wanted to see her people so that was good.

He had become very jealous of who I talked to or where I went. My sister had a guy she was dating that called looking for her; when the phone rang I asked him to answer it; it my sister's man, looking for her, so he handed me the phone I told the guy that she hadn't called me I told him when he sees her to tell her we were going to Arkansas; he said ok, and he cracked a joke I laughed and said bye. I hung up the phone, and the first thing SB said was, why did you want him to know that you were leaving? I said, "What are you talking about?" I said that is my sister's man. He said OK, so I forgot about it.

We got on the road and I was thinking everything was cool. We were just riding and talking, but he never would say anything to me. He would just make remarks to my mother or he would say something to my daughter. When we stopped to eat or use the restroom, he would talk to them not me. I asked him what was wrong with him and he never said anything back; I knew then that this was going to be a hell of a trip.

We got to Bodcaw, Arkansas where we dropped off my

mother. Then we went to Toilette, Arkansas where we took my daughter over to her father's people house I kissed my daughter and told her we would be back in a few days so we got back on the road to Little Rock, Arkansas where his people lived (and to get my birth certificate). As soon as we took off, he started talking irrationally he said, "You must think I'm a damn fool I know that call was your Nigger and both of you think you're slick." I said, "That was my sister's man, and is that what you've been tripping on all this time man you're crazy!" Are you for real? You don't know a truth when you hear one I asked him, "Are you that paranoid?" He said, "I ought to shoot you and push you out on this highway and let the animals have you for dinner." I said, "You are crazy" I told him it would be better than tripping with you the next few days. I said I don't believe that you seriously believe that my sister's man was calling for me! That was truly a nightmare of a trip.

I started to see what everybody was saying about this man he was something different. I see what pastor was talking about, now I didn't say another word to him but he kept trying to bait me, but I never responded. The only thing I said to him was: do what you're going to do I was tired of listening to him, he said, "If I did not have your mother and daughter with me I would have done something to you." I said oh God! What the hell have I got myself into now? I said that's what happens when you are disobedient.

I started repenting and asking God just to get me back home. The rest of the trip is not worth talking about; I did make it back home in one piece, thank the Lord. I told God to move this man out of my life. He told me as long as he was alive that I would never see anyone else. I said God where do I get these fools from? He kept bothering me. He tried to apologize to me about what had happened. I told my sister's boyfriend what happened and he went and talked to him, so like a fool I went back for more.

My mother and I ended up riding with SB to Denver, to my niece's wedding (the daughter of my sister under me). On the way there we had a blowout. It scared my mother so bad that she grabbed my hair and held on to it like it was a safety net. We were on that highway for about four hours waiting to get help finally a patrol car came by.

It was late when we got to Denver; my mother was so tired and mad that she started cursing him out about driving so fast. Remember I mentioned how she would curse people out? She didn't mind doing it either.

When we got to Denver we stayed with a friend of my sister's (they were really close; they had been old running buddies from the streets). The wedding was the next day and everyone was getting ready.

My oldest sister's daughter came with her husband I think they had two kids by then, she got married after her mother (my sister) died. It's a blessing; they are still married. My nieces wedding was beautiful and the reception was very nice (we all were having fun).

After the wedding and reception was over, there was still three hours left on the three rented limousines so my niece said that SB and I could take one and see the city of Denver. We got in the car and all hell broke loose; he started accusing me of all kinds of stuff even though I was with him all night and did not dance with anyone other than him he acted a plum fool! He was just nuts. I said to myself, that's what I get, I felt real stupid (again). I already knew how he was and he had not changed, one bit. That entire apology was a lie! That was a wasted limo ride I couldn't even enjoy the scenery for listening to him fuss. I think that man did not like himself. That pipe made him crazy. He said he was not doing it again, but that was a lie also. I was so ready to get back to Wichita but we had another day to be there.

When we got ready to leave the next day there was a snow storm coming our way; we left early so we could beat the storm. My mother did not ride back with us; she said she didn't like his driving. My niece was going to Wichita to see her father and her grandmother.

We got on the road and drove about 200 miles when the timing belt broke on the car. It was a loaner car (from a car lot where I had just bought a car that had some things that needed to be fixed so they gave us another car to drive out of town).

It was getting dark from the snow clouds coming and I just knew we were going to get caught in that storm. I was trying to watch out for my niece and her husband to drive through because I was going to get in their car with them. SB was standing on the side of the road trying to flag someone down, and a man finally stopped. He took him down to the next stop so he could call a tow truck. I was hoping to be gone when he returned, but it did not happen.

Later, I found out that my niece had gone another way. So we got towed to a place and they confirmed that the timing belt had broken, and that it was going to cost a whole lot to get it fixed. I called the car lot and told them what happened and they said they'd get the car. They should have given me a better car; they were a little upset I did not care. We asked about the bus station so we could catch a bus the rest of the way home. The man who stopped to helped us took us to the bus station; SB bought our tickets for the next bus which was getting ready to leave as we got there, but they waited for us I was glad, I just really wanted to get home. I had one of the worst headaches that I can remember; that man really got on my nerves. He tried to be loveable with me but I really did not want him to touch me.

We got to Wichita about 11:00 PM that night. I forgot who came and picked us up, but I went home and I told him I did not want him to stay at my house. My daughter was not there but I told SB they were bringing her home. After that trip I got my first cell phone I said I will never ride on the road again without one. They had some of those funny kinds of big phones back then that also had pagers I got both so that when people paged me, I could call them back. Back then they didn't have [anytime minutes]. I had a plan that had only 300 anytime minutes; and no text or anything else.

SB would not leave me alone. He had a beautiful daughter that I just loved, and she loved me also. One day he came by my house and told me to come and ride with him (to his daughter's house) I said I did not want to, but he had said something crazy about what he would do if I did not get in the car, so like a fool, I did. (I was scared of him (by then) and I did not know what I was going to do to get away from him). He was drinking real heavy that night; I think he hated rejection. On the way to his daughter's house he was going 100 miles per hour I was begging him to slow down and he would not. I was praying, "God please help me, don't let us have a wreck." His daughter stayed way on the other side of town. We arrived at her house and he was talking crazy; his daughter got mad at him; he went in the kitchen to fix himself (another) drink; I was begging him not to do that. I said, "God, you have to intervene in this." SB poured the drink into a glass and turned the water on to put a splash of water in it and all of that liquor jumped out of the glass! If you could have seen how that stuff flew out of that glass your mouth would have been opened! He dropped that glass and looked at me and I could tell he was scared. He said, "Let's go right now;" he didn't try to fix another drink. I think that made him a little sober. He drove back like he had sense. I said, "Thank you, Lord."

When I got home he came in my house and he was getting ready to light a joint I told him, "Don't light that in my house I do not want any of that stuff around my baby." He said, "I will go in the room," I said no! I did not want that smell in my house. So he was going to do it anyway, when he went to light the joint, the door slammed shut! That scared the hell out of him. I said, "God, I thank you" he said, "I'm leaving" I said bye. He told me, "You had better watch yourself you will never know if you will get shot going into your house." I did not say a word, but what I did was: I called those sisters that were at my church, the ones that we were divinely connected. I called the one that had helped pay all my bills and she called her sister on a three way, that sister called the other, and that one called the other one, until we all were on one line connected like a conference call. I told them what had been going on, and why I had not been to church in the last couple of Sundays. They said that's all right God knows that you love him, and that you are one of His. Those sisters got to praying, oh God, the power of the anointing that are on those mighty woman of God is a blessing I thank God for bringing them into my life.

I went to church that Sunday (the praise and worship service was awesome). I was so jacked up that I pressed in. I went back to evening service and God just showed up and showed out! That word was so awesome and the fire of the anointing that hit that sanctuary was glorious! The pastor was walking around prophesying to people, he was so drunk in the spirit that he went out, and he got back up, he came charging over there to me, and he said to me, God Said, "No Weapon Formed Against You Shall Prosper; you have been ordained by the Holy Ghost and Nothing Can Hurt You. Your House is covered by the Blood." He said it with such boldness, I can't even describe it I just came unglued! Fear of SB left me that night.

He came by my house the next day talking about shooting me I said to him with the boldness and the confidence that I had in God. God said: no weapon formed against me is going to prosper I said, you are the weapon, and I believe if you take that gun out to shoot me, I believe that it will backfire and shoot you. He said, "You're crazy." I said yes, "Crazy for Jesus." He left my house that day and never came back.

He started dating a girl that I knew back in the day. I was visiting his mother about 4 months later and he walked up, he and I talked (outside) for a minute, he really didn't know what to say to me. He asked me why I was still coming around his people? I told him that your mother and your grandmother are both dear to me. They love God, and these are the kind of people God put in my path. If I didn't get anything else but that out of that relationship I know that God gave me two divine connections. Seems like everyone I have met in my life in some way I met them just to meet with people God intended for me to know. As I said before, I am drawn to people's mothers, and they are drawn to me.

His new girlfriend was there and she was mad about me being there she thought I was there to see him. His brother's wife was also there (they were visiting from Minnesota), she told her that: Carolin doesn't want him, and that she did not have anything to worry about. She was so right, my life went on I was back where I needed to be, back with the Lord. I thank God for His grace and mercy. I know I had been living dangerously again.

About 7 months later I got a phone call saying, "Girl, you better be glad you left that man alone." He had shot and killed the man that his girlfriend was taking care of, shot her and then got in a high speed chase with the police, he ran his car into a tree and killed himself. I'm thankful that God covered me! He killed an elderly man in a wheelchair, because she was spending too much time with him, that was her job! That was crazy to me. I went to his funeral because of his daughter you no; that man had a sneaky smile on his face it was weird to me. That was the end of that man. I said I was not going to let anything or anyone else pull me away from God anymore. I was growing stronger in God through every trial that I had been going through. My daughter was growing up, and she saw a lot that we were going through.

For the next few years we fell on hard times again. All the things that I was getting I was putting my trust in man instead of God; I feel that's why I kept going back down. All the things that you think are a blessing are not, if you get them the wrong way. I was taking odd jobs not staying on any of them because of my arm. I could not work very long because of the pain that I had. I was still fighting for disability, and I was going through a lot of other physical problems during that time. I was restricted from doing a lot of things, although I did not follow the restrictions. I would take care of people. A lot of times I would still be hurting but I would still work.

They started sending me to therapy; they wanted my pain to be psychological they were trying everything under the sun to not give me disability.

I was still praying and believing God for change, I knew I needed to change what I was doing. I know God did not like a lot of things I was doing and still being in the church. My pastor's wife would try to keep me encouraged, a lot of the people were, even my pastor, he was always praying with and for me. Satan tried to make me think that things were better for me when I was in the world; the enemy has a way of trying to make you feel that way to get you back where he wants you to be. I did not go back into the world, but I kept making choices that kept me in the bondage that I was in.

My daughter was in high school (by now) and I wanted her to grow up knowing the Lord. One day when I got to the school to pick her up, she asked me if she could drive, she was so excited! My baby had just gotten her drivers permit. I said OK, so she got in on the driver's side and I told her to put on her seat belt and adjust the seat where it needs to be. She was smiling and happy so we took off and about a block from the school she went to make a turn and a car hit us; she was supposed to wait, it was her fault. I got out of the car; the store on the corner had called the police. I started walking back and forth in the middle of the street praying in the Holy Ghost. She was just crying and looking at me. I told her to stop crying but she was so shaken that she could not stop. I said, why are you crying like that, she replied because you're not. I told her that I was all right, and to stop it now.

The police came and I got the ticket. I needed to get the car towed because it was not drivable. I went to the corner store and got the phone book and I prayed that I would find someone that would not cost too much and take it to a body shop that would be fair. I only had liability on my car; my insurance would fix the other person's but not mine. I was shaken also but I didn't want her to know it I knew I had to be able to get her back and forth to summer school and her part-time job; the accident happened on the last day of the school year (but she had failed two classes and I was already praying for the money to send her to summer school and now I also need money to fix the car.) I had just been talking to her about trusting God and having faith (I was being tested in it like big time).

I found an auto body shop and they had their own tow truck so they sent someone to pick up my truck. I talked to the owner and I asked him to fix it just enough so that I could drive it (and not fix the wrecked part of it). He said that he would get back with me when he figured out how much it would cost.

When we got home I wanted to keep what I felt inside

because I did not want my daughter to know that I was worried, but at the same time I was still trying to trust God. I went downstairs and started praying and calling out to God in a way that I was praising and worshipping Him. I let her go over to my sister's house around the corner so she could be with her cousins. I laid down on the floor and I said to God I have been praying and saying I trust you and people have been telling me to really trust you so I am really going to step out on the faith that I been praying and telling my daughter to have. So I said, "God what's up?"

That evening I received a phone call from a girl that I had not heard from in a long time. She said that I was on her mind and so she decided to call me. I told her what was going on and she told me that she had another car that I could use for as long as I needed it. God started working that same day. Praying for something and really believing what you pray for makes all the difference.

When I was in prison I had a really close relationship with God; things flowed for me there. You can still be in prison when you are free. Since I have been out of prison I have had a lot of challenges along the way but we will be tested in our life in order for God to purify our faith. "Trials are a must" (sometimes); everything we go through builds character in us; we either grow from it or we allow it to take us down. God blessed us with the money for summer school and I was able to get her to school and to work. I didn't have the money to get my car out of the shop when it was ready. So he said when I get the money, my car would be there. I would get a few dollars and I would take it to him.

One day the man called me again, and I told him I did not have it. I was still fighting that disability case so our funds were limited I ended up getting on welfare and they gave me food stamps I think it was $323.00 a month, plus a $175.00 of food stamps. I had applied for a program that helps pay your rent; that program really came through for me, and it was a blessing. My life began to revolve around the system.

I never got help from my daughter's her father or his family (since she was little). My father and mother would help me out some. I said to myself, my life really sucks, but I had peace of mind even though I did not have a lot; I knew that God had something more for me. I was ministering to a lot of other people and yet my life was hell. I said how can I minister to people so effectively and tell them how to get out of bondage and yet I could not minister the word to myself? I was connecting with a lot of people in this church. It was an awesome group of loving people going there; I loved everything about that church.

One day the lady called me and said that she had wrecked both of her cars and that she needed her truck. So I took it to her and she brought me back home. I said, "OK God, what next?" So I called my father and asked him to use his truck. He said I could use it for a few days, but he would need it back. It was the Fourth of July weekend and after that Sunday I had to give my father's truck back to him.

I got a phone call that evening, and it was the man from the body shop he said again, that my truck was ready and he told me he had went on and fixed the wrecked part also. I told him that I still did not have the money to get it. He was visiting a lady across the street from my house; he said he told her: I know that girl needs her truck. That's when he said he called me. He asked me how much money I had and I told him I had about a $180.00 dollars left from that welfare check, and I still had bills to pay. He told me to bring him the $180.00 and I could have my truck. I was so over-joyed that I could not speak, I just cried thanking God.

My truck cost $1288.00 but he gave it to me for what I had! "That's God" He made a way for me, and I even got those bills paid.

People began to plant seeds in my life. Things seemed to be turning around for me. This one lady and I became real good friends; I don't know how we got the way we were, but I just loved her and her mother. We began talking about going into business together so we started going out of town buying clothes and selling them. I took my next welfare check to buy those clothes she had her money, but that was all I had. Everyone in church was buying clothes from us I ended up tripling my money (we went back and forth, buying and selling). I started tithing from my money.

We would take the merchandise to clubs; peoples work places and different churches. (Those church women loved the hats and the suits; especially those Pentecostal women; we would sell out quickly.) I think we went to Texas every two weeks; sometimes we would go every week, it depended on how much we sold. We would buy suits, hats, purses, jogging suits, jewelry, and other things. We'd drive her Lincoln up there (she was a fast driver) she didn't like for me to drive. I didn't care, because I did not like driving.

One time we were on the highway and she was tired so I took the wheel. I tried to speed and follow this car I did not want a ticket so I thought that if I followed the guys in front of me they would get stopped first. That was a hell of a way to think huh? So, anyway, I was going about 80 (at least I thought I was). The people up in front of me had to be going at least 95 to 100. I saw the highway patrol turn his car around and I said to the lady I was with: he had to have clocked one of them! He got behind me and turned his lights on me I was mad. I told her that's why I don't drive fast. He got to the window and told me he clocked me at 93. I said, "It is no way I was going that fast (I said to him) those people in front were driving faster than me; Why did you stop me"? He replied, "Because I wanted to." I was getting ready to say something slick, and my friend said, "All right space ghost, you will be going to jail if you don't calm down." In Oklahoma, they usually make you pay the ticket before you leave the scene, but they did not do that to me. (She had this beautiful color Lincoln and that's why I feel like they stopped me. That ticket was a $130.00!

I was really mad about it but it could have been worse, I could have gone to jail. I told her again that's why I don't like to drive fast. We got back to Wichita and I was still talking about that ticket. She said you need to let that go and just pay it. I made the money to pay the ticket, but I thought it was a waste to pay them that much. The clothes that we would get would sell fast.

Money was good for a while. The people at the clubs would

buy a lot of the jogging suits and a lot of the jewelry. People had begun to put in orders for things, and that was good.) I still was not where I needed to be with God; it seems like I'm there one minute, and then I'm not; I said, "I am not going to give in to the world like I was any more."

No matter what I did I kept serving in the church and the pastor's wife and I we kept running together. As I said before I really enjoyed her friendship and she was so easy to talk to. We had a lot of fun having lunch, going to pray for people, going shopping and going to garage sales and just enjoying the Lord. I kept singing in the choir and doing everything that I could to stay busy in the church. I was enjoying all the powerful men and women of God (learning from them).

The enemy never stops trying to destroy our lives. That's why we need to know God's will for our lives. We have to learn obedience, and think positive about life and where God is taking us. The next section tells us about the benefits of Positive thinking and the fruits of Obedience.

Obedience

We have to always obey the Lord. We should obey God and His word because we love Him. Let's look at 1 John 2:3, 4 "Now by this we know that we know Him, if we keep His commandments." V4. "He who says, I know Him and does not keep His commandments, is a liar, and the truth is not in Him." We all must learn obedience. Read Deuteronomy 28:1-14, it will show you the blessings for being obedient. Deuteronomy 28:15-68 shows the curse of disobedience.

We all should conform to God's purpose for our lives. We should feast on God's Word daily and live according to [IT] in order to build a personal relationship with HIM. Genesis 3:5, say's "For God doth know that in the day ye eat thereof, then your eyes shall be opened, and ye shall be as gods, knowing good and evil. In this scripture Satan mislead Eve. He made her think that she could become a god by defying God's word and His authority. (The LORD God had made a covenant with Adam; Eve and Adam broke it.) We have to keep God in our plans. We have to obey God and leave him in our plans.

Be A Positive Thinker

Proverbs 23:7 says: "As he thinks in his heart so is he" God wants us to be positive thinkers. The way we can do that is to develop His thoughts. Philippians 2:5 states "Let this mind be in you that was also in Christ." This is really powerful if we allow God to control our thinking. We should develop this attitude of humility that the Bible teaches. We know that our battles start in our minds. Our thoughts control everything about our lives. Our mind can be very selfish and prideful. Our attitude should not be dependent on people nor our immediate circumstance. Philippians 4:11, 12 say: "Not that I speak in regard to need, for I have learned in whatever state I am to be content." V12. "I know how to be abased, and I know how to abound everywhere in all things I have learned both to be full and to be hungry, both to abound and to suffer need."

Our thoughts are not gained through our own personal effort. We have to think on and meditate on positive things, such as those found in: Philippians 4:8: "Finally, brethren, whatsoever things are true, whatsoever things are honest, whatsoever things are pure, whatsoever things are lovely, whatsoever things are of good report; if there be any virtue, and if there be any praise, think on these things." So the word of God is telling us how to think; because our thoughts determine what comes out in our mouths and also our actions. We just need to ask God to keep our minds focused on [what is good]. God will help us do what is good if we put our trust in Him and not ourselves.

To God be the Glory!!!

Chapter 10

The Loss of my Father and Mother

My father was a great man of faith. Although we did not go to the same church we were always communicating. I loved talking with my father; he always told us that we needed to stay with the Lord. When he passed away he was still married to the woman that he had dated after he and my mother separated. Although he had a whole new family (three children with his new wife and three stepchildren) he never neglected us. He was getting on in age but he stayed active as long as he could. (I know! That's where I got my spunk; my mother would always tell me how I was: "like those Morgan's!")

I had a close relationship with my parents and I was always there for them and they were always there for me. My two younger sisters had moved to Colorado and my sister up under me would be in and out of prison a lot.

I would go to Arkansas with my dad; whenever he needed a driver (I was the one who would go). One time my father, my cousin (the pastor) and my daughter and I went to Arkansas; actually, I called my cousin [uncle] because he was an older man.

We left Kansas in the evening (my cousin started off driving), in Oklahoma we stopped to have a bit to eat; when we finished eating, I got behind the wheel; my daughter was entertaining the passengers and then they all fell asleep. As I was driving I came upon a major detour in the road (due to road construction) instead of me waking them up and asking which way I should go, I decided to guess, and I followed the detour back to the highway that I was on at first.

I had been driving for about 3 hours and my uncle (as I called him) awoke (he nick named me "quizzing" I don't know where he got that name from); he asked me where we were? I told him I didn't know I was just driving on the highway we were already on.

We came to a sign that said: "Fort Smith." He said: "We're not supposed to be going to Fort Smith!" He woke my father and told him we were going the wrong way. I had gone over 100 miles out of the way. They had me pull off the road and my "uncle" took the wheel. My father told him what road to take to get back on track they banned me from driving the rest of the trip (I was glad, I did not like driving any way) we were on the highway, three extra hours.

We reached: Hope Arkansas around 4 AM. They dropped me off at my grandma's house (one of my uncles lived there since she passed away); I missed seeing her there; my uncle and cousins were at the house I enjoyed the time I spent with them I love being back in the country (fresh air; old times). We were there for four days; I don't remember who had died but we went to a funeral. They used to call my father "Big Baby" and some called him: "Shorty." He was a happy man, always laughing and joking with people, but he had a serious side when it was called for.

There was lots of love in Arkansas, the people were so friendly and caring and they always were looking out for one another. We went to the old church that we attended when we lived there. Most of our people were buried in the cemetery in the back of the church; as I'm writing I'm thinking! I believe it was my aunt Easton who had died, she was a great woman of God I used to love going to her and Uncle Marvin's house. They had a field full of fruit trees and a huge garden; they even had a cotton field. When we were little we would go over there and help pick cotton. People think I shouldn't remember those day's but I do; I remember a lot of things (I did not mention in this book), but they will forever be in my heart.

It was time to leave and go back to Wichita and I really wished we could have stayed a little longer, but we had to get back home. Time went by and I was still holding on to what faith I had (as I stated before) I had some great friends at church. I grew very close to two of the families and also my pastor and his family; we had cookouts, fashion shows and even (yearly) Super Bowl parties (things like that). You can have fun: enjoy the Lord and still stay saved. I learned that being a Christian doesn't have to be boring; living for God is a joy if you allow yourself to be led by the spirit.

A few years passed and my father's health began to deteriorate. Even though his body was weakening he held on to the word of God. I would take him to his doctor appointments and spend quality time with him when my stepmother was at work.
My father retired from Cessna Air Craft, but even after he retired he continued to work for the (family) construction company (they'd let him do little odd jobs that would not hurt him; he had to stay busy). He worked until he was 82 years old. Dad lived a very active and full life. The doctor gave him about two weeks to live but he would tell the doctor that he was not going anywhere until God said so. He spoke it with confidence and a boldness of knowing who he was in Christ (and the faith that he had in God's word). He believed what the word said and he kept active doing things as long as he could.

At age 84 he got to where his only (outside) activity was going to church. When I'd visit him we'd sit on the porch and talk; I could talk to him about anything. He was on our prayer board at church and my pastor and his wife would take time to visit him. Near the end, my father was attending my cousin's church because his church (of many years) was having difficulties and finally it closed down. The pastor passed away leaving his wife alone.

[Time Passed] I began to be even more active in my church. I was doing things that I enjoyed, and that was pleasing to the LORD helping other people became a joy to me. My father was a fighter and it was a blessing to see the strength and the faith that he walked in during that time period. I continued to sell clothing and I kept catering and I was still fighting my disability case (all this kept me busy). I still had problems with my arms and also my leg; I fell through a porch (I think I did mention it before), I have had over 8 surgeries throughout my life. I believed God for healing my body, although (I was not using wisdom) I know I was not doing a lot of things that I was supposed to do in order to help myself and my daughter. I was very active, so the thought of being confined to where I couldn't do anything made me angry and depressed.

(Once I had a brace on my neck; a brace on my leg and I had a cast on my right wrist and I was still outside trying to plant flowers with my left hand and I was sitting down digging dirt; the mailman came through, he stopped and looked at me and said: "I have seen it all;" he had to laugh, he said: "you don't let anything stop you!") Everyone was in love with my yard; it was beautiful (if I must say so myself).

I've gone through a lot and my daughter has been with me all the way; she was in her Junior Year in high school and she had begun to see a boy that was off into the gangs (which I did not know at the time). She got hung up on that boy to the point that she was lying and everything. She had begun to change and I knew she had begun to have a sexual relationship with him; it got to where she was defending him to me. I took her to a psychologist (the one that I had gone to in the past when the company was trying to tell me that my pain was psychological). I was so hurt over the things my daughter was doing because of that boy. I would go off on him and she would get mad at me; she really thought that she was in love. He was also messing around with lots of other girls; the boy gave her a STD and I had to take her to the hospital, but that still didn't stop her from being with him; she ended up getting pregnant she was in her Senior year now and I was really hurt about that but there wasn't anything I could do about it; he also had another girl pregnant.

My daughter would cry about him a lot; he was doing her so bad. Her health was good during her pregnancy that was a blessing. He did not come by to see her anymore; I guess he had to keep being the whore that he was; that's what I called him. He wouldn't listen to his own mother or grandmother when they tried to talk some sense into his head. I told my daughter that a man who disrespects his (own) mother couldn't have respect for any woman (he comes in contact with).

I had known his grandfather from the streets he chased women also. I told that young man that I did not like him; I told him that I had to love him because that's what God tells us to do, and I would still minister the word to him out of obedience to God.

My daughter was home a lot and she became more focused on her school work; she was still my baby. I tried to persist in leading her in the right direction. She'd go to church with me and my pastor's wife would minister to her (and many of the other women of God at the church). When my daughter got too big, they put her in home-schooling, which was good. She graduated at midterm but, they let her walk with her class on graduation day (at the end of the school year). She graduated with honors (she was on the honor role). What a blessing!

It truly was God's Grace and Mercy!!!

My father took a turn for the worst and he began to go in the hospital a lot. I would visit him; I'd sit by his bed and read the Bible to him because he loved hearing the word of God.

My brother's from California came to see him. My sister up under me was in prison; the rest of my sisters and brothers were [around]. Everyone came into the room where he was; the doctors said it was not good. My father looked at all of us and said: "I'm tired now;" I knew [then] that he was ready to go. His work on earth was: Well Done! He did not want to be in the hospital so my step mother had their den set up like a hospital room; she took him home (she was a nurse so she knew how to care for him).

I really respect her for taking care of my father the way she did; my brothers had a whole new respect for her. My mother would go and visit him. My mother, my stepmother, my father and my stepfather were all friends (they got along very well) they would all gather at my house for dinners and they would laugh and talk with one another: They all were living for God.

My stepmother had become a Jehovah's Witness but that did not make a difference to me; she was still a wonderful person. She tried at times to change me over but I was happy being a Christian. Her oldest son had also become a Jehovah's Witness. All of her kids by my father and the three she had before she met him went to: Kingdom Hall but it was all good. I loved all of my sisters and brothers they were all [whole to me] not considered half we all got along, and we all loved my father that's what was important. After she took my father home I would go over and help her with him. He got to where he was [just] there and I knew that it was a matter of time.

January 30, 1999 my daughter went to the hospital (she was having a hard time, she dilated to 6 and she could not go anymore. Her water had broken and the fluid was getting in the baby's lungs so they ended up giving her a C-Section). They gave her a block I was scared, but I did not let her know I got in front of her and we were praying so she would stay calm; they took her into the operating room and prepared her for the surgery I called the baby's daddy's people. They wanted a girl so bad because only boys were being born in that family. They let me stay in the room with her so I sat on a chair in front of her, keeping her focused on God; she would repeat the prayers I would say with her. At one point she almost passed out but God brought her through and here comes this 8 pound 9 ounces girl! She was so pretty to me, big baby. They cleaned her up and I was the first to hold her then I handed her to my daughter and then I went out there to tell the daddy's people.

They were so happy to have a little girl in the family. She came out looking just like my daughter; you can also see a lot of him (but she looked a lot like my daughter when she was born).

While they were in the hospital my daughters friends would come to visit her and the baby; they would get mad at me because I did not let them hold the baby (very much). I made them wash their hands because I did not want any germs on her; I guess you could say I was an over-protective grandmother.

They were finally ready to be released from the hospital I prepared everything for her and the baby. She had lots of stuff already from the baby shower, plus things from people that I had done volunteer work with during the Christmas Season. Also 15 families from Boeing had adopted me and my family during Operation Holiday (they all gave me lots of things for her and the baby). During that same time frame I was also taking care of my youngest sisters 3 daughters. My sister had gone to Colorado and was supposed to come right back, but she ended up being gone for almost a year. God was looking out for my life big time (I don't talk about that much) I kept a lot of kids back then; they always had a home with me, and to this day they are all still close to me and they will forever be in my heart.

I took my grandbaby to see my father because I really wanted him to see her before he died. He looked over at her I don't know if he really saw her or not, but I wanted to take her over there anyway. I went home, and that early evening I was standing in front of my sink washing dishes and I felt something that felt so peaceful go by me I knew my father had just died. The phone rang about 15 minutes later and when I saw it was my stepmother I told her I felt my father die before she even told me. This was February 6, 1999; my father passed away 7 days after my granddaughter was born. God had called my father home I was so hurt; my father was like a rock to me; I am really missing my father (still) to this day.

It was time to plan the funeral; my stepmother and her oldest son wanted to have the service at the Jehovah's Witness Hall. He had tried to take charge but I stepped in and said: "No! I know that he was your husband and you have a right to do what you want, but, my father was not a Jehovah's Witness and that was not the way he lived so why do you want to do that to him?" I asked her son: "How can you preach a funeral for my father based on him being married to your mother?" The rest of our brothers and sisters had a problem with their idea also. We talked to her and she finally agreed to let us do his service. She said: she could not come to the funeral, because: "Jehovah's Witnesses do not go into churches," which for me was hard to understand.

I began to make the funeral arrangements for my father; my mother volunteered to help me. We went over to my cousin's house (the one I called my uncle) and we were putting information together about his passing; my cousin then told me some things that I didn't know about my dad (he had done a lot of stuff) I even found out that we had another brother and sister. My mother was surprised also she said: "The old buzzard." I told mama, that was a long time ago; she said: "it was when we were still together." I started laughing, she really got mad. The girl was my age and the boy was the same age as my brother (right before me).

My stepmother helped as much as she could and I really respected her for how she allowed us to do the funeral. I shaved my father's and cute his hair and made sure that he looked nice. My older brothers had already gone back to California, but they came back to help me with everything. We had the funeral at our cousin's church; his nephew preached the funeral. My pastor said the prayer and he delivered a prophetic word to our entire family. Everyone spoke with such love for my father. The prison allowed my sister to attend the funeral but she had to come with a guard, but he was nice enough to let her move around and not look like she was being secured. My pastor complimented my father, he said that: "he was a well-respected man." The things that were said about him were a blessing to us all. My sisters and brother that my father had with her came to the funeral. The only ones that did not come into the church were his wife and her oldest son. She did go to the cemetery with the rest of the family for the final viewing.

It was something, trying to get use to him not being here. Things settled down, for a while then all hell broke loose. My daughter had been doing ok [as long as that boy wasn't around]. SG, was there consoling me; he would always show up whenever something important happened in my life, and then he'd disappear (again).

I had bought a big Van to drive back and forth to Texas (to buy clothes); one day my daughter asked if she could borrow it I told her that it was ok, so she and her cousin left the house.

That evening it rained very hard. They hadn't returned or called, and I began to worry about them; because it was getting late. When they finally drove up, my niece was behind the wheel; she ran into the house and said something was wrong with my daughter. I ran out to the Van and when I saw her [I knew exactly what it was] I put my daughter in the back seat and I drove to the hospital like a bat out of hell! On the way there I called my pastor and he and his wife, and they said they'd meet us there. When I pulled up to the hospital door, I ran in screaming. I told them that my daughter had overdosed! They rushed out to the Van with a stretcher; they wheeled her in and started to working on her right away. My pastor and his wife got there just as they were going through the double doors (with her) my pastor started praying, binding death off her; he said she would be all right. All of a sudden we heard her scream! The pastor said: "You hear that! "It is just like a baby being born." He had been speaking into her life a lot I told them that they were two special people that God put in my life; they were always there for me.

The doctor came out and told us that they had pumped her stomach and that she would be alright. They asked me if I knew what she had taken (I did not have a clue) I kind of knew she was depressed, but not to that degree. They said they'd have to keep her for observation [in the psych ward for 3 days]. My pastor prayed with me and we went in to see her; the pastor prayed for her; they went home and I went to home to changes clothes and then I went back up to the hospital to stay with my daughter.

I was so mad at that boy that I could have killed him. She was crying and telling me she didn't want to live. Do you know how hurtful it is when your baby says something like that? She was suffering from post-partum depression (according to the doctor).

(When I rushed my daughter to the hospital my niece stayed at the house with my grandbaby.) I tell you I just ran out the door and when I saw my child, fear tried to set in. It was raining so hard, all I could do was drive and pray I told the devil he was a lie, he was not going to get my baby. I asked God to help her to see [that life is worth living]. I prayed that He would move that boy out of her life. Words cannot describe how I was feeling. This was on a Friday and I went to church that Sunday; I was praising God and crying I could not stop crying. My Pastor did not tell the congregation what had happen, but he told some of the women to just go over to where I was; he said: "Just love on her nothing else and you don't need to know what's going on."

I know that God knows what's going to go on even before we

know. I just thank Him for how He keeps us in our right mind, even when the enemy tries to make us go crazy. I never would have thought in a million years that my daughter would do something like that. I am grateful for my niece for getting her home (to me) so fast. My niece said that she saw my daughter "looking real weird" and that she was driving crazy (not staying on the road) so she asked her to let her drive; she was scared but, thankfully she didn't panic "God had it all covered."

Sometimes we have to look beyond what we see in a person and see what God sees. I was so focused on disliking that boy and yelling at her about him that I missed seeing what she was going through. I went back up to the hospital to talk to her to find out what was going on in her head. She grabbed me: hugging me, crying and saying that she was sorry and she wanted to go home. I told her that even if I wanted to take her home, by law when someone tries to kill themselves they have to go through all the procedures I told her that I'd stay there with her. She said that she had taken some of the old pills that the doctor had been mailing to me for pain after I had the accident on the job. The company doctor was mailing them to me monthly and I would just throwing them in a box not taking them, because they were drugs. I know (now) that I should have destroyed them a long time ago. The enemy used those prescription drugs to try to make my daughter kill herself (but, God be the glory; it didn't work). I felt guilt about that for a long time I went home and threw all those pills in the trash. When my daughter returned home I did not want her out of my site. My father was dead and then this happened; it did not stop there.

About a month later, a good friend of mine came over with another friend that we both had known for a longtime: They were high on heroin. They were talking to me about being tired of doing what they were doing so I ministered to them the way God spoke to my heart, and I told them that I wanted to keep in touch with them (I really wanted to help them.) One of them was an old running buddy of mine from back in the day (a month went by and I had not heard from her).

One day I received a phone call telling me that she was dead I was told that her [live-in-boyfriend] shot her in the chest and, watched her die (before he called the police). They said she had dragged herself from her bedroom to the hallway where she died. I said: "That sick bastard!" I was so mad and so hurt it was all over some damn dope! All I thought about was him standing over her waiting for her to die. How in the hell can someone do that? I tried to call her daughter to see how she was doing. She had a husband that was locked up (and I know he was hurt); I don't know why she was with that guy and letting him stay there in her house. They had her funeral that following week. I said: "Lord, this has been a year!!!"

But it did not stop there. My mother took sick about mid-August; she had gotten where she had to have people coming in to take care of her. My stepfather had left my mom and married a younger woman (the home-wrecker); my mother's heart was broken. [The home-wrecker] was the daughter of one of her friends at the church; they all belonged to the same church. She was a hussy; she had been cheating on her husband with my stepfather; it's very sad that (two families were broken because of them).

My mother got real mean when she got sick she already was a curser. She would make all the home care workers mad to the point that they did not want to visit her. I would go over and clean her house and take the abuse that no one else would put up with; my mother acted like she hated me for who I was; I always had respect for her and my father. She always said I was too much like my father's people, plus, I would call her on things when I knew she was wrong.

My mom would come to our church and she'd talk about everybody in the building; she said we all were going to hell for wearing pants to church. But she liked my pastor and she would try and tell him stuff about me. I don't know why things went so wrong with her and her relationship with God. Pastor told me that, the God in me was fighting with the devil that was trying to destroy her he said you are the closest thing for her to lash out at. I don't

know why my other sisters and brothers were not around to help. Sometimes SG would visit her (as I said earlier she loved him); he would always take her side, right or wrong and she liked that.
He said he did it to make her feel good. I told him that, that was not helping her. He used to call me super religious Carolin who thinks she's all that. I told him my mother needed to come to terms with what's going on so she could get better. I was fighting for my mother's soul the enemy was really trying to destroy her.

We went to the hospital one night and the doctor told me that there was nothing else they could do for her but I did not want to accept that because I knew that God had healed her from cancer over 40 years ago. The doctor said that she had a lung disease that they could not do anything about.

My niece (who was like a daughter to my mother) came down and took her back to Colorado with her; she said there was a good lung hospital there. When my mother was in Colorado things were going good for her until she wanted to go back to Wichita.

After she went back home, her health began to decline. She was staying in an apartment on 21st in Shady Brook she did not like living there. She said: "there were too many sick people there." Her sister stayed in the same building and she would try and help mama as much as she could; she was older than my mother. She'd try and talk to my mother about her meanness. I felt bad for mama because she would run everybody away (from her), but! No matter what she said to me I would never leave her without care.

SG continued to help with her, from time to time. I said to her: "you are always talking crazy to me and talking about me to other people" I also said: "when everybody else is gone I will be the only one who will always be here for you." I said that because one day I had left her apartment and when I returned, a friend of hers who had come to help me give her a bath, was already there, I overheard mama talking (bad) about all of her kids, especially me I was so mad when I went in I said: "how dare you talk about us like that." The lady left and mama tried to grab me (she tried to pull me towards her). I told her that she was wrong and she started crying and asking me to forgive her; she said she was sorry I was so hurt I had to leave before I said something real crazy I did not like to disrespect my parents.

I went back later, because she had no one else. My daughter and one of my nieces would often help me with her. My mother would call me on the phone to come over there in the middle of the night and when I would get there she would tell me something like: "I need a glass of water" I was so tired of her treating me like that. I called my aunt who lived in her building and I cried about it, she said: "Baby, your mother knows she's really sick and she knows that you are the only one who is there for her, it is not that she resents you; it is that you are there for her to take her frustrations out on; she loves you, she really does." I remembered what my pastor had told me something similar a few weeks prior to my aunt's remarks.

I talked to the doctors about her and they said that she should no longer live alone, so I decided to move her to my house. I had the third bedroom set up for her. We put a hospital bed in there with an air mattress so she would not get bed sores. SG gave me a chair that would lift her up so when she sat in the chair it would not be hard to get her out of. I found another agency that sent nurse's aides to help with her care but after a month she ran them off also I told her that she couldn't keep doing that. Her church would send food to the house because she'd call and tell them that I was starving her. She wanted all the [kinds of food] that the doctor told her she could not have and I would not give it to her. One of the ladies from her church would come over sometimes to give me a break so that I could run errands (that was very helpful).

Mama got bad and we had to take her back to the hospital this was about January, 2000; the doctors came in and told me that it was near the end and they were going to send hospice to talk with me. I began to cry; I had a lot to grasp at that time. The doctors told my mother everything.

When we returned home, hospice came over that evening and we got things set up. A Registered Nurse came over to do the paper work and sign the intake forms and whatever else we had to do, then I called everybody to tell them what was going on.

My sister was still incarcerated. In prison you are given a choice; you can go home for a bedside visit or you can wait until they die to go to the funeral she wanted to see mama before she died. I called and made the arrangements for my sister to come (ASAP); they brought her there within 3 days; the doctor had given her less than three months to live but she lived five months.

My sister immediately went into the room and began combing her hair, doing her feet and doing everything she could to comfort her. My sister I can say: she was one of the greatest beauticians that walked this earth. People loved the way she did their hair (black, white or whatever nationality they were, she could do and take care of anyone's hair. She could help people grow hair back that was all broken off). My mother was telling her that I was treating her bad, taking her money and doing with it what I wanted and that I wasn't feeding her (and a lot of other stuff that I was not doing). They let her visit for about 5 hours.

That evening they took her back to prison; my mother got real feisty with me that night she started to rattle the rails on her bed so it would keep us awake, my nephew and my daughter were there and they both had to go to school the next day. My nephew was the son of my oldest sister who passed away. My daughter was in college by then. Mom had raised my nephew; so, when she took sick I had to take him. I still could not understand why my other sisters would not help take care of mama!

My mother belonged to a Seventh Day Adventist Church; it was one of the members who would come over on (some) Sundays so I could go to church. I had missed a lot of church when all of this started, but my pastor's wife would always come over with some of the members, to pray with me.

Every time I would go to church my mother would call an ambulance to take her to the hospital (you are not supposed to go to the hospital after you are on hospice). The lady would come to the church to get me and I would have to leave and go to the hospital. I would be so angry with my mother because she was doing that just to make me mad. I got there and some of her church people were there and they looked at me like I was crazy.

My mother had told them all sorts of lies about me. There was one lady that stood up and said to my mother: "I am not going to sit back and let you do that baby like that because none of what you're saying is true and you know it. She is the only one that has helped you and she is the only one that has taken care of you and none of the rest of them is anywhere to be found." She also said: "you ought to be ashamed of yourself: God loves the truth and I'm not going to let you do her like that another day you are my friend and I love you, so you stop that."

A friend of mama's came over one day and told me to go get some air and she would visit with my mother. My mother looked at her and asked: "what are you doing here with your mule looking a>>?" It was funny, she told my mother: "Sitting with you with your ugly a>>." They got to throwing insults to each other. She was one of the ladies my mother used to hang out with when she and my father divorced. It was a joy to see some laugher even if it was but for a moment.

My sister who lived in Colorado came to visit our mother; she told me that she'd stay with her while I took a break so I went to Bible study that night when I got back my mother was calling out to my sister; she had given her money to buy herself a bottle of liquor and she came back drunk and passed out at the foot of my mother's bed. My mother had gone to the bathroom on herself (I was so mad at my sister) my mother said: "Don't leave me here with her drunk behind anymore" she was no help whatsoever."

Things were really getting bad and I was getting tired. I got to a point where I would just lay in bed and cry at night I kept saying to God, "If this is for me to continue to do, You will have to give me the strength to go on, because I'm tired," she was wearing me and the kids out. I know it was the enemy trying to destroy her soul. I told the devil, "You have destroyed her body, but I'll be damned if I let you take her soul." My pastor's wife or somebody from the church would always call me at the time when I felt I could not go on another moment. I did not want my mother to die as bitter as she was so I fought for her soul.

That next Sunday, she called the ambulance again and the lady came and got me again. The hospital admitted her; she was there for 3 days the doctor told me that hospice could no longer take care of her needs they said that my mother was overbearing and that [you cannot call to go to the hospital while on hospice] I did not understand that but that was their rules so they told me to think about putting her in a home. Well, I did not want that, but I could not take care of my mother by myself. I was still going through some health problems, and lifting her and trying to get her up and down had become more than I could handle (I just could not do it).

I had gotten so stressed from lack of rest and none of my siblings wanted to help. I believe that my sister who was in prison would have helped if she had been home. It was the hardest decision I had to make; but I had to put her in a home. I found a place that had room for her and the hospital transported her there in an ambulance. She begged me to take her home and I told mama that I could not take care of her by myself I know how hurt she felt because everyone was there for my father; but not for her they did not like her fussing and cussing all the time. My thing was, she's still my mother, when all is said and done. God said to honor thy father and mother that your days will be long; so that's what I did for both of my parents no matter what I felt; I did it for them because I loved them.

I tried to visit her every day because in those places they seem to neglect you if you don't have people coming to check on you. She still talked about me to everyone that came to see her. My pastor went to visit her and she told him that I had mistreated her and threw her in there, but everyone knew I had done the best I could for her. My pastor told me, "It was the anointing that the [enemy tried to fight against you] for how you took the stand to put your mother first you denied yourself." I prayed and I asked God to heal her or take her. I was tired of her suffering the way she was; I asked God to: "let her make peace with You before she leaves this earth;" she was not herself and I knew that.

My niece came from Denver to see her and she asked her to take her back to Denver; my niece told her that if she could she would, but she was not in any condition to take that ride. Mama said: "Y'all are going to miss me when I'm gone." Mama told my niece that if she left her there she would not see her anymore. Well, my niece had to return to Denver.

It was on a Wednesday; I was sitting on my back porch: the time was 7:30 AM the phone rang it was the Nursing Home calling to tell me that my mother had passed away during the night: the date was: May 31, 2000 she only lived two weeks after she went to the nursing home.

I called both my pastor and the assistant pastor, who owned a funeral home; they met me at the nursing home. They walked into the room with me, and my mother was lying in a body bag half zipped. I walked over to her and she looked like she was in more peace than I had seen on her in such a long time. After I looked at her and they zipped the bag all the way, I broke down and cried. The assistant pastor embraced me as they prayed for my comfort. It hurts even now to write about this because she suffered so much. But she died [in the Lord] and I knew it and I said, "All I went through was worth seeing that peace on her at the end." I said to God, "I lost my father a year ago and now my mother I thank you for the time you gave me with the both of them."

I knew it was going to be me getting the funeral together, so when I went home I called my niece in Denver and she called my sisters that were there with her. I called the prison to tell my sister and then I called my brothers. My church was a great support to me. I had a hard time making her funeral arrangement but God came through for me. I won't go into all I had to do because that's not important; the only thing I can say is that God will always be there to strengthen you in your time of great need.

My aunt who had lived in the same building as my mother came out to help (as much as she could) although she was not in the best of health herself. I called our relatives in Arkansas and they were making plans to come. I requested that Mama Pumpkin my spiritual mother (the one who had helped me when I got out of prison) sing, she was in Florida at the time but she came. My pastor agreed to do the prayer and my mother's pastor did the eulogy. As I had mentioned before my mother was a member of the Seventh Day Adventist Church. They don't believe in eating meat (I don't know why) all I know is: my mother did not live like that, she loved her meat and she ate it all the time and some of the other ladies did too. Her church wanted to do the food so they did the cooking. The married guy I used to date came over and offered to fix food for the family at my house.

Two days before my mother's funeral more drama came into my life; I got a call saying that my daughter was taken to the police station to be questioned about a murder. At the time I was sitting at the table correcting some information on my mother's obituary (the corrections needed to be done by the next day). Two of my friends were there from the church helping me do some other things when I got the call, that something was terribly wrong; I started SCREAMING they grabbed the phone and said: "she'll be right down." One of the ladies took me downtown to where they were interrogating my daughter; as we were walking up, my daughter was walking out and I just grabbed her and hugged her. She told me the story; it was not what I was told on the phone.
I believed her because I know my daughter and she would not cover up something like a murder, they apparently believed her also because they let her go. I said, "God, I cannot take too much more." My friends were praying for me because they knew I was on overload because I did not have the help of the rest of my family until my niece arrived from Colorado; she got there as fast as she could.

I had not seen SG, for a while, but when the Hearst drove up I saw him standing on the corner looking; I was glad to see him (he's really a good person). My mother had a beautiful funeral; most of my friends from the streets were there and many people from my church were also there. Even though she fussed and would curse you out, people that knew her, loved her for the person she was. She was well known for her cooking all over town.

I had to get her final affairs in order; then there was the issue of her worldly possessions (I had her car and all of her furniture and stuff). I cashed in what she had on her policy to help bury her.

My sisters thought that I had more (but I didn't). If they would have been around they would have known that. When people die, some family members go crazy over material things. I felt that they did not deserve anything (even if I would have had something to give them). They were too busy to even help take care of our mother.

I kept my mother's car [because] I had to finish paying off the loan on another car that was attached to my mom's credit (my mother had cosigned a car loan made for my baby sister's daughter but after my niece wrecked the car, she stopped making the payments on it; my mom's car was already paid for, but the bank had used it as collateral when she cosigned for my niece; the bank would not release the title until my nieces car loan was paid so, I kept making the payments on the car that was wrecked and abandoned by my niece, until it was paid off. I felt justified in keeping both cars (my mom's and the one that would have ruined her good name with the bank). My baby sister thought she was entitled to it but I told them that if they paid for it or gave me the money back for the loan that they could have it. She had the nerve to get mad! I gave her daughter my mother's furniture because, she would come over and help bathed my mom and she'd do things with my daughter to help mama. I had purchased the furniture for my mother, the Christmas before she got sick; almost everything she had I got her. My sister who was in prison had given her lots of things also.

Out of anger my baby sister went into my basement, she took my mother's television, and she broke some things and destroyed my baby picture. I was so mad at her for doing that; my pastor's wife said that I should just pray for her.

After things settled down a bit I began to be active in the church (again). I had really missed fellowshipping. I had my own car, but I let it go back because I did not need three cars. I kept my mother's car and I had the car that once belonged to my niece. I got it fixed and continued making payments on the loan and I kept up the insurance on both cars.

Three months or so had gone by since my mother died I was

really praying a lot. I had gotten myself to where I was doing ok WHEN here come SG again! He came over one day; he was looking pretty wild. He had gone all the way back to being [of the world]. He had been drinking and getting high, he had lost the store and was about to lose his house. He was still messing around with the woman who was responsible for my house getting burned down (way back when). (I am glad that I got out of that store but I felt bad for him.)

I ended up cutting his hair and fixing dinner for him. He was behind on his mortgage and all of his utilities had been cutoff so I let him stay in my 3rd bedroom. He said that he wanted to get back to where he was [with the Lord]. He had done so much for me before he got himself into the situation that he was in; as I said before I really loved him I felt that God had a purpose for us together I felt he was called to preach. His whole family was men and women who loved God.

I tried not to get myself back involved with him in anyway, other than ministering to him. He still had respect for me as always, I appreciated that. God had a great call on my life and I knew that the enemy was trying to really move me from where God wanted me to be. The pastor had prophesied in my life that the enemy was scared of me. He also told me that it was a great anointing on my life and that the devil was literally trying to cut me off at the knees! He told me that people did not understand why I praised God the way I did. He said, "If they only knew where God had brought you from they would be praising God too." I keep saying it but I enjoyed serving at the church.

SG started going back to church and he was also looking for a job. He and my daughter got along very well; he would not disrespect her at all. My nephew was staying with me and he would talk with him a lot. People saw a man in my house, but we were not sleeping together, I had been teaching my daughter and nephew that sex (outside marriage) is not ordained by God I was trying to teach them to respect themselves (I had become celibate and had been since 1995). My daughter slept in my room with me along with the baby. God was really dealing with SG; I was glad because I knew that God could change him. He finally found a job, working security at Wal-Mart. He earned enough money to pay his bills and get himself together, so he moved back into his house. He had a friend who would always try to set him up with women.

The womanizing started all over again. He invited a woman to church one Sunday but he wasn't there himself because he had to work. I went to his job as usual to take him a sandwich and I saw her leaving the security car parking spot and she saw me; SG got really short with me [like I had messed up something] I guess I was cramping his style. Next thing I knew, they were together and he had moved her into his house.

I had a key, so one day I went over there and he had changed the locks. I had the [keys] because I would go over there to work on the clocks with him (we had been trying to get that off and running again). I called him, and he said he had other things that he wanted to do. I didn't say anything; I just hung up. I called my pastor's wife and I told her what he had done. I guess he wanted someone he could have sex with (It hurt but what can you do)! Some men can be dogs!!! She said: "I told you a leopard never changes his stripes, they just move them around." Things did not work out the way he thought they would. People told that lady that the only person he really loved since his wife died was Carolin.

I ran into him and her one day and you could have bought him for a nickel he was so embarrassed; he didn't know what to say. He tried to tell me [they were business partners].

I used to pray that God would let him see who He was in him. His family was mad at the way he treated me. I personally felt that he was running from himself; he was trying to forget about his wife who had died. He was a man who had loved being married; he had a heart of gold, but he was a hell of a person to deal with. The woman, who moved in, turned his house upside down; she was trying to remodel it and she did; it was a mess.

SG took out a 2nd mortgage he had put her name on the mortgage; that made them co-owners (he ended up being indebted to her) things did not go well for them. I don't know why; but, he ended up back to me. And again, I don't know why, but I kept taking him back! I knew in my heart, that he really cared for me. He wanted a better paying job after we got back together).

One day my daughter came in when he was at my house; she told him that she had seen a help wanted sign at apartment complex on 23 in Oliver. He went over there and applied for the job and he got it he was hired as a maintenance man; he was very good at fixing things. They really loved his work and he had favor with the boss and the people who owned the building. He asked me to marry him and I said yes; so the next day we went ring shopping. He was attracted to the biggest ring in the place (the shiny object). I on the other hand wanted something less ostentatious (I did not like over-sized rings) all I wanted was something delicate and small. SG was the type of person who wanted people to think that he was important; I felt that people should be able to see who you are in Christ: the Holy Spirit will make you shine (we were exact opposites).

I always admired his first wife after she became a woman of God. I know he had gone through a lot with her death and all, so we would talk about her life and the things that I was going through. As I mention before I felt that she and I had a lot in common as far as ministry.

He finally decided to go through her things and share them with family. I began to plan the wedding; he said that I could have the kind of wedding I wanted. As I said before, I really loved his kids. There always was a special bond between his daughter and son and myself and his grandchildren. My granddaughter was with us a lot when my daughter was at work and also when she was trying to get her nurses aid license. So my grandbaby grew up calling him her papa, he was all she knew. She really loved him and always wanted to be around him. His grandkids my granddaughter basically grew up together.

We would take trips to visit his children and go shopping at a name brand discount store. He would buy me anything I wanted. He became a true father head in my family his flaw was his temper. His daughter would always tell him that he needed to calm down I would also tell him not to let things get to him; he would blow things all out of proportion and then he'd apologize.

His temper got so bad that it would stress me out and I would say to myself do I want to live like this the rest of my life!
I remembered how he was before, and it [stayed] in the back of my mind.

I loved ministering to people; I would go to different places praying for people and he would go with me. He would always let me pray for the people; he would just stand back and watch. One day he told me that when we got married that I was going to have to stop a lot of that, and that I would have to learn to submit to him; the problem was not submitting; it was how he came to me wanting me to put God second; after him. That's the way I took it and I was not going to do that. He did an awful lot for me but I was not the type of woman who would be willing to put a man over the MAN. I was not going to stop doing what I loved best (and that was putting God above all others even a husband).

SG would serve in the church and he was faithful in whatever he committed himself to do (he did excellent work and he did it in a timely manner). He was a very neat and clean person; his house was always clean and in order. He was fun loving and playful; he'd keep you laughing; but sometimes he would make people mad.
He was an ideal man [with the exception of his temper] and his desire to take total control of our relationship after marriage.

He was there for me through some of my trials and tests and I'm grateful for that I have great respect for him. He was an important part of my life. God will always be with us through any storm. Having gone through the death of my sister, my parents and my best friend made me stronger (I still miss them all).

I wrote this next chapter on prayer. The power of prayer helped me. It really took me from Prison to Purpose in chapter 12. God watched over my life for all of these years because of prayer. Prayer is a much God given purpose to all who will embrace its power; keep praying people around you; the ones that you know can tap into the spirit ram. Prayer is a daily lifestyle we should always keep in communion with God. The next section talks about grief. Sometime in our lives we will all have to cross that path.

Grief

Grief is oh so real. God wants and expects us to grieve when we are broken-hearted. We have to express our grief. If we don't, it will bring some complex emotions and it can cause physical illness. Grief is not forever, but we go through it when we lose someone who is dear to us. Jesus can identify with us because He is a man of sorrow and knows grief. He also understands when we are hurting. Our grief is healed by our promise of God's unfailing grace. Let's look at 2 Corinthians 12:9: "And he said unto me, My grace is sufficient for thee; for my strength is made perfect in weakness." God sent strong men and women around me and he gave me His word. Although many of them are gone, God will always be there for us. Here are some scriptures to look at. How Jesus handled it. Matthew 14:13-14 2. Don't be ashamed to grieve 2 Samuel 1:11, 12. Finding the freedom to grieve Genesis 50:1-11.
We will all face death one day.

IT TRULY WAS GOD"S GRACE AND MERCY

Chapter 11

Prayer

This Chapter will be a blessing to all who allows God to minister to their spirit man; the power of prayer has helped me to endure and to learn from my own trials and tests. I was raised around prayer from both sides of my family, they believed in the power of prayer.

I thank God for all the things that my parents did for us when we were young. We can overcome any obstacle in our path through prayer and petition to God. God's word is more powerful than any two-edged sword Hebrews 4:12 that might try to cut through our joy.

The enemy tried hard to demolish me, but, because of: God's mercy and His grace. I have been tried and tested, and I thank God that I have come out on the other side of righteousness.

I have been scorched, banged up and bruised but not nearly as much as our LORD and Savior Jesus Christ was when He came here to pay our sin debt on the cross. You see, anything that comes into a child of Gods life has got to come through God's hands first. Yes, that's right; Satan has to get permission from God first. In Job 1:11 the action against Job was attributed to the hand of God. There is nothing that Satan can do to us that falls outside of God's dominion. Job 1:12 tells us that Satan's power is limited by God. God's full intention for our lives is to allow testing to prove His (Gods) strength and not our own. God has promised that everyone who believes on Him will not be tempted beyond what they can bear.

We should not fear Satan because God's Word is more powerful than anything that he could ever say or do to us. Speech is powerful. The spoken word can encourage or discourage. We have to open our mouths with wisdom which requires [studying His word]: Proverbs 16: 20 say "He who heeds the word wisely will find good and whoever trusts in the Lord, happy is he. When we pray God's will we are repeating His promise to us (we are only repeating what He already said). God Only responds to His Own Word (His own will). Prayer brings peace and contentment into our lives and it gives us the strength to avoid yielding to temptation (whatever the temptation may be).

God has a plan for all of our lives if we listen to Him. Proverbs 19: 20 (KJV) says: "Hear counsel, and receive instruction, that thou mayest be wise in thy latter end." Jesus spoke the Word when He was tempted by Satan. "Then Jesus led up of the Spirit into the wilderness to be tempted of the devil" Matt 4:1 (When Jesus was tempted (by Satan) He said: [Matthew 4:4] "It is written..." In Matthew 26:41 He tells us to watch and pray. 1Thessalonians 5:17, says to: "pray without ceasing." It is really very important that we should always pray for one another. James 5:16, tells us to: "Confess your trespasses to one another and pray for one another, that you may be healed. The effective fervent prayer of a righteous man avails much."

Prayer is a powerful weapon that we all can use in our lives. Jesus gave us a model prayer; Matthew 6:6,7 says: "But you, when you pray, go into your room, and when you have shut your door, pray to your Father who is in the secret place; and your Father who sees in the secret place will reward you openly." V7 "And when you pray, do not use vain repetitions as the heathen do. For they think that they will be heard for their many words." God knows what is in our hearts and He hears our prayers through our Mediator (His Son Jesus). [Continual prayer is the secret to accomplishment.]

The goal is not to have a fixed time to pray. The goal or purpose is for us to communicate with God. Sometimes we need to fast and pray. Fasting combined with prayer, allows our bodies to be totally dependent on manna from heaven rather than groceries from the A&P. Matthew 17: 16-21 says, "Lord, have mercy on my son, for he is an epileptic and suffers severely; for he often falls into the fire and often into the water." V16 "So I brought him to Your disciples, but they could not cure him." V17 "Then Jesus answered and said, O faithless and perverse generation, how long shall I be with you? How long shall I bear with you? Bring him to Me." V18 "Jesus rebuked the demon, and it came out of him; and the child was cured from that very hour." V19 "Then the disciples came to Jesus privately and said, Why could we not cast it out?" V20 "Jesus said to them, Because of your unbelief; for assuredly, I say to you, if you have faith as a mustard seed, you will say to this mountain, Move from here to there, and it will move, and nothing will be impossible for you." V21 "However, this kind does not go out except by prayer and fasting;"

1 Timothy 4:4-5. "For every creature of God is good, and nothing to be refused, if it be received with thanksgiving:" V5 "For it is sanctified by the word of God and prayer." We must pray with confidence: True confidence rooted in the Lord's capabilities and His relationship with His children is a quiet strength that brings "great reward", a lasting security that is fully satisfying.

The Woman's Study Bible helped me a lot to study the word of God for my life.

Prayers in action

These are some things that prayer is to me:

Prayer is gratitude; Father I thank You for all of the adversities and trials that You allowed to come into my life in order to mold me into the person that you want me to be.

Prayer bestows upon us a: Thankful spirit. Father I just thank You for who You are. I'm grateful because You changed me. You have given me love and a heart to reach others.

Prayer is God given to us all: Heavenly Father, without You, I am nothing. We pray to Him expressing our total dependence on Him. I thank God for giving me hope where there was none. He changed my hopelessness into hopefulness. God has given all of us the power to make the impossible reality. [God Has] a plan and purpose for our lives and every day I thank Him for what He is already doing in my life and in the lives of the people He gives me to pray for and with and for those He allows me to intercede for to Christ.

Prayer is an Attitude adjuster: It should always occupy a place in our [hearts] and in our homes.
Prayer is and should be a lifestyle: It should be the first thing we do when we awake.

Praying and getting results: we have to become pure, clean and open before God when praying for ourselves and others.
All we need to do is pray God's word from our heart and we will always get results. Sometimes God says: "Yes," "No," "Grow," or "Not now." But He always answers our prayers. We always have to come to God with a sincere heart not just lip service. We have to pray Gods will because He knows what's best for His children. We are His children we have to allow God to build His character in us. We have to remove our flesh and self. God will accept us just as we are; we must come clean before God. We cannot come before him puffed up. John 15:3 Jesus said, "Now ye are clean through the word which I have spoken unto you." God's word helps us to become who He [says] we are (through Him).
When we pray we are admitting that we are nothing without God; our best is as filthy rags.
The name of Jesus makes Satan tremble (there is power is His name). We are righteous because of Christ.
James 5:16 says, "The effectual fervent prayer of a righteous man avails much."

1. ***Prayer helps us to overcome temptations***. Read Genesis 3:1-6 and Matthew 26:40-41 say's "Then he came to the Disciples and found them sleeping, and said to Peter, What? Could you not watch with Me one hour?" V41 "Watch and pray, lest you enter into temptation. The spirit is indeed willing, but the flesh is weak."

2. ***We must balance our prayer with actions.*** Exodus 14:15. "And the Lord said to Moses," Why do you cry to Me? Tell the children of Israel to go forward."

3. ***God keeps His promises to us.*** 1Samuel 1:11 Hannah made a vow to the Lord, she said, "O Lord of hosts, if You will indeed look on the affliction of Your maidservant, and remember me, and not forget Your maidservant, but will give Your maidservant a male child, then I will give him to the Lord all the days of his life, and no razor shall come upon his head."

4. ***Make sure that you really want what you pray for.*** Moses interceded to God for the people. Numbers 14:17-19. "And now, I pray, let the power of my Lord be great just as You have spoken, saying," V18 "The Lord is longsuffering and abundant in mercy, forgiving iniquity and transgression; but He by no means clears the guilty, visiting the iniquity of the fathers on the children to the third and fourth generation." V19 "Pardon the iniquity of this people, I pray, according to the greatness of Your mercy, just as You have forgiven this people, from Egypt even until now"

5. ***The Disciples asked Jesus to teach them how to pray.*** Luke 11:1, "Now it came to pass, as He was praying in a certain place, when He ceased, that one of His disciples said to Him, Lord, teach us to pray, as John also taught his disciples."

Our Words are our Battle Ground

Proverbs 18:20 tells us that, "Death and life are in the power of the tongue; and they that love it shall eat the fruit thereof."
Luke 6:45 says that: "A good man out of the good treasure of his heart bringeth forth that which is good; and an evil man out of the evil treasure of his heart bringeth forth that which is evil; for out of the abundance of the heart his mouth speaketh."

What we speak and where we are is the fruit of what we have spoken with our mouth in faith; whether it was spoken negative or

positive. Our mouth speaks whatever is in our hearts.
The environment we create or that we change is by the faith filled words that we speak.

God has given us the power through the [words we speak] to change everything in our lives.

You can tell what is in a person's heart by what and where they spend their time.

God's Word spoken in faith, can change our destiny (from eternal damnation to eternal life with Jesus Christ, our LORD and Savior). Philippians 4:13 tells us that: "I can do all things through Christ which strengthens me." We have to keep our priorities straight remembering to be grateful for everything God have given us.

Words are so important. We have to think before we speak, Proverbs 15:28
What we speak reveals what's in our hearts Matthew 12:34-36
Let our speech always be with grace. Colossians 4:6
Why we should use them carefully, Psalm 15:3-4
We have to use the power that has been given to us. Don't let your words destroy you. Make them work for your good.

Love with a Pure Heart

1 John 3:16: "By this we know love, because He laid down His life for us. And we also ought to lay down our lives for the brethren." V17 "But whoever has this world's goods, and sees his brother in need, and shuts up his heart from him, how does the love of God abide in him?" V18 "My little children let us not love in word or in tongue, but indeed and in truth." V19 "And by this we know that we are of the truth, and shall assure our hearts before Him." Love is the most positive evidence to see if a person is really in Christ. In Matthew 5:8 Jesus affirms the "pure in heart" is the true happiness in loving God with our whole hearts. Psalm 51:10
says: "Create in me a clean heart, O God; and renew a right spirit within me." We must ask God to cleanse us from within; clear our hearts for new thoughts, not things that destroy us. 1John 3:3

says: "Anyone who has this hope in Him purifies himself, just as He is pure." A pure life will not and cannot exist without a pure heart set on God.

*We have to love, it is not an option. 1John 3:11: "For this is a message that you heard from the beginning, that we should love one another." *We have to demonstrate our love. 1John 4:7 "Beloved, let us love one another, for love is of God; and everyone who loves is born of God and knows God." *Love will cause a person to respond with love to others. 1John 4:21 "Beloved, if our heart does not condemn us, we have confidence toward God." God is the definition of real love. Without God, love does not exist. That's why we can read John 3:16 and know that He really and truly loved us all. There is nothing that you and I can do to change God's love for us. That is why I am so grateful that He loved me and saved me, from myself. 1John 3:1 says: "Behold, what manner of love the Father hath bestowed upon us, that we should be called the sons of God; therefore the world knoweth us not, because it knew Him not." We are all God's children and by Him loving us, it should really encourage us to strive to live as Christ did.

The Lord's Prayer

This is how Jesus taught His disciples to pray: Matthew 6:9-13

"Our Father which art in heaven:" ***We have to recognize who God really is.***

"Hallowed be Thy name;" ***Praise Him just for who He is in our lives.***

"Thy Kingdom come, Thy will be done in earth as it is in heaven:" ***Doing God's will, will reveal our purpose.***

"Give us this day our daily bread;" ***We are petitioning God to meet the needs in our lives***. "And forgive us our debts, as we forgive our debtors." ***We are asking God to forgive all of our failures and debts against Him as we forgive others their failures and debts against us.***

"And lead us not into temptation, but deliver us from evil;" ***We are asking God to help us avoid temptation and to give us strength to overcome it.***

"For thine is the kingdom, and the power and the glory, forever. Amen."

We have to praise Him. In order for our prayers to work we have to learn to walk in forgiveness, be pure before the Lord in all areas of our lives. We have to become clean before Him. We cannot go before God any kind of way. God's Word says: that it is a person's heart that determines whether we are clean or not.

God has to build His character in us. We have to bind the flesh by the power of the Holy Spirit so that God can manifest His Glory. I always ask God to help me decrease so he can increase in my life. God is beginning a process of completing our salvation. 1Peter 2:1-5 "Wherefore laying aside all malice, and all guile, and hypocrisies, and envies, and all evil speaking." V2 As newborn babes, desire the sincere milk of the word, that ye may grow thereby:" V3 "If so be ye have tasted that the Lord is gracious." V4 "To whom coming, as unto a living stone, disallowed indeed of men, but chosen of God, and precious," V5. Ye also, as lively stones, are built up a spiritual house, a holy priesthood, to offer up spiritual sacrifices, acceptable to God by Jesus Christ." God's word nourishes us and helps us to grow in Him. In John 15:3 Jesus said: "Now ye are clean through the word which I have spoken unto you."

Chapter 12

From Prison to Purpose

My purpose was born out of all the pain and the trials that I brought upon myself. Learning, forgiveness and extending mercy to others as God has extended His mercy to me was my new birth.

People will hinder your progress if you're not firmly rooted and grounded in God's grace and love. We can't blame others when we make our own trails and bumps in the road. God does not direct evil against us; all though he may allow us to go through some trials that have resulted from our own sinful choices or from the sins of the world in which we live. Gen 50:20 says: "But as for you, ye thought evil against me; but God meant it unto good, to bring to pass, as it is this day, to save much people." (See: Jeremiah 1: 5-10).

God brought good out of all the evil and negativity that He allowed to come into my life. The evil in our lives will bring good for those who trust in Him. God taken away all of the evil in my life and replaced it with good. God's gift of mercy towards me was extended to me when I placed my faith in Him; God canceled all of the judgments against me, and He remembers them no more. Everything that we go through ***before*** we surrender to God and ***accept*** His Son Jesus was done outside God's grace, but thank God we saw the light in time, before it was too late. Our purpose as Christians is to learn from our mistakes.

I was still at the church that I had attended since 1995.
I was still with SG although our relationship was not good. It was up and down all the time; more than I should have allowed. We attended a singles ministry at the church an awesome couple presided over it. SG didn't like it because he felt that we were not single (because we were engaged to be married) I on the other hand thought that until we said I do, that [I] was still single and God was still the head of my life.

A man from the church planned weddings (and or made wedding dresses) he was a very gifted and talented man of God, and he was married to a very sweet woman. I had a visual idea of the dress and veil that I wanted him to make for me so I gave him a description and he said that he could do it; so we gave him a down payment.

I reached a point where I was becoming more and more stressed although I couldn't quit put my hand on the problem. I really loved SG (I mean really). I couldn't understand why he would always fly off the handle. I had a loving relationship with his children and grandchildren; my daughter and grand baby loved him; so what could be the dilemma! (My mother would have been happy had she lived to see us planning our wedding.) A lot of people thought we belonged together (I did too).

An apostle would attend our church sometime and she would always prophecy [to him]. I knew he had a calling on his life, but he didn't take it seriously all he wanted to do was stay in the shadow just serving, doing things not ministering. As I said before, we would go places and he would always put me up front to pray or whatever was needed as far as ministry was concerned I was puzzled by that, but if anyone needed anything to be done he was the man to call.

I could not forget that he told me that I wouldn't be doing "all that ministering once we got married," and that I would have to learn to submit to him as my husband. That really didn't set with me to well. The problem with that was I know how to submit to a man of God: Paul said: "Be ye followers of me, even as I also *am* of Christ" 1 Corinthians 11:1. I felt that he was not doing all that he knew God wanted him to do. The apostle told him one time that God was going to take running out of his feet. He went out under the power and he wept; later that day he was back to his old self again; I would get so mad at him.

His brother (who was our pastor) told me that he was high maintenance (for attention) and that I was not going to be able to serve in the ministry the way I desired. My pastor said, "Sister, you love God too much I don't think it would work. I love my brother but I have to tell you the truth." (All of this kind of talk was weighing heavy on my heart; I had a lot on my mind.) I was receiving prophecy after prophecy I was hesitant to receive some of the chatter. You know: the devil is terrified of those who love the LORD. I've been told that: "I bankrupted the devil." Some people have said that I was being held back.

One Sunday evening I went to the singles ministry (he didn't go with me) I was so stressed that the woman of God who was over the ministry watched me. (Her husband wasn't with her that time.) After it was over, she said, "Sis, can I talk to you?" I said: "sure" so, we went outside; after everybody left. She looked at me and took both of my hands and she said: "you know I love you and brother man with all my heart and what I'm getting ready to say doesn't change my love for him," I said: "OK." She said: "You don't want to marry that man, do you?" She said: "planning for a wedding should be a happy event, knowing you're marrying the person you love, but! I don't see that in you." I told her: "No, I don't." I told her why; she said she knew it all along. She said that God showed her that I had an anointing of deliverance on my life she told me that she sees me praying for people and God was delivering sick people, people getting out of wheel chairs, women getting pregnant that the doctors said they would never have kids, a lot of things were spoken into my life from her, and also my pastor. She told me that I needed a man of God that could pray me through after I have [put out] so much from being on the missions that God was sending me on; she said, "Baby, he is not the one." I just looked at her with tears in my eyes because I knew most of what she was speaking was true. I just wanted him to change and I thought he would.

After we finished talking I left and went to where he was and I really didn't have that much to say. We went out to dinner that following weekend; we were sitting and talking. He grabbed my hand and looked at me and said, "Are you ready to spend the rest of your life with me?" It was like I froze! He looked me in the eye and said, "You can't even answer that; you are taking too long." I can't really remember how the conversation went after that but the wedding was canceled. He was so up and down with me that I just couldn't deal with the stress that I was under from being with him. I can still say he was a good man and I really did love him, but I knew that I had to be obedient to God. My pastor told me to leave the fruit on the tree because it was not ripe, yet. We continued being friends. It was like we always found ourselves around one another. He would always get mad at me about old boy friends (I remained friends with everybody I dated in the past). I always had men in my life that were [just friends].

I started doing a lot more in the church I tried to serve as much as I could. I started going to different places speaking about my past life (as God was leading me to give my testimony) I went back to the El-Dorado County Jail and spoke there.

I met up with five (white) men who were involved in Prison Fellowship and I began to go to some of their meetings I liked what they were doing. They had a special program (for the prison in El-Dorado). Some of the men that had been in prison were singing in the program. I was introduced to the men by the young woman that I talked about earlier in my book (that I met when we were inmates in the same jail) they were going into the county jail there, just like the people who came to see me. It was amazing! I was the only woman that would go into the jail with them.

The following week I went to the women's side and they went to minister to the men. I was talking to a woman who said that she and her boyfriend had received fifty years for killing her mother. She set it up and he killed her. I was kind of blown away by what she told me, but I didn't let her see my shock. When you are witnessing for God you have to (try to) leave all those emotions out. She was very hurt by what she had done and she wanted to give her life to the LORD. I gave her what God told me to say to her; the rest of them that were there were listening then I started to sing and it was so amazing! One of the jailers remembered my voice and came in and said: "It's you! I recognized that voice right off!" He said: "I was one of the ones that worked here when you were in here back in 1979 you made a great impression on all of us here." He said he'd talk to me when I finished with the ladies.

I was telling them about my stay in that same jail; we prayed and then I left. The men that went up there with me said that when I began to speak everyone stopped to listen. Someone turned on all the speakers; that day I was able to minister to both the men and the women. God is awesome! I was glad that God used me that evening. To have one of the guards remember me after all those years! It was overwhelming. All we have to do is be willing and ready and God will place the right people in our path (at the right time). Doors were opening for me so that I could witness.

I ended up speaking at Junior High schools, High Schools, and the Youth Residents Hall. God was allowing my testimony to be heard in many places. God used my past to [jerk the hearts] of young people in need of the guidance that I rejected all those years ago, when I was their age. WOW! I couldn't comprehend a lot of it but if God said it, I had to believe it.

As I mentioned before my daughter's baby's father was in a gang. There was always something going on with that young man. He thought I was crazy because I would tell him what the Lord said (in His Word) and I'd tell him how I felt (in a nice-nasty way). I don't think there's such a thing as nice nasty but it sounds appropriate to me.

I began to have a lot of contact with gang members. My nephew had gotten involved in gangs real bad (my deceased sister's son). I had moved to a bigger house on the other side of Oliver Street, one of my brother's friends owned the house and said that I could move in with the intention to let me buy it, it was a beautiful home and I really loved it. I always got nice places in order to make sure the kids had a safe place to stay. I tried to help them to do something with their lives; the girls would listen, but the boys in our family were hardheaded; I don't know what to say about them. I always tried to be everyone's sanctuary but I ended up regretting a lot of stuff (I did).

My sister got paroled to me she and I hadn't had a real relationship for a long time because she used to use my name and I went to jail in her place a few times. She couldn't understand why I was no longer angry about it. God had changed my heart; I was a new creation in Christ I told her that I forgave her with all my heart; I don't think she believed me. You can't live and be effective for Christ when you are holding bitterness and un-forgiveness in your heart. My desire was to grow spiritually and be a representative for Jesus. 1 Corinthians 5:17 says" If anyone be in Christ he is a new creation, old things have passed away and behold all things become new." My sister really couldn't understand my new-life. The house was big enough that she had her own room and the hall bathroom. There were two full baths and a half bath I told her that she could live there as long as she did not bring any kind of trouble to my house. I meant all of it because I love all my family. My baby sister has been strange ever since mama died.

Around 3 AM one morning the phone rang; it was a young woman from the Chicago gang; they were looking for my nephew I told her he was not there; she said, "When you see him next he will be cut up in little bitty pieces." I said, "Young lady can I say something to you?" She said, "No, B>>> let me tell you something, you can die too!" I told her that I was not scared of her, because my house and all its contents had been ordained by the Holy Ghost; she hung up and I prayed the 91st Psalm over my house I said, "ANGELS TAKE YOUR POST!" I also quoted Isaiah 41:10 then I made a phone call to my pastor. He prayed and agreed with me and we rebuked death off of my nephew.

That same night my sister came in with this girl; she said that the girl's nephew had been beat up by gangs and was in the hospital in a coma she said that she was trying to cheer her up. I told her about the phone call that I had just received and she started talking real crazy. She said I know plenty of gang members and that she was going to go get a gun from one of them and she would wait for them to come there. I told her no she will not bring that mess to my house because my grandbaby was there (my daughter was at work and God had already covered me). She told me I was crazy. I said this is my house and that's what I believe. I asked her, "How can you cheer anybody up talking like that?" God told me to get that young lady and bring her into my room and pray for her, so I did; after I prayed, they left and I went to bed. I didn't let fear take me that night.

The next morning the lady that I had prayed with the night before call me and asked me to come to the hospital because they were getting ready to turn the life support off her nephew and she wanted me to pray with his mother I said OK. I didn't want to go by myself, so I called my pastor's wife she said, "Baby, I would go with you but I can't right now" so she prayed with me and told me I would be OK. I started driving towards the hospital and fear came over me. I tried to call another one of my prayer partners, she said: "Sis, you know I would go but I can't at this moment." I was talking to the LORD and He began to minister to me (He took me again to Isaiah 41:10). He said I did not give you a spirit of fear. It seemed so powerful when the WORD came to me. Then he took me back to Jeremiah 1:5-10 I said OK Lord; I had to repent from questioning Him. I knew if He was sending me (to minister to the mother at the hospital) that everything has already been set.

I knew that more gang members would be up there. When I arrived the first person I saw was my sister and her friend, so she showed me where his mother was and I went over to sit beside her. I said, God I am trusting in you, because I don't have a clue as to what I'm supposed to say (to this lady). God said give her part of your testimony, so she will know that you weren't just another person coming to her to talk about God. There was a person up there from some church; they were sitting and crying with her. I'm not going to lie, that pissed me off! The Holy Ghost arose up in me and the confidence of God came over me; I was able to speak with the power of knowing that His glory was going to reveal and shine in that hospital that day.

There was a young woman in there that was so bitter, that I really hurt for her. His mother had told me she herself had a physical problem that she had been bleeding for more than a month. God told me to lay hands on her and pray healing in her body. I said Lord, what if I do and nothing happens? God said just do it and quit questioning me. I asked those gathered if anyone else wants to pray? (There were about 4 people in the room,) and they all accepted my invitation except that bitter young lady

(I prayed for her anyway).

After we prayed; I did what God said, I asked her if it was all right to go see her son; she replied yes. I went into his room and began to sing to him all of a sudden, I heard someone coming down the hall praying in the Holy Ghost it was my prayer partner. I was so glad to see her; God knew when I would need help.

All of those gang members that were his friends came up there at the moment she arrived; the hospital employees were scared. They smelled like weed and some of them were talking crazy. The hospital was afraid to tell them that all of them [could not be in there at the same time] so, they called security and let them tell them.

Two of the gang members went into the room with me and my friend. One of them leaned over the patient and the other one stood on the other side of the bed. My friend asked them their names and the one who was leaning over him did not raise his head, but gave us his name. She looked at the other one and asked him name and he told her, she told him that she had a son that had his same name. She prophesied some things to him and he just looked at her. She said you have been told that before, haven't you? He said, yes.

We finished in there and God told me to pray for all of those gang members. I said, "God they are not going to listen to me" God said just do it. So I walked to where they all were, I told them that I wanted to pray for them, and I told them: if any of you want to come in this room come. [At my amazement] all of them came in (except that same young lady). [The Holy Spirit] told me to tell them not to retaliate against the other gang. I spoke to them about all the senseless killing among them and I asked them why they continue to allow the enemy to destroy them? They respectfully listened. God got the glory in there that day and many were blessed.

I began to thank God for the spirit of obedience in me, that day at that moment. I said bye to his mother then we left, this was on a Tuesday and that following Friday at the club on 13th street in Wichita Kansas two more of them were killed in a shootout.

Guess who was in the middle of it all? My sister! She said she had to get up under a car. One of the ones that was in the room with me and my friend got killed, and one other one.

They turned the machine off of the young man that was in the hospital and his mother wanted me to come speak at his funeral (it was not for me to do); I declined. She told me that when she went to the doctor, her bleeding had stopped and the doctor could not find anything wrong. God proved Himself to her that day.

The next week or two some gang members came over to my house. My nephew and other gang members all over town were playing with fire. Black on black crime was running amok; kids were robbing members of other gangs at gun point; their young lives were indeed spiraling out of control. I talked to the three who came to my house; I told them that they were jeopardizing their future; they listened.

The next day, my nephew showed up and I told him that he was playing with his life and everyone around him. I ended up sending him to Colorado with my niece. The heat was on in Wichita and I wanted my nephew out of the line of fire. When He got to Colorado he started causing all kinds of trouble; he was a very troubled young man. I was so tired of all the drama!

We were having special services at our church one week and I was running late the first night. I got dressed for the meeting but at the last minute I changed into another outfit. That night an apostle and his wife were there. He kept looking at me and I was wondering; why is this man watching me that way? After his wife finished speaking; he went up front with her and he said a few words and then he came over to me; he said, "I know you said to yourself, why is this man looking at me that way" he said, that two days before they came there, he saw me in a vision and everything that I had on was the way he saw me: He said that I was standing still and whatever was happening around me, I just stood there: He said I was asking God why things were coming at me so hard. God told him to tell me because He knew I could handle it and, that young man has caused you so many heartaches; but you whether the storm you were going through.

After he spoke to me I came unglued and started screaming and praising God; I never heard the rest of what he was saying but my spirit man received it. I calmed down after a while and he told me that God was going to use me to set some young people free. It was an anointing night; everyone was blessed.

That Saturday night he preached about how the enemy was trying to destroy all of our young people so they started praying for young people and I went up to stand in for my daughter. They were saying that the enemy was trying to swallow up all our young people in this big hole so he could destroy their future. His wife came over to me and told me that my daughter was [coming in]; she told me not to worry because your integrity is going to draw her. I just began worshiping and praising the Lord for what He was doing for everyone in that service that night.

I didn't know that at the same time she was speaking to me, that my daughter was being shot at. I was at church that Sunday; my phone was in my car; my daughter had tried to reach me (she had made over 10 calls to me). After church I listened to my messages and my daughter was on there saying, "Mama, call me, I almost got killed last night." I hurried and called her and she told me what had happened and all I could do was cry.

I got to the house and I began to praise God and I was crying tears of joy because God was showing me as I was praising Him how [His angels of protection] were batting those bullets from around my child. She and her boyfriend both said that they knew my prayers were covering them. Then she said, "Mama now, I know that Psalm 91 really works (he said the same thing). I was so blessed by his testimony of knowing that the power of prayer works. He ended up getting out of the gang. Praise the Lord!

It pays to be consistent with our kids, not only the young people, but everyone that God put's in our path. You can give them the word, but if you're not living it, what good will it do? God is so good to us and we should cherish Him. I just praise and thank Him for all He has done in the lives of the young people that he has put in my life. It has been a blessing to be able to minister to them and see their lives change.

The man who inspired me to write this book started to attend my church that's where I met him. He serves faithfully and the ministry is blessed to have him; he serves in all areas in this ministry. I got to know him as a friend, and as a teacher of the word I really believe that people are truly blessed by his teaching. I got to know him as a wonderful friend and true man of God. He supports and encourages everyone in the body of Christ. He takes care of his mother and father and always makes sure they are comfortable. That is truly a blessing to have a son like that. I have much respect for his friendship (as I said at the beginning of my book). He was faithful in taking good care of his grandmother until she died; she lived to be a 100 years old and that's a blessing from God. I thank God I was able to attend her 100th birthday party.

I have had a lot of blessings come my way for being faithful and obedient to God. I hated to leave this ministry I served as a deacon and as a minister of the word of God. I was sad when I had to leave, but God said that it was time to go. My pastor and my dear friend (his wife), was upset and hurt, but I had to do what God told me to do.

I left and went and sat under this apostle for one year. God said it was time for [me] to go out. I served in Wichita Kansas for many years. I took care of people, I cleaned their homes and I ministered to the sick; I visited hospitals, nursing homes, jails, prison and I have preached at women's conferences.

I have seen and done things that I know that I am still here only by the grace of God. I had been going back and forth to Denver from Wichita since 2002. God told me in 2006 to pack up and move to Colorado. I did not want to at first, it took a minute, but I awakened one morning at 5:00 AM and I said yes! To God's will.

I had a garage sale for three weeks straight and what I had left, I gave away. When I was living [in] the world I did not like Colorado, but after I put my trust in Jesus it became a blessing.

I left Wichita on November 1. 2006; when I got to the sign that said leaving Kansas, welcome to Colorado, it was like a weight lifted off of me. I just cried because I knew it was what God wanted me to do. Denver Colorado began a new journey for me. It took me to another level; my time there is still not complete.

When we really listen to the Holy Spirit, God will give us instruction: What we should do and where we should be, when we are obedient to Him, as I stated in the beginning of my book.

I thank God for giving me the ability to write this book, and Colorado is where God graced me to do it. I am so thankful to God for all He has done in my life and the people that He placed all around me for each season and time that He allowed me to walk in, and the place that He has me now. But there is always room for growth and improvement. I can never say this enough. **(Always be teachable, and never be above correction.)**

The next few pages will tell what it means to follow Jesus. How we surrender in love. Being prepared to serve, Using God's gift of time, and stepping out through faith in Christ Jesus.

Following Jesus

Following Jesus is the definition of commitment. It demands a choice. Either we deny ourselves and follow Him, or we deny Him. Either we go our own way, or we follow Jesus. When Jesus prayed to His Father in the Garden of Gethsemane He demonstrated that the Father's will, took precedence over His human (flesh and blood) will. Jesus also demonstrated His love for mankind when He took up His cross (for you and for me) in obedience to His Father.
Being committed builds our faith and helps us to develop character. It helps us to be spiritually disciplined. Proverbs 16: 3: "Commit thy works unto the Lord, and thy thoughts shall be established." We must trust God as if everything depends on Him while working as if everything depended on us. It is a lifetime venture. It requires work, our time and most of all our determination. In Matthew 16:24 Jesus says "If any man will come after me, let him deny himself, and take up his cross and follow me."

Surrendering to God in Love

When we surrender we voluntarily yield to the authority of another. The word of God teaches us to surrender our lives to God,

God's way...Philippians 2:5-11 says: "Let this mind be in you, which was also in Christ Jesus." V6. "Who, being in the form of God, thought it not robbery to be equal with God?" V7 "But made Himself of no reputation, and took upon Him the form of a servant, and was made in the likeness of men." V8 "And being found in fashion as a man, He humbled himself, and became obedient unto death, even the death on the cross." V9 "Wherefore God also hath highly exalted him, and given Him a name which was above every name;" V10 "That at the name of Jesus every knee should bow, of things in heaven, and things in earth, and things under the earth;" V11 "And that every tongue should confess that Jesus Christ is Lord, to the glory of God the Father." God illustrates the blessing that follows obedience when we surrender. God's word should overpower anything. Total surrender to God requires us to have an understanding and the knowledge of what the Bible teaches us. We have to obey God's Word. God promised us in His word that when we surrender to Him; that He will strengthen and bless all who are obedient [to Him].

Be Prepared to Serve

We have to be ready to serve God's people. We are to be a light to the world. Here's a few scriptures that will help us on our journey. 1. We have to treat others as we want to be treated. Matthew 7:1 says: "Therefore all things whatsoever ye would that men should do to you, do ye even to them; for this is the law of the prophets."

1. ***We should never compromise our faith.*** Romans 1:16. "For I am not ashamed of the gospel of Christ; for it is the power of God unto salvation to everyone that believeth; to the Jew first, and also to the Greek."
2. ***We should listen to their problems.*** Galatians 6:2, "Bear ye one another's burdens, and so fulfill the law of Christ." The body of Christ functions only when all the members work together for the common good of the Father.
3. ***Pray for them and their needs.*** James 5:16. "Confess your faults one to another, and pray one for another, that ye may be

4. healed. The effectual fervent prayer of a righteous man availeth much." We must help others to come to know Christ. It's not just about us.
5. ***We should always count on God's help***. 1 Thessalonians 5:23. It says: "And the very God of peace sanctify you wholly; and I pray God your whole spirit and soul and body be preserved blameless unto the coming of our Lord Jesus Christ."
6. ***Stay away from evil***. 1Thessalonians 5:22. "Abstain from all appearance of evil." Never let evil get a foothold. Let us allow God's strength to help us avoid temptations.
7. ***We have to walk in Love***. Ephesians 5:2 "And walk in love, as Christ also hath loved us, and hath given himself for us an offering and a sacrifice to God for a sweet smelling savor."

Christ had a love for us that made Him sacrifice himself for us. Our love should be that same kind of love, a love that goes beyond affection to self-sacrificing.

We are free in deed because of Christ. Galatians 5:1 says: "Stand fast therefore in the liberty wherewith Christ hath made us free, and be not entangled again with the yoke of bondage."

If you have a testimony, why sit on it? Why not ask God to increase your territory! Ask God to give you a heart to reach the lost? Remember people always matter.

Use God's Gift of Time

In Matthew 6:33 God says: "Seek first the Kingdom of God and His righteousness, and everything else will be added unto you."

God redeems our time as well as our souls. Colossians 4:5 "Walk in wisdom toward them that are without, redeeming the time." This tells us to be wise in our contacts, making the most of our time so we have the chance to tell others about Christ.

God will help us determine how to use our time. Psalm 55:17 says "Evening and morning and noon I will pray, and cry aloud and He shall hear my voice."

Ecclesiastes 9:10, says: "Whatever your hand finds to do, do it with all your might: for there is no work or device or knowledge or wisdom in the grave where you are going."

Allow God to direct your path. Proverbs 3:5, 6, "Trust in the Lord with all thy heart and lean not to thy own understanding. V6 "In all thy ways acknowledge Him and He shall direct thy path."
Here are some things we need to know:

>Make decisions that count.

>Accomplish the task at hand.

> Use clear communication with a goal in mind.

> Be in a right environment that will help achieve your goal

> Do what's important

> Don't waste time on foolishness

Stepping out on Faith

Faith: It is you and I wanting more out of life: John 10:10, says "I have come that they may have life, and that they may have it more abundantly." The greatest power in this world is to have a positive idea. We walk the walk of faith when we seek God's guidance. God promised us that He will guide us. We have to open our minds consistently and constantly to God. God will give us a strong and powerful will to proceed only on a determined path. Faith is steady, it is stable and it is steadfast. It is a process to open our conscious and subconscious mind through prayer. God will direct us in the way we should go. Psalm 25:4 says: "Show me your ways, O Lord; teach me Your path. Lead me in your truth and teach me. For You are the God of my salvation."

Faith is stepping into the unknown. We have to run and leap into everyday life with expediency. We have to believe in God, and trust that He will always be there for us. God has a plan and purpose for you; don't miss what He has for you. If you fall get back up. We can't allow ourselves to give up. It took me many, many falls but I never stopped trying to please God. Trials only come when we need to be held accountable; it makes us strong. People will continue to persecute us, but that's ok. They did it to Jesus (God the Son) while He was one of us. No matter how much we learn there's still more to learn. But we must not ever abandon the basic truth that: only through Christ Jesus are we saved. The sacrifice He made for OUR SIN is permanent and nothing will ever change that. We have to love people because that's what Jesus, did no matter what they did to Him. 1John 3: 11-15, "For this is the message that ye heard from the beginning, that we should love one another. V12 Not as Cain, who was of that wicked one, and slew his brother. And wherefore slew he him? Because his own works were evil, and his brother's righteous. V13 Marvel not, my brethren, if the world hate you. V14 We know that we have passed from death unto life, because we love the brethren. He that loveth not his brother abideth in death" So no matter what people do to us love them and God will bless you for it. I have made my share of mistakes and I have learned through a lot of them. 1995 was when I finally got off the roller coaster and truly stop going to the clubs the bars and truly surrendering my total life to God so He could change me to the woman He called me to be. I still make mistakes: who doesn't! But God loves us for who we are. Don't let people look down on you. As I said before we are all somebody in the eyes of our Lord and Savior Jesus Christ. God loves you

May the Lord truly bless you!!!

God is blessing RBT Ministries and WWAP Ministry to reach out in the Communities and the Nation to help spread the good news through training, nurturing, education, fellowship, and helping us to, understand and know our identity

Contact information:
Minister Caroiln J Morgan: Director and Founder of Women With a Purpose Ministry.
In-house Director: RBT Ministries
email: cmorganwwapmia@gmail.com cmorganrbtmin@aol.com
websites:www.womenwithapurposemin.com
www.rhymingbibletruths.com